MobileMe for Small Business

PORTABLE GENIUS

MobileMe for Small Business

PORTABLE GENIUS

by Brad Miser

WILEY

Wiley Publishing, Inc.

MobileMe for Small Business Portable Genius

Published by
Wiley Publishing, Inc.
10475 Crosspoint Blvd.
Indianapolis, IN 46256
www.wiley.com

Published simultaneously in Canada

ISBN: 978-0-470-43641-7

Manufactured in the United States of America

10   9   8   7   6   5   4   3   2   1

For general information on our other products and services or to obtain technical support, please contact our Customer Care Department within the U.S. at (877) 762-2974, outside the U.S. at (317) 572-3993 or fax (317) 572-4002.

Wiley also publishes its books in a variety of electronic formats. Some content that appears in print may not be available in electronic books.

Library of Congress Control Number: 2009922583

WILEY

About the Author

Brad Miser has written more than 30 books on technology with the goal of helping people learn to get the most out of that technology as easily and quickly as possible. In addition to *MobileMe for Small Business Portable Genius*, Brad has written *My iPhone*, *Teach Yourself Visually MacBook Air*, *Absolute Beginner's Guide to iPod and iTunes*, *Teach Yourself Visually MacBook*, *MacBook Portable Genius*, *MacBook Pro Portable Genius*, and *Special Edition Using Mac OS X Leopard*. He also has been a coauthor, development editor, or technical editor on more than 50 other titles.

Brad has been a solutions consultant, the director of product and customer services, and the manager of education and support services for several software development companies. Previously, he was the lead proposal specialist for an aircraft engine manufacturer, a development editor for a computer book publisher, and a civilian aviation test officer/engineer for the U.S. Army. Brad holds a Bachelor of Science degree in mechanical engineering from California Polytechnic State University at San Luis Obispo and has received advanced education in maintainability engineering, business, and other topics.

In addition to his passion for silicon-based technology, Brad enjoys his steel-based technology, a.k.a. his motorcycle, whenever and wherever possible. Originally from California, Brad now lives in Indiana with his wife Amy; their three daughters, Jill, Emily, and Grace; and a rabbit.

Brad would love to hear about your experiences with this book (the good, the bad, and the ugly). You can write to him at bradmacosx@me.com.

Credits

Senior Acquisitions Editor
Stephanie McComb

Project Editor
Jama Carter

Technical Editor
Paul Sihvonen-Binder

Copy Editor
Gwenette Gaddis Goshert

Editorial Director
Robyn B. Siesky

Editorial Manager
Cricket Krengel

Vice President and Group Executive
Publisher
Richard Swadley

Vice President and Executive Publisher
Barry Pruett

Business Manager
Amy Knies

Senior Marketing Manager
Sandy Smith

Project Coordinator
Kristie Rees

Graphics and Production Specialists
Jennifer Henry
Andrea Hornberger

Quality Control Technician
Melanie Hoffman

Proofreading
Joni Heredia

Indexing
Broccoli Information Mgt.

The probability that we may fall in the struggle ought not to deter us from the support of a cause we believe to be just; it shall not deter me.
—Abraham Lincoln

Acknowledgments

While my name is on the cover, it takes many people to build a book like this one. Thanks to Stephanie McComb with whom this project had its genesis and who allowed me to be involved. Jama Carter deserves lots of credit for keeping the project on track and on target; I'm sure working with me was a challenge at times. Paul Sihvonen-Binder did a great job of keeping me on my toes to make sure this book contains fewer technical gaffs than it would have. Gwenette Gaddis Goshert transformed my stumbling, bumbling text into something people can read and understand. Thanks also to my agent, Marta Justak, for managing the business of the project and being a support for me during the writing process. Lastly, thanks to all the people on the Wiley team who handle the other, and equally important, parts of the process, such as production, sales, proofreading, and indexing.

On my personal team, I'd like to thank my wife Amy for her tolerance of the author lifestyle, which is both odd and challenging. My delightful daughters Jill, Emily, and Grace are always a source of joy and inspiration for all that I do, and for which I'm ever grateful.

Contents

chapter 1

How Can MobileMe Benefit My
Business?   2

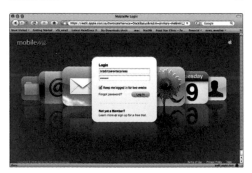

chapter 2

How Do I Set Up MobileMe for My
Business?   14

chapter 3

How Can I Synchronize Information
Using MobileMe?   52

chapter 4

How Can I Get the Most Out of MobileMe iDisks?   100

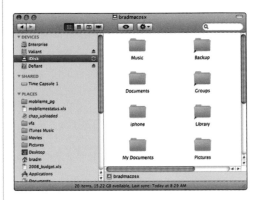

chapter 5

How Can I Take Advantage of
MobileMe Chat Features? 128

chapter 8

What Can I Do with the MobileMe
Web Contacts Web Application? 242

chapter 9

How Can I Use MobileMe's Calendar Web Application?   260

Introduction

Running a small business is a challenge. You have to do more of everything than people working in larger organizations. Unlike those larger organizations, you don't have dedicated specialists for each area of your business; you and your team must be jacks-of-all-trades and be able to take on new challenges to make your business prosper. One particular area that can require a lot of effort for your team and expense for your business is setting up and maintaining a collaborative environment that you and your team can use to communicate among yourselves and with customers (or potential customers) and to share resources related to your business. Likewise, maintaining your own email, file sharing, Web hosting, and other technical services is expensive, time consuming, and takes your focus off growing your business.

Apple's MobileMe service is a perfect addition to your small business because, for a relatively small annual fee, you gain access to a suite of very useful services that you can take advantage of to run your business better and more efficiently. Think of MobileMe as your own IT network staff and you won't be too far off the mark. MobileMe puts vital resources and tools in your hands while minimizing the amount of time and expense you need to implement and manage those tools and resources. MobileMe helps you spend less time (and money) on the technology needed to run your business so you can give more attention to making your business successful.

The purpose of this book is to provide a resource when you are wondering how to do something better, how to do it more easily, or even how to do it at all. Each chapter is organized around a question, and within each chapter are answers to that question—answers that are task-focused so you learn by doing rather than by just reading. The steps are very specific and, I hope, quite complete. If you start at step 1 and work through each step in sequence, you'll end up someplace you want to go. Thus, the book's title of *Portable Genius*; it is intended to be your companion to guide you on your in-depth exploration of MobileMe as part of your small business. After you've been through a topic's steps, you'll be prepared to go even further by extending what you've learned to other tasks.

We've designed this book to provide a broad range of topics that interest most MobileMe small business users. You need to start with Chapter 1 to learn what you can do with MobileMe and then proceed to Chapter 2 to establish your MobileMe accounts, but after that, the topics in this book are in no particular order. You can jump to any chapter without having read the preceding ones. After you have your MobileMe accounts, I recommend that you take a look at the table of contents and decide which question you'd like answered next. Turn the appropriate page and off you go!

How Can MobileMe Benefit My Business?

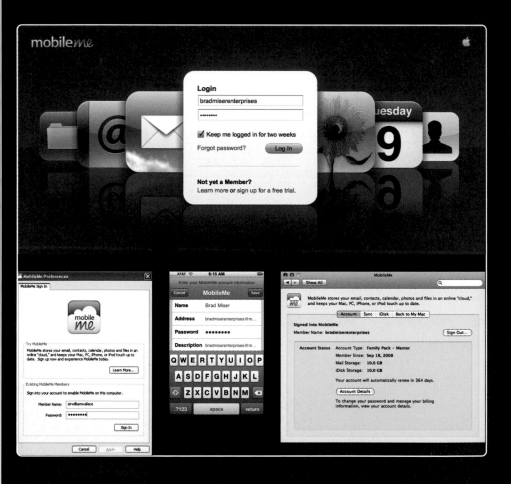

Today's businesses are becoming more and more virtual; instead of office spaces, businesses are using technology to enable their team members to work together without physically being in the same place. This is especially true for small businesses, where the expenses associated with maintaining an office are often hard to justify. Implementing technology appropriate to your business is key to enabling a virtual organization to function effectively. While Apple's MobileMe service is marketed toward consumers, it actually provides a number of services that enable businesses to function effectively and virtually without the costs associated with traditional IT support.

Understanding MobileMe

MobileMe is a set of services that are delivered over the Internet. While Apple markets MobileMe primarily to consumers, it can be a great asset to your small business when you understand how you can deploy MobileMe effectively, which just happens to be the point of this book. Using MobileMe, you can take advantage of powerful technologies for your business that previously necessitated expensive and complex IT resources (in-house or outsourced) that required lots of your time and money. MobileMe services, including the required hardware and software, are all provided and maintained by Apple. All you need to access them is a MobileMe account and a supported device with an Internet connection. And, MobileMe is quite inexpensive to deploy even if you have quite a large small business. Some of the most significant benefits MobileMe provides to your small business include the following:

- Synchronize information on Macs, Windows PCs, and iPhones.
- Store files online using a virtual hard disk (called an iDisk in MobileMe lingo).
- Text, audio, and video chat.
- Publish Web sites.
- Email using email applications on desktop computers or iPhones and via the MobileMe Web email application.
- Manage contacts online via the MobileMe Web Contacts application.
- View calendars on the Web.

Later sections in this chapter provide an overview of each of these capabilities, and chapters throughout the rest of this book are dedicated to the details.

Although MobileMe provides these sophisticated services through complex technology, you don't have to worry about that complexity. You can easily configure, use, and maintain MobileMe for your small business with the information in this book. You don't need to be an IT or technology expert either; MobileMe is well designed so you can focus on using MobileMe effectively in your business rather than spending a lot of time trying to understand how MobileMe's tools work.

To use MobileMe, you must have one or more MobileMe accounts. Chapter 2 contains details of obtaining MobileMe accounts for your business. You can use a number of options to deploy MobileMe for your business, and that chapter helps you choose and implement the option that is best for you.

You can access MobileMe services with any of the following devices:

- Macs running Mac OS X with the latest version of Safari or Firefox
- Windows PCs running XP or Vista with the latest version of Safari or Firefox (MobileMe is not fully compatible with Internet Explorer)
- iPhones running version 2.0 or later of the iPhone software

Synchronizing Information on All Your Devices via the MobileMe Cloud

You probably use more than one computer or other device to operate your business. For example, you might have desktop computers, laptop computers, and an iPhone. As you use each of these devices, you make changes to important information, such as updating a contact's information, creating a bookmark, or responding to an email. Ideally, you want to have the same information available to you on all the devices you use, and even better, you want your devices to be synchronized with as little action from you as possible. MobileMe can do this for you.

When you obtain a MobileMe account, you gain access to the MobileMe cloud; this is an area on Apple's servers where your information can be stored. Each device that is synced with MobileMe connects to the cloud and transfers information to and from it. Because all the devices are connecting to the same cloud, they all have access to the same information. MobileMe software on each device ensures that the most current information is available on each device, as shown in figure 1.1.

You can choose which devices and the specific kinds of information on those devices that are synced with the cloud by configuring each device you want to include in the synchronization process. You can synchronize Macs, Windows PCs, and iPhones. Chapter 3 provides an explanation of how to configure each kind of device for MobileMe synchronization.

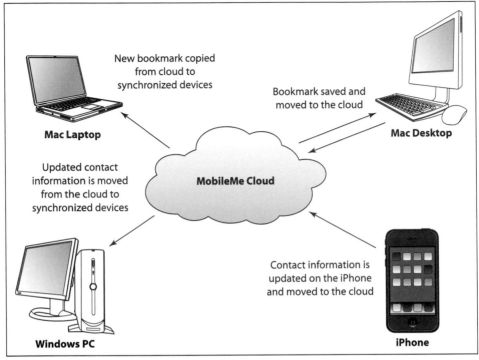

New bookmark copied from cloud to synchronized devices

Bookmark saved and moved to the cloud

Mac Laptop

Mac Desktop

Updated contact information is moved from the cloud to synchronized devices

MobileMe Cloud

Contact information is updated on the iPhone and moved to the cloud

Windows PC

iPhone

1.1 MobileMe synchronizes information on Macs, Windows PCs, and iPhones via the MobileMe cloud.

Storing and Sharing Files Online with MobileMe iDisks

An iDisk is a virtual disk space in which you can store files, much like you store files on a hard drive internal to or connected to a computer. The benefit of an iDisk is that it is located on Apple servers that you can access over the Net, which means the files stored there are available to any Mac or Windows PC that can connect to the Internet. This is very useful for working with your own files because you can use file synchronization between the iDisk and computers to ensure that the most current version of any file is available to you. Even better, you can use the Public folder on your iDisk to share files with others. For example, if you are collaborating on a document with one of your team members, you can store that document on your iDisk, and both you and your team member can access it from there. Or you can place documents you want to make available to customers there and send them a link to download those documents to their own computers.

You can access your iDisk from your computer's desktop and by using the MobileMe iDisk Web application, as shown in figure 1.2. On a Mac, you can keep a copy of your iDisk on your computer so that you can work with its files even when you aren't connected to the Internet, and you have the local version synchronized to the online version automatically or manually.

On a Windows PC, you can connect to your iDisk just like other drives and devices available to you over a network. With Safari or Firefox, you can access your iDisk using the iDisk Web application, which enables you to work with the disk similarly to how you use it from the desktop. Taking advantage of an iDisk is covered in Chapter 4.

1.2 Files stored on your iDisk are available from your desktop and from any computer running Safari or Firefox.

Using MobileMe to Communicate

A major challenge in running a virtual business is ensuring that effective communication is happening between you and your team members. Your MobileMe account provides chatting capabilities that you can access via the Mac's iChat application or the AIM application on Windows PCs, as shown in figures 1.3 and 1.4. Using these applications, you can easily text chat with team members; for even more effective communication, you can audio and video chat as well. On the Mac, you also can control a team member's Mac or share control of your Mac with her, and using iChat's file sharing, you can conduct online presentations and share files. In Chapter 5, you learn the ins and outs of using these tools to communicate effectively.

1.3 To keep in touch with team members with a Mac, use your MobileMe account and iChat to text, audio, or video chat.

1.4 You can also use your MobileMe account to chat on a Windows computer using the AIM application.

Publishing Web Sites with MobileMe

One thing every business needs — no matter what that business's products or services are — is a Web site. With a MobileMe account, you can easily publish one or more Web sites; you don't have to worry about any of the hardware or software that is required to put the sites on the Web because

MobileMe handles all that complexity for you. You can instead focus on creating a Web site that effectively represents your business and enables your customers, potential customers, and partners to get information and interact with you. You can use many applications to create the Web sites you want to publish via MobileMe.

If you use a Mac, a good choice to create your Web sites is the iWeb application because it is tightly integrated with MobileMe and allows you to create Web sites using templates that you can easily customize to design your site. Publishing a Web site with iWeb is literally a one-click operation, as shown in figure 1.5. If you don't have iWeb or you use a Windows PC, you can use another application to create your sites, such as a Web creation application or applications that can save their output as a Web site; for example, Microsoft Office applications can do this.

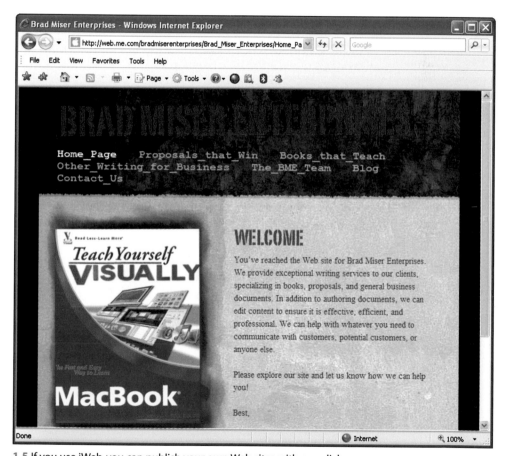

1.5 If you use iWeb, you can publish your own Web sites with one click.

When you publish a Web site, the default URL begins with web.me.com; you should register your own domain so that your URL starts with something more identifiable with your business. After you have registered your domain, you can easily configure MobileMe to publish your sites using that domain.

Publishing and managing Web sites via MobileMe is explained in detail in Chapter 6.

Touring Your MobileMe Web Site

As part of your MobileMe account, you have access to your own MobileMe Web site. You access your site by moving to me.com and entering your MobileMe member name and password. Once logged in, you can use the following tools:

- **Email.** The MobileMe Web email application is a full-featured tool that you can use to create, send, read, and organize email, as shown in figure 1.6. The primary benefit of this application — as compared to an email application installed on your computer — is that you can use it from any computer with an Internet connection and Firefox or Safari. You can use this application with your MobileMe email accounts, and you can configure an external email account in it too. Along with the kinds of features you'd expect from an email application, you can create and use email aliases, which are very useful for temporary addresses that you can use for specific business purposes or to limit your exposure to spam or other Internet hassles. MobileMe's email tools are described in Chapter 7.

- **Contacts.** The Contacts application enables you to access and manage contact information being stored in the MobileMe cloud. Like the other MobileMe Web applications, this means you can get to your contact information from just about any computer. (Of course, when you sync computers via MobileMe, your current contact information is always available locally too.) You can create, manage, and organize your contacts using this application within Firefox or Safari. Using this tool is explained in Chapter 8.

- **Calendar.** While a bit more limited than the other MobileMe Web applications, you can use the Calendar application to view your calendars, providing you quick access when you aren't using one of your own computers or other devices. You can post calendars you manage in Outlook or iCal to the MobileMe cloud, and they become visible in the MobileMe Web Calendar application. You also can create and manage calendars within this application. Working with calendars is covered in Chapter 9.

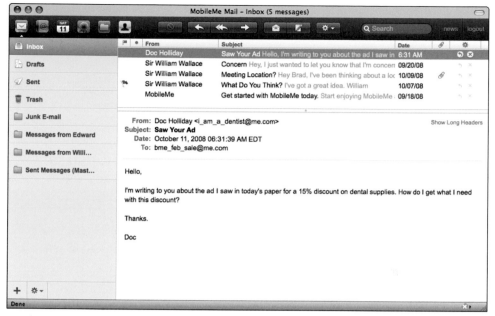

1.6 The MobileMe Web email application enables you to work with your email from any computer with an Internet connection and a supported Web browser.

- **Gallery.** Use the Gallery tool to publish photos to the Web. This tool isn't as useful for business as some of the other MobileMe services (for example, you are better off publishing photos related to your business via Web sites). However, you might find creative ways to use the Gallery as part of your business, and you can always use it for personal purposes. So for details about using the Gallery, see Appendix A.

- **iDisk.** With the iDisk Web application, you can access your online iDisk to manage the files stored there or add new files to it. This works similar to accessing a disk from a computer desktop, except of course, you can use your iDisk from any computer with a working Internet connection and Safari or Firefox. Your iDisk's capabilities are covered in Chapter 4.

- **Account.** Use the Account application to manage your MobileMe accounts. For example, you can add more disk space or create and manage Family Member accounts, as shown in figure 1.7. This tool is explained in detail in Chapter 2.

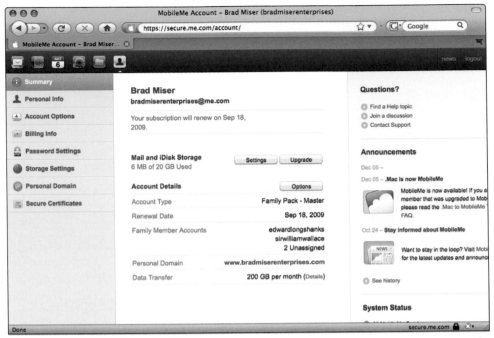

1.7 In addition to the applications provided on your MobileMe Web site, you can use its Account tool to manage your MobileMe accounts.

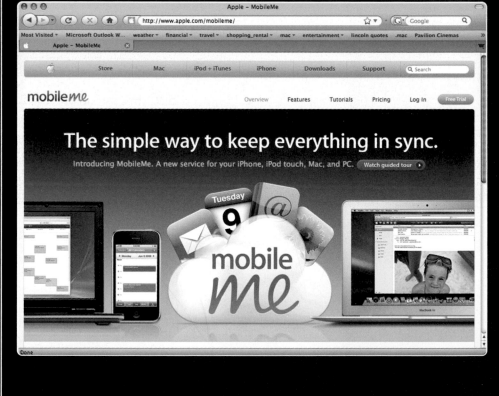

To get your business started with MobileMe, you create MobileMe accounts for yourself and your team. You can choose from two types of MobileMe accounts: Individual and Family Packs. Both can be useful. Which you choose depends on your strategy for rolling out MobileMe for your team members. After you have created the accounts, you configure those accounts on the devices you and your team members use, including Macs, Windows PCs, and iPhones. You can also use the .me Web site for MobileMe applications and to manage your MobileMe accounts. The details are in this chapter.

Choosing and Setting Up MobileMe Accounts

To take advantage of all that MobileMe offers, you need to have a MobileMe account. You can choose from two kinds of accounts. Each kind includes specific resources and has different fees associated with it. After you've decided on the accounts you want to use for your business, you can create them for yourself and your team members.

Both kinds of MobileMe accounts include the following resources:

- **Online disk space.** Each MobileMe account includes access to disk space on Apple servers. This virtual space is incredibly useful for general file storage and is also used to deliver all the other services that MobileMe offers. For example, you share this disk space for your iDisk and for your MobileMe email. It also is where you store all the content for a MobileMe Web site.

- **Monthly data transfer.** MobileMe accounts allow you to transfer a specified amount of information through them each month. This is important because it determines how much data your Web site is able to serve on a monthly basis.

- **Email account.** Each MobileMe account includes an email account; these email accounts have the domain *.me.com*. The email addresses are something like *yourmembername*@me.com, where *yourmembername* is the name of the account you create. The email account shares online disk space with the iDisk. You can configure these email addresses within standard email programs, such as Outlook or Mail. You also can access them through the MobileMe Email Web application.

- **Email aliases.** In addition to the primary email account, you can configure email aliases for that account. These are "pointer" addresses to which you can receive and from which you can send email. They redirect email to the primary account while hiding that account's "real" address. Email aliases are useful for creating addresses for such purposes as sending a special offer from your business or shielding yourself from spam and other Internet attacks. Alias accounts can be created and managed as you need them.

- **iDisk.** Your iDisk is where documents and other files are stored under your account's online disk space; this space is shared with the email account. An iDisk can be mounted directly on the desktops of both Windows PCs and Macs so you can use it just like the computer's hard drive. Also, you can use the MobileMe iDisk Web application to work with your iDisk.

Web site. Each MobileMe account can have its own Web site. If you use a Mac, you can create and publish a site easily using iWeb. If you use a Windows PC, you also can publish a Web site to your MobileMe account; it's just a bit more work.

◉ **Photo gallery.** The Gallery is a tool you can use to post images for easy online viewing.

◉ **MobileMe cloud.** Perhaps the most important part of every MobileMe account is its ability to share information using the MobileMe cloud. Each device can access this cloud to keep email, contacts, calendars, and Web bookmarks in sync automatically. For example, you can configure a Windows PC, Mac, and iPhone so that the same emails are available on each device. As you make changes on one device, those changes are reflected on the other devices automatically.

The two kinds of MobileMe accounts, shown in figure 2.1, are:

◉ **Individual account.** As you suspect from its title, this kind of account is designed for individual use. It includes 20GB of online disk space and up to 200GB of monthly data transfer. The cost of an Individual account is $99 per year.

◉ **Family Pack.** This account starts with an Individual account and adds the ability to create and manage up to four sub-accounts, called Family Member accounts (for a total of five accounts). The master account includes 20GB of online disk space. Each of the four Family Member sub-accounts has 5GB of online disk space. The total data transfer for the master account under a Family Pack account is the same as for an Individual account, or 200GB per month, and each Family Member account has 50GB per month of data transfer. The cost of a Family Pack is $149 per year.

Note Sales and other taxes are added to all MobileMe costs, including the annual subscription and any upgrades you purchase.

In addition to the default resources included with each account you create, you also can upgrade the online disk space and monthly data transfer for your accounts. You can add 20GB of online disk space (for a total of 40GB) and 200GB of data transfer (for a total of 400GB) for an additional $49 per year. Or you can add 40GB (total of 60GB) of online disk space and 400GB (total of 600GB) of data transfer for $99 per year more.

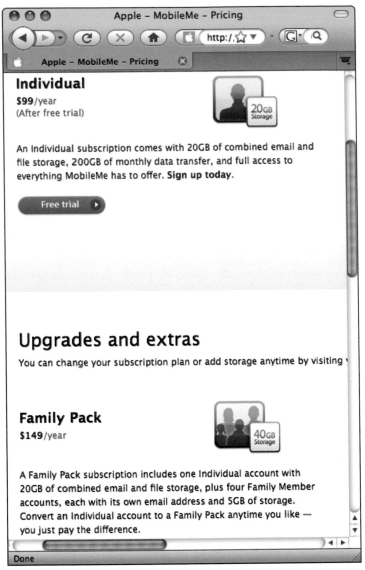

2.1 You and your team can access MobileMe via Individual or Family Pack accounts.

Choosing accounts for your business

The type of accounts you should create depends on how you and your team are going to use them. If a person is going to be storing a lot of data on his iDisk or publishing a large Web page, an Individual account is the way to go because these accounts include the largest amount of storage space and monthly data transfer. For those team members who are primarily using MobileMe for email and information synchronizing (such as for contacts and calendars), providing a Family Member account can save you money compared to obtaining an Individual account for each of the same team members.

To determine which accounts you should get, first identify those team members that are definitely going to need lots of online disk space, such as those people who create large or many documents or who are going to be maintaining Web sites for your business. Each of these people will need their own Individual accounts.

For people who are primarily going to be using email and who don't need that much online disk space, consider using a Family Pack account so that you can provide up to four more people with Family Member accounts. This will save you almost $350 per year as compared to paying for five Individual accounts.

Be aware that you can only have a total of five accounts under each Family Pack so you'll need one master account (that includes the same resources as an Individual account) for each group of up to four Family Member accounts. The master account is also responsible for managing the four sub-accounts associated with it.

You also can convert Family Member accounts into Individual accounts; if someone using a Family Member account needs more disk space, you can upgrade the Family Member account to an Individual account. So, if you have any doubt about whether someone will need a Family Member or Individual account, start with the Family Member account (assuming you have a Family Pack account of course) because it is less expensive, and you can always upgrade it.

Setting up Individual MobileMe accounts

All MobileMe accounts start as an Individual account. To create an Individual MobileMe account, go to www.apple.com/mobileme and click the Free Trial button in the upper-right corner of the window. Then follow the steps as you are prompted; see figure 2.2.

Caution After you've created an account, the member name can't be changed. So double-check the member name before you finish the sign-up process.

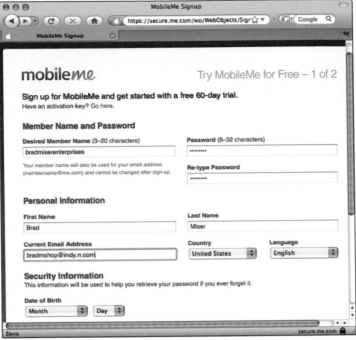

2.2 The most important step in creating a MobileMe account is selecting a member name.

1. **Enter the member name for the account.** The member name comes into play in a number of ways. One is that you use the member name to access your MobileMe account. Another is that you use it to configure MobileMe on your devices, such as a computer. The member name is the first part of your email address and is also included in the default URL for your Web site. For these reasons, make sure your member name has meaning for your business and that people will be able to remember it so they can send you email and move to your Web site more easily. Your member name is between 3 and 20 characters, and it has to be unique to your account.

Genius

When choosing a member name, consider writing out variations of the email address and Web site to see how they look and whether potential customers or your business contacts are likely to associate them with your business. The email address will be *membername*@me.com, while the default Web site URL will be web.me.com/*membername*. Because the member name must be unique to your account, consider creating a couple of versions that work for you in case one of them is already in use by another MobileMe account.

2. **Enter a password in the Password field.** Your password can be between 6 and 32 characters; for better security, include both letters and numbers in your password and make it at least 8 characters long.

3. **Re-enter your password in the Re-type Password field.**

4. **Enter your first and last names in the relevant fields.**

5. **If you have an existing email address, enter it in the Current Email Address field.** Apple can use this address to contact you.

6. **Choose your country and language on the two pop-up menus.**

7. **Configure the month and day of your birth on the two pop-up menus.**

8. **Enter a question in the Secret Question field.** Should you forget your password, you'll need to provide an answer to this question to reset your password. Use something factual, not obvious, and memorable, such as your mother's maiden name or the city where you were born. Don't use something you might not remember, like your favorite movie.

9. **In the Answer field, type the answer to the question.** You'll need to supply this exact answer to be able to reset your password.

10. **If you don't want to receive marketing and general informative emails from Apple, deselect the Please keep me informed with updates from MobileMe and Apple check box.**

11. **Click Continue.** Your information is checked. If MobileMe finds any problems, such as your member name already being in use, the fields you need to change are highlighted in red and you see an explanation of what needs to be fixed at the top of the screen. Make any changes required, and click Continue until you move to the second screen, where you enter a credit card for the account.

    You must associate a valid credit card with the MobileMe account. This card will be charged when the free trial period ends (unless you cancel the account prior to that time, of course).

12. **Follow the prompts to complete the information associated with your credit card.**

13. **Select the check box at the bottom of the screen.** Doing this indicates that you have read and agreed to the MobileMe Terms of Service and Apple's Privacy Policy (you can actually read these documents by clicking the links at the bottom of the screen).

14. **Click Sign Up.** The information you entered is checked. If any of it needs to be corrected, the related field is highlighted in red and you see an explanation at the top of the screen. Correct the information and click Sign Up again.

When you have successfully created the account, you see the Sign Up Complete screen, shown in figure 2.3. Here, you see your member name and the email account associated with it. The account is ready to use. (If you click the Continue to Setup button, you move to the MobileMe Setup Web page. This Web site provides information about configuring MobileMe on devices. Because you already have this book, you don't really need to visit that Web site, but you can click the button if you want to check it out.)

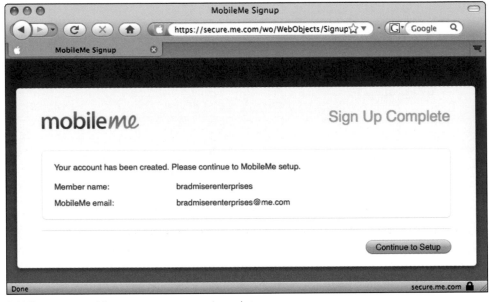

2.3 When you see this screen, your account is ready to use.

The account you create is a trial account and behaves as if it is a full account, meaning you have access to all of MobileMe's functionality. The credit card you provided when you created the account isn't charged until the end of the free trial period. At that point, the account is converted to a full account automatically, and your credit card is charged. (You can cancel the free trial account at any time prior to that to avoid this charge.)

Setting up a Family Pack account

Earlier, you learned that a Family Pack account can be a cost effective way to provide MobileMe services to your team members. All Family Pack accounts begin as Individual accounts. You convert an Individual account into a Family Pack account and then configure the Family Member accounts under the Family Pack account.

The first task in setting up a Family Pack account is to access your MobileMe account configuration tools on the me.com Web site. If you are starting with a trial account, you must first convert that free trial account into a full account (the steps to do so are explained in the section on converting a trial account into a full account later in this chapter). When you have a full account, you can convert it into a Family Pack account.

Note

MobileMe is fully supported by two Web browsers: Safari and Firefox. Safari is installed on all Macs. If you want to use Firefox on a Mac, you need to download and install it (see the section on downloading and installing Firefox later in this chapter). Because Internet Explorer is the default Web browser on Windows PCs, you need to install Safari or Firefox before using the MobileMe Web site on a Windows PC (see the section on downloading and installing a compatible Web browser later in this chapter).

Accessing MobileMe account configuration tools

To log into your MobileMe Web site to access the account configuration tools, perform the following steps:

1. **Log into www.me.com by entering your member name and password.**

2. **If you select the Keep me logged in for two weeks check box, you can access your account again without reentering your account information.** You shouldn't select this box if you are using a public or other computer that isn't under your control.

3. **Click Log In, as shown in figure 2.4.**
   You move into your MobileMe account.

4. **Click the Account button, which is on the right end of the MobileMe tool-bar.** (It's the one with the silhouette.) When prompted, enter your MobileMe password again.

5. **Click Continue.** You move to the Account tools screen. Along the left side of the screen, you see different tabs, such as Summary, Personal Info, Account Options, and so on. When you select one of these tabs, information about and controls for the related area appear in the center pane of the window.

2.4 To access your MobileMe account, you log into the me.com Web site.

6. **Click the Account Options tab.** You see various options and upgrades for your account.

If you are using a free trial account, move to the next section. If you are already using a full (paid for) account, skip to the section on converting a full Individual account into a Family Pack account.

Converting a free trial account into a full Individual account

You can convert only a full (paid for) Individual account into a Family Pack account. If you are using a free trial account, you have to wait until the end of the free trial period or skip the remaining part of your free trial to be able to create a Family Pack account. If you skip the remaining part of the free trial period, your credit card will immediately be charged the annual subscription fee.

To convert a free trial account into a full Individual account, do the following:

1. **In Account Options, click the Skip Trial button, shown in figure 2.5.** When you are prompted, enter your account password again. Then click Continue. (You move to page 1 of the Reactivation or Upgrade screen.)

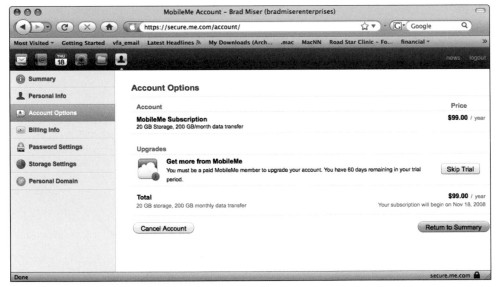

2.5 You can convert only a full Individual account to a Family Pack, so you need to forfeit the remainder of the free trial period to create one of these accounts.

2. **Review the name, email address, country, language, and contact preference information; change any information that needs to be updated, and then click Continue.**

3. **Select a credit card type, and enter its information as prompted.** This can be the same card you used initially or a different card.

4. **Review the name, address, and phone number information for the card; change any information that needs to be updated.**

5. **Read the information in the About Your Subscription section and if you agree with it, select the I have read and agree to the MobileMe Terms of Service and Apple's Privacy Policy check box at the bottom of the screen.**

6. **Click Sign Up.** The information you entered is checked. If any of it needs to be corrected, the related field is highlighted in red and you see an explanation at the top of the screen. Correct the information, and click Sign Up again. When the information is verified, you see the Confirm Your Information screen that shows the account you are updating, the credit card that will be charged, and the amount that will be charged (fees plus taxes).

7. **If the information is correct and you're ready to transform your free trial account into a full account, click Sign Up.** Your credit card is charged, and your account is converted into a full account. You move to the Sign Up Complete screen that shows the member name and email address. Your account is now a full Individual account that can be converted into a Family Pack.

8. **Go back to me.com.** You should still be logged in to your account; if not, log in again.

9. **Click the Account button, and enter your MobileMe password.**

10. **Click Continue.** On the Summary screen, you see that your account is now a full Individual account that expires one year from the time you converted it from a free trial account.

Converting a full Individual account into a Family Pack account

To convert an Individual account into a Family Pack, do the following:

1. **In Account Options, click Upgrades.** You see a sheet with the upgrade options on it. Next to the description of each option, you see its additional cost per year.

2. **Click the Add the Family Pack to your account radio button, and then click Continue.** You a screen like that shown in figure 2.6.

3. **To use the same credit card you entered originally, leave the Use my existing credit card radio button selected; to use a different card, select the Use a new credit card radio button and provide the information as prompted. Click Continue.** You see the selections you made on the Confirm Your Selections sheet.

2.6 Adding the Family Pack to your account adds $50 to your annual fee.

4. **If the information on the confirmation sheet is correct, click Upgrade; if not, click Cancel to stop the process or Back to go to previous screens to correct information.** After you click the Upgrade button, your upgrade is processed. When that is complete, you see the Upgrade complete sheet.

5. **Click OK.** The sheet closes, and you return to the Summary screen. It now shows Family Pack — Master as the account type and indicates that you have four unassigned Family Member accounts. You can create up to four sub-accounts at any time.

Creating Family Member accounts

To provide others with access to MobileMe through a Family Pack account, you create a Family Member account for each person. Here's how to do it:

1. **Log into your MobileMe account.**

2. **Click the Account button, enter your password (if prompted), and then click the Account Options button.**

3. **Click the Set Up Account link, which is located under the text "Family Pack."** You see the Set Up Family Member Account sheet, shown in figure 2.7.

Set Up Family Member Account

⦿ Create a new account
   Create a new account for a friend or family member.

◯ Convert existing account
   Use an expired .Mac or MobileMe account as a Family Member Account.

Account Details
Enter the information below for the account you're setting up.

Member Name (3-20 characters)
`sirwilliamwallace`

Password (6-32 characters)   Confirm Password
`••••••••`   `••••••••`

First Name   Last Name
`William`   `Wallace`

Password Question (e.g. What's my pet's name?)   Password Answer
`Who is my nemesis?`   `Longshanks`

Date of Birth
`May` ▼   `7` ▼

[Cancel]   (Continue)

2.7 When you create a Family Member account for someone else, you enter information similar to what you entered when you created your own account.

Genius

If you select the Convert existing account option, you can re-create an expired .Mac or MobileMe account as a Family Member account. This is a good way to reuse an email address for an account that has lapsed for one reason or another. (By the way, .Mac is the previous name for MobileMe.)

4. **Select the Create a new account option.**

5. **Enter the member name for the account.** Like the member name of the master account, the member name for the Family Member account is the first part of the person's email address; it also is part of the URL to his Web site. So make it something related to the person for whom you are creating the account. The member name must be unique and be between 3 and 20 characters.

6. **Create a password for the account by entering it in the Password field.** The password can be between 6 and 32 characters; for better security, include both letters and numbers in the password and make it at least 8 characters long.

7. **Reenter the password in the Confirm Password field.**

8. **Enter the person's first and last names in the relevant fields.**

9. **Configure the month and day of the person's birth on the two pop-up menus.**

10. **Enter a security password question and a security password answer in the relevant fields.** The person for whom you are creating the account will need to know the answer to the unique question if she ever forgets her password.

11. **Click Continue.** The member name you create is checked. If it isn't unique, you are prompted to select or create a new member name. (If you aren't prompted to choose a different member name, you move directly to the Set Up Complete sheet on which you see the information for the account you created and can skip to Step 13.)

12. **If prompted, select one of the suggested member names or enter a different member name.**

13. **Click Continue.** The member name you selected or entered is checked. If the name is unique, you move to the Set Up Complete sheet on which you see the information for the account you created, as shown in figure 2.8. If the name isn't unique, you must repeat Steps 11 and 12 until it is.

Genius

To show the password, security question, and security answer on the Set Up Complete sheet or the Print page, click the Show Security Information link. You can see what you have typed rather than the dots that hide these details. The person who will be using the account needs this information to be able to use the account.

14. **Click Print.** You go to a Web page showing the account's information. Print this page. You need this for the person using the account.

15. **Close the Web page. You return to the Set Up Complete sheet.**

16. **Done.** The sheet closes, and you see the account you created listed under the Family Pack section on the Account Options screen. The account is ready to use.

Set Up Complete

The following MobileMe account has been created:

Name	**William Wallace**
Member Name	**sirwilliamwallace**
Email Address	**sirwilliamwallace@me.com**
Password	··········
Security Question	··········
Security Answer	··········

Show Security Information

To get the recipient started with MobileMe, copy and send him or her the above information (remember to include the password). You may also print this page by clicking below.

A setup guide is available at http://www.apple.com/mobileme/setup

Print...   Done

2.8 William can now use MobileMe.

You can repeat these steps to create up to three more accounts for a total of four Family Member accounts. Each Family Member account can be used just like an Individual account (except that they don't have as much online disk space). For example, a Family Member account can be configured on a Mac or a Windows PC as described in the following sections.

Configuring a MobileMe Account on a Mac

Because the MobileMe software is built into the Mac OS, setting up a Mac to access MobileMe services is easy. After you have a MobileMe account, you log into that account on the MobileMe pane of the System Preferences application. The second, but not required, part of the process is to download and install the Firefox Web browser application; you only need to do this if you prefer to use Firefox instead of Safari.

Logging into the MobileMe pane of the System Preferences application

When you log into a MobileMe account on a Mac, you can automatically access its iDisk from the desktop. The associated email account also is configured in the Mail application automatically.

1. **Choose Apple menu ⇨ System Preferences.** The System Preferences application opens.

2. **Click the MobileMe icon**. The MobileMe pane appears.

3. **Enter the member name of your MobileMe account.**

4. **Enter the password for your MobileMe account.**

5. **Click Sign In.** You log into your account and see information about it similar to that in figure 2.9. The account is ready to be used from the Mac's desktop.

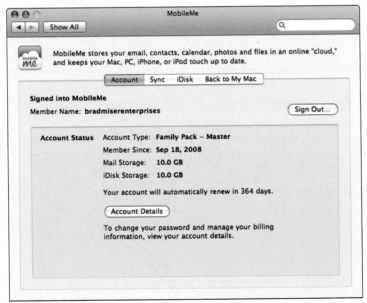

2.9 This Mac can access an iDisk and other resources associated with this MobileMe account.

After you sign into a MobileMe account, you see that the MobileMe pane has four tabs. On the Account tab, you see information about the account, such as its current status and disk space allocation. On the Sync tab, you configure synchronization using the MobileMe cloud. On the iDisk tab, you can manage your iDisk. You can use the Back to My Mac tab to access a Mac across the Internet as if it were on your local network. You learn more about these tabs throughout this book.

Logging into a MobileMe account on a Mac isn't required to use that account's resources because the account can always be accessed through the Web (as you learn throughout this book). But it does make using MobileMe more convenient because some resources, namely iDisk and email, are available to you automatically.

Each user account on a Mac can have a different MobileMe account configured for it. So, if you share a Mac with other people who have their own user accounts, each person can configure her MobileMe account under her Mac user account. For example, you might configure a Family Pack's master account under your user account while someone else who uses your Mac might configure a Family Member account under his Mac user account.

Downloading and installing Firefox

Safari is Mac OS X's default Web browser, and you can use that browser to access MobileMe Web services, such as its email or calendar applications. However, some Mac users have a personal preference for the Firefox browser for its faster speed, better extensibility, and other features. If you want to give Firefox a try, download and install it with the following steps:

1. **Go to www.firefox.com.**

2. **Click Free Download.** The installer disk image downloads to the Mac. When that process is complete, you are prompted to continue to download the file because it contains an application.

3. **Click Continue.** When that process Is complete, you are prompted to accept the license agreement.

4. **Click Accept.** You see a Finder window showing the disk image and containing the Firefox application icon.

5. **Open a second Finder window.**

6. **Move to the Applications folder.**

7. **Drag the Firefox icon from the disk image folder into the Applications folder.** The application is installed on the Mac.

8. **Unmount and delete the disk image file.** Firefox is ready to use. The first time you launch it, a setup application enables you to transfer information, such as your bookmarks, from Safari.

Configuring a MobileMe Account on a Windows PC

To use MobileMe on a Windows PC, you have to install and configure the MobileMe control panel. This control panel is installed when you update iTunes to the current version or install iTunes on your PC if it isn't installed there already. (iTunes is also required to use an iPhone.)

When the control panel is installed, you configure it to access your MobileMe account. To use the MobileMe Web site, you must download and install Safari or Firefox.

Note

The Windows sections of this book are based on Windows XP. If you are using Windows Vista, the details may be slightly different for you and your screens may look a bit different too. Likewise, different flavors of XP may have slightly different details. However, you still should be able to accomplish the steps with relative ease.

Updating iTunes

The MobileMe control panel is installed when you update iTunes to the current version. If you already have iTunes installed on your PC, make sure you are using the current version by choosing Help ⇨ Check for Updates and following the onscreen instructions.

When you are using the current version of iTunes, you can skip to the section on logging into the MobileMe control panel to log into MobileMe.

Downloading and installing iTunes

iTunes is Apple's digital audio and video application that became very popular with the introduction of iPods. When you download and install iTunes, you also get the MobileMe control panel. Downloading and installing iTunes is a snap:

1. **Go to www.apple.com/itunes/.**
2. **Click Download iTunes.** If you do not want to be on mailing lists, deselect those options.
3. **Click Download Now.**
4. **At the security warning, click Run or Open.** The application installer downloads to the PC.
5. **At the next security warning, click Run.** The application installer runs.
6. **Follow the onscreen instructions to complete the installation of iTunes.**

Logging into the MobileMe control panel

You can use the MobileMe control panel to configure a Windows PC to access a MobileMe account by performing the following steps:

1. **Choose Start ➪ Control Panel.** The Control Panel folder appears.

2. **Double-click the MobileMe control panel.** The control panel opens, as shown in figure 2.10.

3. **Enter the MobileMe member name in the Member Name field.**

2.10 This Windows PC can access an iDisk and other resources associated with this MobileMe account.

4. **Enter the password in the Password field.**

5. **Click Sign In.** The account's configuration is registered, and information about the account is displayed in the control panel. The account's resources can now be accessed on the Windows PC.

When you are logged into a MobileMe account, the MobileMe control panel has three panes. The Account tab provides general information about the account, such as its current status and disk space allocation. The Sync tab is for synchronization of the account. The iDisk tab lets you work with the account's iDisk. You learn more about these tabs throughout this book.

Downloading and installing a compatible Web browser

The current version of MobileMe is not fully compatible with Microsoft's Internet Explorer Web browser. You need to use Safari or Firefox for MobileMe to work correctly on your Windows PC. If you don't have one of those browsers installed, the following sections tell you where and how to get them.

What you choose is a matter of personal preference. Because they are both free, you can try each of them to see which you prefer.

Downloading and installing Safari

Safari, Apple's Web browser, is available for Windows PCs. To download and install it using Internet Explorer, perform the following steps:

1. **Go to www.apple.com/safari.**

2. **Click Download Now.**

3. **Select the Safari for Windows XP or Vista radio button.**

4. **Deselect the Keep my information check box.**

5. **Click Download Safari.**

6. **At the File Download dialog box, click Run.** The installer starts to download to your PC.

7. **At the Security Warning prompt, click Run.** The Safari installer launches.

8. **Follow the onscreen instructions to complete the installation of Safari.**

Downloading and installing Firefox

Firefox is a well-respected Web browser for both Windows PCs and Macs. To download and install it using Internet Explorer, follow these steps:

1. **Go to www.firefox.com.**

2. **Click Free Download.**

3. **Select the Firefox for Windows XP or Vista radio button.**

4. **At the File Download dialog box, click Run.** The installer starts to download to your PC.

5. **At the Security Warning prompt, click Run.** The Firefox Set Up Wizard launches.

6. **Follow the onscreen instructions to complete the installation of Firefox.**

Configuring a MobileMe Account on an iPhone

iPhones are amazing devices. In addition to their cell phone functionality, they are also digital entertainment devices and, effectively, mobile computers with email, Web browsing, and thousands of third-party applications. Because you can do so much so easily with an iPhone, they are great additions to your small business, especially if you travel. MobileMe email, calendar, and contacts automatically synchronize on iPhones so you have current information with you at all times.

Adding a MobileMe account to an iPhone

To set up the MobileMe account on the iPhone, follow these steps:

1. **On the Home screen, press Settings.**

2. **Scroll down the screen.**

3. **Press Mail, Contacts, Calendars.** The Mail, Contacts, Calendars screen appears.

4. **Press Add Account.** You see the Add Account screen, as shown in figure 2.11.

5. **Press mobileme.** You see the MobileMe account screen, as shown in figure 2.12.

2.11 Adding a MobileMe account to an iPhone is a great way to stay current while you are on the move.

2.12 After you enter the MobileMe account's information and press Save, you have instant access to email, calendar, contacts, and bookmarks.

6. **Enter your name, your MobileMe email address, and your MobileMe password.**

7. **Change the default description, which is your email address, if you want to.** This description appears on various lists of accounts.

8. **Press Save.** Your account information is verified. When that process is complete, you see the MobileMe screen. From here, you choose which elements of your MobileMe account you want synchronized on your iPhone; see figure 2.13.

2.13 You can choose which elements of the MobileMe account are synchronized on the iPhone.

9. **Ensure that the Mail status is ON to sync your MobileMe email to your iPhone; if it is OFF, press OFF to change the status to ON.**

10. **To access your MobileMe contacts on the iPhone, press OFF next to it so its status becomes ON.**

11. **To use your MobileMe calendar on the iPhone, press OFF next to it.** Its status becomes ON, and the MobileMe calendars are moved to the iPhone after you save your changes.

12. **To move bookmarks being synchronized on MobileMe onto the iPhone, press Bookmarks OFF so its status becomes ON.**

13. **Press Save.** The account is synced to the iPhone. You return to the Mail, Contacts, Calendar screen where you see your account on the Accounts list. The account is ready to use.

Determining how MobileMe information is moved onto an iPhone

After you have configured your iPhone to access the MobileMe account, use the information in this section to determine how MobileMe information is moved onto the iPhone. You can choose from a couple of options.

You can use Push, which means that information is moved from the MobileMe servers onto the iPhone as changes occur. So the information on iPhone is always current. As you make changes on your iPhone, information is pushed onto MobileMe servers. The downside is that frequent communication must take place between the MobileMe servers and the iPhone, which causes the iPhone to use its battery faster.

You can also use Fetch. With this option, iPhone periodically requests information from the MobileMe servers. At that point, the information is downloaded from the servers onto the iPhone and information changed on the iPhone is moved onto the MobileMe cloud. Synchronization can happen according to a schedule, or you can do it manually.

If you have more than one account configured on the iPhone, such as multiple MobileMe accounts or a MobileMe account and an Exchange account, you can use different options for each account.

To configure how MobileMe information moves onto the iPhone, do these steps:

1. **On the Home screen, press Settings.**

2. **Press Fetch New Data.** To use Push, ensure that its status is ON (if it is OFF, press OFF to turn Push on). To use Fetch only, ensure that the Push status is OFF (if it is ON, press ON to turn Push off). See figure 2.14.

3. **Select a schedule for information to be fetched.** For example, select Every 15 minutes, Every 30 minutes, or Hourly if you want information retrieved at those intervals automatically; or to retrieve information only when you want it, press Manually.

4. **Scroll down the screen, and press Advanced.** You see the list of accounts that are active on the iPhone, as shown in figure 2.15. Under the account, you see the kind of information being provided.

   For MobileMe accounts, you see one listing for Contacts, Calendars, and Bookmarks (you only see the services whose status is ON) and another for Mail; you can configure the two groups separately. For each kind of information, you see how that information is being moved onto your iPhone, such as Push or Fetch.

5. **Press the account and services you want to configure.** You move to the Select Schedule screen.

6. **Press Push to use Push, or press Manual to use the Fetch schedule.**

7. **Press Advanced.** You move back to the list of accounts.

8. **Repeat Steps 5 through 7 until you've configured all the accounts.**

9. **Press Fetch New Data.** The MobileMe information is moved onto the iPhone according to the settings you selected.

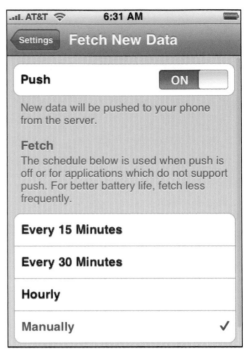

2.14 The Fetch New Data screen contains the settings that determine how information is moved from MobileMe onto the iPhone.

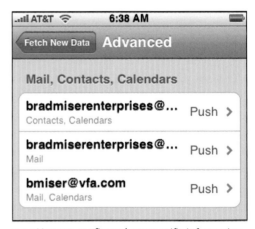

2.15 You can configure how specific information from a MobileMe account, such as email, is delivered to the iPhone.

Note Even if you enable Push, you should choose a Fetch schedule because not all accounts support Push. When Push services aren't available, information is retrieved according to the Fetch option you select.

Touring the MobileMe Web Site

The MobileMe Web site is useful for two main functions: managing your MobileMe accounts (covered in the next section) and using the MobileMe Web applications (covered in later chapters). Both of these require accessing your MobileMe Web site. To access your MobileMe Web site, go to www.me.com and log in using your MobileMe member name and password. You move into your MobileMe Web site, as shown in figure 2.16.

MobileMe toolbar   Application window

Selected application (Mail)   Selected application's toolbar   Logout command

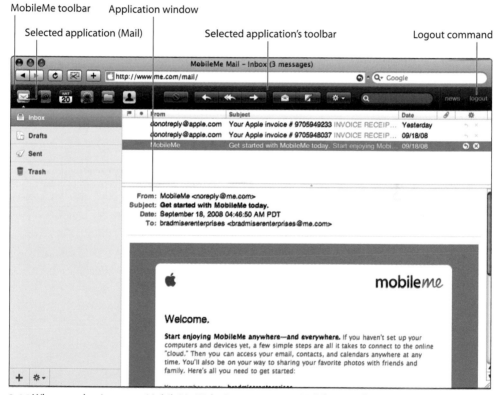

2.16 When you log into your MobileMe Web site, you can use MobileMe Web applications.

Your MobileMe Web site includes the following applications, whose icons appear from left to right in the MobileMe toolbar:

- **Mail.** You use the Mail application to work with email using a Web browser, as explained in Chapter 7. You also configure MobileMe email in email applications (Chapter 3) and, of course, use MobileMe email on an iPhone (see the preceding section).

- **Contacts.** The Contacts application provides information and tools for your contacts. It's explained in Chapter 8.

- **Calendars.** We all need to manage our time, and the MobileMe Calendars application enables you to create and manage your calendars from the Web site. See Chapter 9 for more information.

- **Gallery.** Using the Gallery application, you can publish Web galleries of photos, and other people can view and download photos your post there. You can even allow other people to post photos to your gallery. The Gallery is covered in Appendix A.

- **iDisk.** The iDisk application enables you to work with your online disk space. That's covered in Chapter 4.

- **Account.** The Account application is what you use to manage your MobileMe accounts. See the next section for details.

When you select an application by clicking its icon, you see the application's tools on its toolbar. The window changes to become the application's window. Each application has its own window. For example, when you click the Mail button, you see the Mail application window that has the mailboxes pane on the left side, the messages list in the top part of the right pane, and the reading pane on the lower-right part of the window.

If you use a computer in a secure location, you can remain logged into your MobileMe account for up to two weeks. You even stay logged in if you move away from your MobileMe Web site or quit the browser. Of course, this works only if you selected this option when you logged in. When you return to me.com, you move back into your site automatically. (If more than two weeks has passed since you logged in, you need to log in again. You also may need to log in again if you shut down your computer or clear the Web browser's history or cache.)

To log out of your MobileMe Web site, click the Logout command. You move back to the Login window.

Note If you remain logged in, MobileMe continues to work most of the time. At the time I was writing this book, the login behavior was somewhat inconsistent. Occasionally when you move back to me.com, you may have to log in again even though you selected the check box to remain logged in. This is likely a bug that I hope will be resolved by the time you are reading this.

Managing MobileMe Accounts

As you work with MobileMe, you may need to change your account. For example, you may want to upgrade your disk space. If you have a Family Pack account, you'll also want to manage its Family Member accounts. For example, when you hire a new team member, you might want to add a Family Member account to provide him with email, an iDisk, and other MobileMe services. You perform all these account activities using the Account application.

Depending on the kind of account, you see different options when you use the Account application. For example, when you manage a Family Pack account, you have tools available that enable you to manage the Family Member accounts.

Note The Account application is an exception to the "remain logged in" setting. When you use this application, you are automatically logged out after 15 minutes of inactivity.

Accessing the Account application

The first part of any account management task is to access the Account application. Log into the me.com Web site, and click the Account button. If prompted to do so, enter your MobileMe password again. You can now move Into the Account application.

Genius You can move to the MobileMe Web site to manage an account from the MobileMe pane of the System Preferences application (Mac) or MobileMe control panel (Windows) by clicking the Account Details button.

Viewing Summary Information

The Summary Information area provides an overview of the account. Access it by clicking the Summary option in the left pane of the Account window. The information you see here includes the following, as shown in figure 2.17:

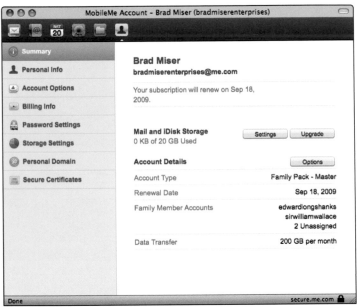

2.17 The Summary Information for an account includes when the account will renew and the amount of disk space it has.

- **Identification.** At the top of the screen, you see the name associated with the account and its email address.

- **Renewal date.** MobileMe accounts are set to renew at the end of each year by default (you can change this if you want). The date on which the account renews next is shown just under the member name. The renewal date for Family Member accounts is one year from the date those accounts were created. If the Family Pack account isn't renewed before that date, the Family Member account becomes inactive when the Family Pack expires regardless of its renewal date.

- **Disk space allocation.** The Mail and iDisk Storage area shows how much online disk space is being used and shows controls to relocate or upgrade disk space. You'll read more on this later.

● **Account Details.** In this section, which isn't labeled when you are working with a Family Member account, you see the type of account (Individual, Free Trial, Family Pack – Master, or Family Pack – Member). You also see the renewal date and the amount of data transfer allowed per month. When you are viewing a master account for a Family Pack, you see the member names of the configured Family Member accounts and the number of unassigned accounts.

Genius

The buttons you see in the Summary Information take you to other areas within the Account application. For example, clicking Options moves you to the Account Options section.

Managing Personal Information

When you select the Personal Information option, you see the following, as shown in figure 2.18:

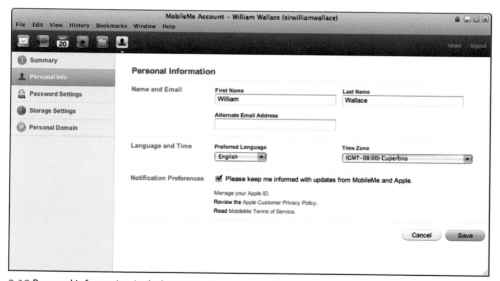

2.18 Personal Information includes name, alternate email address, and time zone.

● **Name.** You can change the name associated with the account.

● **Alternate Email Address.** Apple uses this address to contact you if MobileMe email is unavailable.

- **Preferred Language.** Use this pop-up menu to choose the language you want the MobileMe Web site to use for your account. The selection of languages is limited to those supported by MobileMe and your computer.

- **Time Zone.** Use this pop-up menu to select the time zone. This setting primarily impacts email. (The time zone used by the Calendar is controlled by the time zone preference you set in the Calendar application, as you see in Chapter 9.)

- **Notification Preferences.** If you select the check box, you'll receive emails from Apple, either Apple marketing information or useful notifications about MobileMe services. The Manage your Apple ID link takes you to the My Info Web site where you can change information about your account, such as phone numbers, addresses, and such. The Apple Customer Privacy Policy and MobileMe Terms of Service links take you to fascinating legal documents that you should take the time to understand, but if you are like me, probably don't.

Setting Account Options

In the Account Options area, you can perform two basic tasks: add to the disk space available to your account, or add or remove Family Member accounts (for a Family Pack account).

Note Account Options are not available for Family Member accounts. That's because the Family Member accounts are managed by the Family Pack account under which they were created. Changes to these aspects of a Family Member account must be made from their parent Family Pack account.

Adding disk space to your account

If you have an Individual account, you have two upgrade options: to add disk space and data transfer or to convert the account into a Family Pack (explained earlier in this chapter). If you have a Family Pack account, you can upgrade to increase the amount of disk space available. To add disk space to an account, perform the following steps:

1. **Go to the Account application.**

2. **Click Account Options.** You see the current disk space for the account and any upgrades that have been applied. If you are using a Family Pack Master account, you also see the Family Member accounts being managed under your account.

3. **To add disk space to an Individual account or a Family Pack, click Upgrade (Individual account) or Add Upgrades (Family Pack).** You see the Upgrade sheet, shown in figure 2.19. You see the upgrades available for the account. For example, if you have not upgraded disk space before, you have 40GB and 60GB options. The prices you see are prorated: For example, if you've had the account for six months, the fee will be half the annual fee.

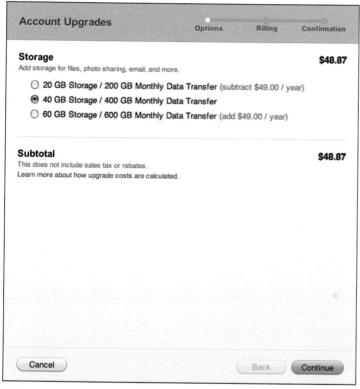

2.19 Because this is a Family Pack account, only the disk upgrade options appear on the Upgrade sheet.

4. **Select the upgrades you want to apply to the account, and click Continue.** The Billing Information sheet appears.

5. **To use the same credit card you associated with your account originally, leave the Use my existing credit card radio button selected; to use a different card, select the Use a new credit card radio button and provide the relevant information.**

6. **Click Continue.** You see the selections you made on the Confirm Your Selections sheet.

7. **If the information on the confirmation sheet is correct, click Upgrade; if not, click Cancel to stop the process or Back to go to previous screens to correct information.** After you click the Upgrade button, you upgrade is processed. When that is complete, you see the Upgrade complete sheet.

8. **Click OK.** The sheet closes, and you return to the Account Options screen. It shows the upgrades applied to your account. If you upgraded disk space, the additional space is available to you immediately, and you see the new disk space totals on several screens in the Account application.

Removing Family Member accounts

You can have up to four Family Member accounts under a Family Pack account, and you can add or remove accounts as you see fit. To be reminded of how to add a Family Member account, see the section on creating Family Member accounts earlier in this chapter.

To remove a Family Member account, do the following:

1. **Go to the Account application.**

2. **Click Account Options.** You also see the Family Member accounts being managed under your account in the Family Pack section, shown in figure 2.20.

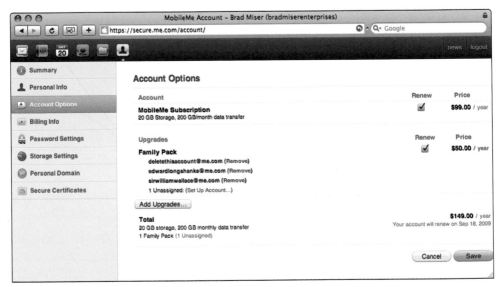

2.20 You can add or remove Family Member accounts as you need to.

3. **Click the Remove link for the account you want to delete.** You see a warning prompt.

4. **Click Delete.** The account is removed, and another account becomes available for you to assign.

Caution When you remove an account, all the information for that account stored on MobileMe servers, including email and files on the iDisk, are deleted. Make sure you've saved any information you want to keep on your computer's hard disk before removing an account.

Upgrading a Family Member Account

You can't upgrade a Family Member account to an Individual account using the Account application. To upgrade a Family Member account to become an Individual account, follow these steps:

1. **Click the Contact Support link in the upper-right corner of the Summary screen while logged in under the Family Member account.**

2. **Click the appropriate country.** The MobileMe Support page appears.

3. **Click Account & Billing, and then click Converting & Upgrading Accounts.**

4. **Click the Upgrading an email-only or Family Member account to a full MobileMe subscription account link.**

5. **Click the MobileMe Upgrade page link.**

6. **Enter the account's password, and click Continue.** The Reactivation or Upgrade screen appears where the account's information is already entered.

7. **Follow the onscreen instructions to upgrade the account.** When that is complete, the account becomes an Individual account and is no longer counted against the Family Pack from which it came.

Managing billing information

The billing information associated with an account determines the credit card where any charges to the account are made including annual renewal or upgrade fees. To change this information, do the following:

1. **Go to the Account application.**

2. **Click Billing Information.** You see the current credit card information.

3. **Make changes to the information as needed, such as configuring a different credit card.**

4. **Click Save.** The next time charges are accrued to your account, the new credit card will be used.

Note

Because all charges are made to the master account for a Family Pack, Family Member accounts do not have Billing Information.

Changing passwords and security

You can use the Password Settings tools to change an account's password and security settings. Here's how:

1. **Go to the Account application.**

2. **Click Password Settings, and enter the account's current information in the Current Password field.** (You may wonder why this is required because the password is already required to get to this screen, but I guess we can't type our passwords too many times!)

3. **Enter the new password in the Enter New Password and Confirm New Password fields.**

4. **Use the Date of Birth pop-up menus to change the birth date associated with the account if necessary.**

5. **To change the security question and answer for the account, change the information in the Secret Question and Answer fields.**

6. **Click Save.** The changes take effect immediately.

The next time you log into the account, you must use the new password.

Allocating disk space

The disk space associated with any kind of MobileMe is shared between email and iDisk. In most cases, you'll want more space allocated to your iDisk so you can store as many files and other information there as possible. However, if an account is primarily used for email, you may want to have more disk space allocated for email storage. Adjusting the space allocations is simple:

1. **Go to the Account application.**

2. **Click Storage Settings.** You see the current disk space allocations.

3. **Choose the amount of space that should be allocated to email on the pop-up menu shown in figure 2.21.** The options you see on this menu depend on the size of the disk available. For example, for a 20GB, the smallest amount of email space is 30MB (which is quite a bit if you get into the habit of copying email you want to save onto your computer). Your options also depend on the amount of disk space being used. For example, if you are using 10GB on an iDisk, you can't allocate less than 10GB to the iDisk. You would have to remove files from the iDisk to set its allocation to be less than 10GB.

4. **Click Save.** The space is reallocated, and new allocations appear on the screen.

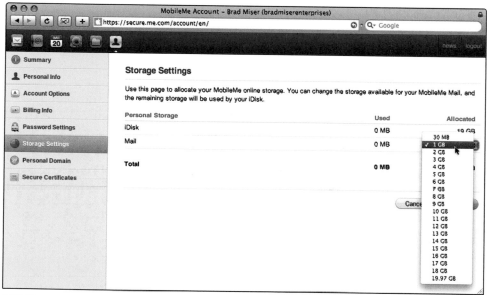

2.21 If you save email you want to keep on your computer, you don't need a very large allocation of disk space for it.

Note

The Personal Domain setting enables you to associate a registered URL to your MobileMe Web site. Instead of using the default URL of MobileMe, you can use the URL you register to customize the URL for your site. This option is explained in Chapter 6.

Revoking secure certificates

When you use iChat for encrypted chats and when you use the Back to My Mac feature, a certificate ensures that the communication to your computer is safe. This certificate is used to encrypt and decrypt information that moves to and from your computer. Most of the time, this process happens in the background and you don't need to think about it. However, if your computer is ever stolen or you believe someone has gained access your MobileMe account, you should revoke the secure certificates.

1. **Go to the Account application.**

2. **Click Secure Certificates to see the certificates that have been created for your account.** The top certificate in each section is the active one. Below that is a list of all previous certificates, which have the Revoked status.

3. **Click Revoke Certificate.** You are prompted about revoking the certificate.

4. **Click Revoke Certificate.** The certificate is revoked and will no longer be used.

If you want to use an encrypted service, such as chatting, again, you use the associated application to re-create the certificate on each computer that uses the certificate.

Caution If your MobileMe account's security is ever compromised, immediately change your account's password and security information to prevent other people from using your MobileMe account.

Forgot Your Password?

It's inevitable: You or a Family Member account user will forget the password associated with a MobileMe account. All is not lost, however. To recover the password, click the Forgot password? link on the me.com Login dialog box. You move to the My Info: Password Retrieval screen. Enter the email address associated with the MobileMe account, and click Continue. You are presented with two options. If you have access to the email account, click the Send email button to have a password reset link email to you. Or you can click the Answer Question button, at which point you have to correctly answer the account's security question to reset the password.

Stopping MobileMe

I don't expect many people reading this book to need this section. You are probably going to like MobileMe so much that you'll use it indefinitely. However, if you want to cancel MobileMe at some point, you have two options.

You can cancel a MobileMe account before the trial period ends. If you do this, you'll be charged nothing for the time you used the account. To cancel a trial account, go to its Account Options screen and click Cancel Account.

Genius

After you've canceled an account, it becomes inactive. You can start using it again by performing the steps to create a new account, except that you choose the Reactivate an account option. This enables you to resume using the email address that was associated with an expired or canceled account.

If you are past the free trial period, you can cancel the account and receive a prorated refund, but you have to contact MobileMe support to have the account canceled. To do this, go to www.apple.com/support/mobileme.

Genius

Accounts renew automatically every year. If you don't want an account to renew automatically, go to its Account Options screen and deselect the Renew check boxes for the parts of the account you don't want to renew automatically. When the end of the current period comes, you'll be warned that the account will become inactive prior to the end time. If you let the account expire, you'll no longer be able to access it. However, you can renew the account to regain access to its email address. When the account becomes inactive, all emails and iDisk contents are lost.

To unregister MobileMe on a computer, perform these steps:

1. **On a Mac, open the MobileMe pane of the System Preferences application; on a Windows PC, open the MobileMe control panel.**

2. **Click the Account tab, and click Sign Out.** The account is logged off the computer, and you lose desktop access to its resources. The MobileMe pane or control panel returns to the single tab configuration.

3. **To log into the same or a different MobileMe account, enter the member name and password, and then click Sign In.**

How Can I Synchronize Information Using MobileMe?

MobileMe provides the cloud — a central Internet location where you can store information. Any device or application synchronized with the cloud stores information on itself and on the cloud. Macintosh computers, Windows PCs, iPhones, and the MobileMe Web applications can all be synchronized with the cloud. Changes to information in one place are automatically made in all the other places that are in sync. You can access the information you need no matter where you are and what device you are using.

Using MobileMe to Synchronize Macs

When you use more than one Mac or a combination of devices, such as a Mac and an iPhone, keeping information in sync makes your working time more effective and makes your working location more flexible. Suppose you add a contact to the Address Book application while working on a desktop Mac. When that Mac is synchronized, the contact you added is copied to the MobileMe cloud, where it immediately becomes available in the MobileMe Contacts application available on your .me Web site. If you have another computer, such as a MacBook Air, that computer also is synchronized, and that contact is copied to the Address Book application on it as well. Likewise, the contact appears on your iPhone, which you can use to make a call to close the next big deal.

However, contacts are just one kind of information you can keep synchronized between multiple Macs with MobileMe. You can keep all this information in sync:

- Bookmarks
- Calendars
- Contacts
- Dashboard widgets
- Dock items
- Keychains
- Mail accounts
- Mail rules, signatures, and smart mailboxes
- Notes
- Preferences

You can sync a subset of this information with Windows PCs and iPhones. That subset includes the most important information, including email, contacts, calendars, and bookmarks.

In addition to selecting the information you want to sync, you can choose the direction in which information is synced, such as from MobileMe to a computer, from a computer to MobileMe, or in both directions.

Before setting up MobileMe synchronization on a Mac, you should configure the information that is to be synchronized. Because this book is focused on the tools you use for small business, the following sections explain how to configure email, contacts, calendars, and bookmarks; the full list of information you can sync for Macs is a bit larger.

After you are managing this information on a Mac, you can configure it to keep that information synchronized with the MobileMe cloud.

Configuring MobileMe email accounts in Mail

Mail is Mac OS X's default email application. Because support for MobileMe email is built into Mail, configuring a MobileMe email account is very simple:

1. **Launch Mail.**

Note

> If you use a different email application, such as Microsoft Entourage, you can still configure it to use a MobileMe email account, but the steps and details are a bit different. To get those details, refer to the application's help system for information needed to configure the application with an IMAP account.

2. **Select Mail ⇨ Preferences.** The Mail Preferences dialog box appears.

3. **Click the Accounts tab.** You see the Accounts pane. In the list on the left side of the pane, you see the accounts that are currently configured. When you select an account on this list, the tools you use to work with the account are shown in the right part of the pane.

4. **Click the Add button (+) located at the bottom of the account list.** The Add Account sheet appears, as shown in figure 3.1.

3.1 Because support for MobileMe email accounts is built into the Mail application, configuring an account is simple.

5. **Enter your name in the Full Name field.** This name is shown as the From name on your email; you should input the same name you used when you created your MobileMe account. This way, the From address is the same whether you use Mail or another application to send email.

6. **Enter *membername*@me.com, where *membername* is your MobileMe member name, in the Email Address field and your MobileMe password in the Password field.**

7. **Select the Automatically set up account check box.**

8. **Click Create.** Your account information is checked as Mail logs into the account. If what you entered contains any errors, you see an error message; you must correct the MobileMe account information and try again. When Mail is able to configure the account, you return to the Accounts tab and you see the MobileMe account on the list of accounts.

The email account is ready to use as is. However, you should do some additional configuration of the account to determine where email is stored so that you maximize your use of online disk space. To do so, perform the following steps:

1. **With the MobileMe account you just created, click the Account Information tab.**

2. **Enter a description of the account in the Description field.** The default is MobileMe, but you should input something unique to be able to identify the account on the list of accounts and in other locations. The rest of this information is automatically filled in by Mail and can be left as is.

3. **Click the Mailbox Behaviors tab.** This tab controls where various messages are stored. It is an important part of managing your online disk space. Use it to prevent saving emails there that don't need to be.

4. **Select the Store draft messages on the server check box if you want messages on which you are working to be stored on the MobileMe server.** If you work on email from different Macs, you can access the drafts from any of them that have the same MobileMe email account configured in Mail. If you deselect this box, you can work on draft messages only while using the Mac on which the messages were originally composed.

5. **Select the Store notes in Inbox folder check box if you want notes created in Mail to be stored in the Inbox in addition to the Reminders section of the Mail Inbox.**

Note Notes are free-form text items that you can create to record snippets of text. You can transform notes into email messages or To Do items. You can create notes using the commands on Mail's File menu and work with them similarly to email messages.

6. **Select the Store sent messages on the server check box to store sent messages on the MobileMe server.** Generally, I recommend that you leave this option unselected so you don't use your allocated MobileMe storage space for sent messages. But if you want to be able to access your sent messages from multiple Macs, you might want to store them on the MobileMe server. Another benefit of keeping the email on the MobileMe server is that it provides a secure backup of your email, which can be very valuable for a small business.

7. **On the Delete sent messages when pop-up menu, choose the time at which you want sent messages to be deleted.** Your options are Never, One day old, One week old, One month old, or Quitting Mail. To keep track of business communications sent over email, delete sent messages no more frequently than one month old. If you leave your sent messages on the MobileMe server, you don't want to choose the Never option because that can use lots of server storage space. If you store sent messages on a computer, it's okay to choose Never because of the large size of a Mac's hard disk.

8. **Select the Store junk messages on the server check box if you want messages that Mail identifies as spam to be stored on the server.** Because this is usually a waste of disk space, I recommend you deselect this box. Wasting disk space on a local hard drive is less of a problem than using your online disk space because you have more of that space available.

9. **On the Delete junk messages when pop-up menu, choose how often you want junk messages to be deleted.** If you have junk messages on the MobileMe server, choose more frequent deletion to save server space.

Genius

If you use Mail's Junk mail tool, you should periodically review the Junk mail folder. The Junk tool isn't 100 percent reliable and might classify some clients' or business associates' messages as junk. Check the Junk folder regularly to make sure you don't miss an important message. Remember to check more frequently than the delete setting in step 9 so you review all Junk messages before Mail deletes them.

10. **Select the Move deleted messages to the Trash mailbox check box if you want messages that you delete to be moved into that folder in your Inbox instead of being deleted immediately.** I recommend that you enable this option just in case you are too fast on the Delete button for your own good.

11. **Select the Store deleted messages on the server check box if you want deleted messages to remain on the server.** I recommend that you don't do this to avoid using valuable server space. This means you can only access deleted messages on the Mac you deleted them on.

12. **On the Permanently erase deleted messages when pop-up menu, choose how often you want to erase messages stored in the trash folder.** The options are Never, One day old, One week old, One month old, or Quitting Mail. I prefer the Quitting Mail option so I don't use much space for deleted messages, but deleted messages do exist for a period of time because I don't quit Mail very often. Most of the others work too, but the Never option prevents you from using disk space on unneeded messages.

13. **Review your configured settings, and make sure they are what you want, as shown in figure 3.2.**

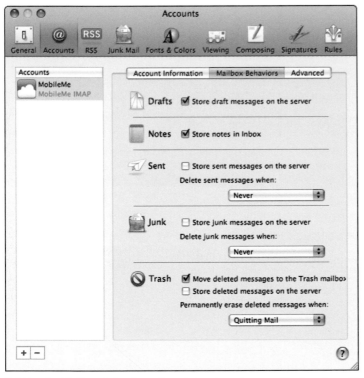

3.2 Use the Mailbox Behaviors tab to determine where and for how long Mail stores various kinds of email.

The last settings you should configure for the email account are on the Advanced tab:

1. **Select the Advanced tab.**

2. **If you ever want to make the account inactive, deselect the Enable this account check box.** The account remains configured, but it isn't checked for new messages, and you can't send messages from it. You can re-enable the account by selecting this box again.

3. **If you want to check for new mail in the account only manually, deselect the Include when automatically checking for new mail check box.** When this box is selected, new email is received according to the schedule you set for Mail to check for new mail.

4. **Use the Keep copies of messages for offline viewing pop-up menu to choose where messages are stored. This way, you can access those messages when you aren't connected to the Internet.** Choosing the All messages and their attachments option or the All messages but omit attachments option places a copy of each message on your Mac. The Only messages I've read option moves read messages onto your Mac. The Don't keep copies of any messages option leaves all messages on the server unless you specifically move them to a folder on your Mac.

5. **Close the Mail Preferences dialog box.**

Note

The settings at the bottom of the Advanced pane are for advanced settings that can be useful for other kinds of email accounts you are managing in Mail. You aren't likely to ever use them when you are working with MobileMe email.

6. **Click Save at the prompt.** The changes you made are saved, and the account starts behaving accordingly. You are ready to use the MobileMe email account in the Mail application.

Genius

After you have configured the MobileMe account on one Mac, include Mail Accounts in the MobileMe synchronization options and sync your other Macs to configure the same email account on those computers. See the section on configuring MobileMe Synchronization on a Mac later in this chapter for details on configuring syncs.

Creating and managing contacts in Address Book

Address Book is Mac OS X's default contact manager application. You can use it for all your contacts, and it includes tools that help you organize and work with your contacts effectively, which is extremely important for a small business. Of course, you also can synchronize the contacts in Address Book with MobileMe so your contact information is available on all your devices.

Address Book uses the concept of an address card, similar to the cards used in the old Rolodex days. Of course, in Address Book, the address cards are digital and are called Virtual Cards, or *vCards*. You can share Address Book vCards with all contact manager applications and add vCards from other applications to Address Book.

You create and manage contact information in Address Book the same way regardless of whether you keep that information synced with MobileMe. This isn't a chapter, or even a book, on how to use Address Book, but you should create at least a couple of contacts in Address Book if for no other reason than to test synchronization with MobileMe. So here are some instructions that will help you create contact information in case you haven't used Address Book before:

1. **Open the Address Book application.** Figure 3.3 shows the Address Book window with three panes. The Group pane shows default collections of contacts and the groups that have been created to organize contact information. For example, All contains all the information managed in the application. Last Import contains the information you most recently imported. To work with contacts, you first select the appropriate group. The Name pane then shows the address cards (vCards) in the selected group. When you select a card shown in the Name pane, the Card pane shows the details for the selected card.

2. **Click the Add button (+) at the bottom of the Name column.** A new, empty card based on the template appears in the Card pane.

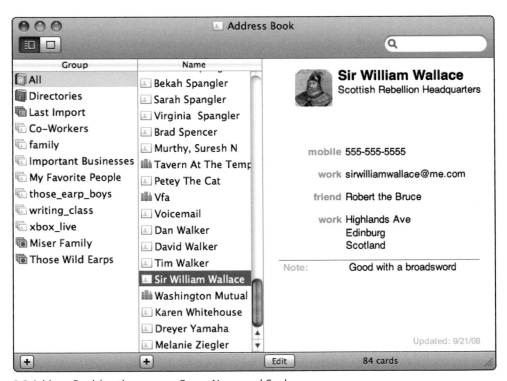

3.3 Address Book has three panes: Group, Name, and Card.

3. **Enter the contact's first and last name in the appropriate fields.** You can press Tab to maneuver between them. If the card is for a company, select the Company check box and enter the company name; first and last name information is optional for companies.

4. **Enter the contact's company in the Company field.**

5. **Click the pop-up menu next to the first field (work by default), select the type of contact information you want to enter, and enter it.** For example, to enter a work phone number, choose work.

Note

When you select a data type, Address Book automatically creates a field of the appropriate format, such as for phone numbers when you select mobile.

6. **Repeat step 5 to create and enter information into each field you want to complete.**

7. **Click the Remove button (the dash with a red circle) next to a field name if you want to remove it from the card.** You can remove fields that don't apply to better tailor the card to the contact.

8. **Click the Add button (the green circle containing the +) to add another field of the same type to a card.** Note that the Add button appears only when you've filled in all the empty fields of a specific type, such as email addresses. A new field appears, and you can select its type and enter the appropriate information.

Genius

If the information you want to enter isn't available on the pop-up menu, open it and choose Custom. Type the label for the field you want to add, and click OK. You return to the card, and the custom label appears on the card. Enter the information for that field. The custom field is added to the card.

9. **Add text for the contact in the Note field.**

10. **Add an image to the card using one of the following options:**

    - Drag an image file from the desktop, and drop it onto the Image well located immediately to the left of the name. The Image sheet appears.

    - Double-click the Image well located immediately to the left of the name, and the Image sheet appears. Click the Choose button, and use the resulting Open dialog box to move to and open a file.

- Double-click the Image well located immediately to the left of the name, and the Image sheet appears. Position the Mac's iSight camera on a subject you want to use for the contact's image. Click the Camera icon; after three seconds, the image is captured.

11. **Adjust the image, as shown in figure 3.4, by doing either of the following:**

    - Click and drag the slider to the left or right to adjust the image size.

    - Click and drag the image around in the image box until the part of the image you want displayed is contained in the box.

12. **Click Set.** You return to the card, and the image is stored on the card.

13. **Click the Edit button.** The card is created. Only fields containing information are shown, as indicated in figure 3.5.

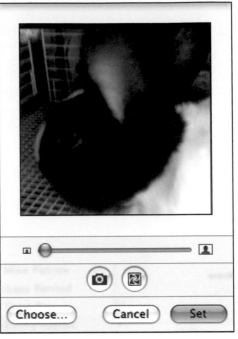

3.4 You can configure images for contacts. These images appear when you receive email from the contact or calls from the contact on an iPhone.

Genius To apply special effects to an image you capture with a Mac's iSight camera or to an image you import, click the Effects button located to the right of the Camera button. Select the effect you want to apply to the image.

Creating and managing calendars in iCal

With iCal, you can manage your own time, which is critical to effectively managing your business, by creating calendars that help you be where you're supposed to be when you're supposed to be there. You also can use To Do items to track important tasks. iCal is very useful as a personal calendar tool. If it could do only that, it would be worth using. However, iCal is designed for calendar collaboration. You can publish calendars for others to view in iCal that they have running on their Macs. You also can enable people who don't use iCal to access your calendars via the Web. And you can subscribe to other people's calendars. Because you can sync your iCal calendars with MobileMe, you can access them at any time from different computers and from an iPhone.

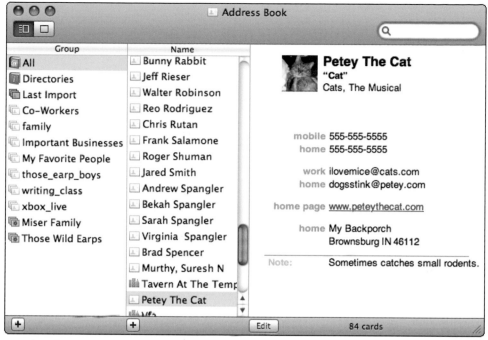

3.5 When the new card has been saved, the Edit button is black (when the card is in Edit more, the button is blue).

Creating calendars

When you use iCal, you deal with two levels of calendars. First is the overall calendar, which is what you see inside the iCal window. This calendar includes all the information managed or shown by the application. On the second level are the individual calendars on which you create events and To Do items. There are many good reasons to create multiple calendars for your events and To Do items. An obvious example is one calendar for business events and one calendar for personal events. However, when creating calendars, also consider publishing your calendars. If you don't want to show some events in a published version, you can create a calendar for those events that you don't publish and another for those that you want to share.

On the other hand, you don't need to create so many calendars that they become unwieldy. In most situations, one to three calendars are ideal.

To create a calendar, take on the following tasks:

1. **Click the New Calendar button (+) located in the bottom-left corner of the iCal window.** A new, untitled calendar appears in the CALENDARS section of the iCal window.

2. **Enter a name for the new calendar and press Return.** The name is especially important if you are going to share the calendar with others, so they will recognize it in their iCal.

3. **With the new calendar highlighted, choose File ⇨ Get Info.** The Info sheet appears, as shown in figure 3.6.

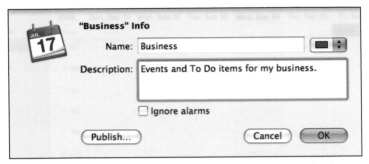

"Business" Info

Name: Business

Description: Events and To Do items for my business.

☐ Ignore alarms

Publish...   Cancel   OK

3.6 Use the Info sheet to configure the basic information for a calendar.

4. **Enter a description of the calendar in the Description field.**

5. **Use the Color pop-up menu to associate a color with the calendar.** When you add events to the calendar, they appear in the color your select. Having different colors for different calendars is useful when you simultaneously view multiple calendars.

6. **Select the Ignore alarms check box if you don't want alarms to be enabled for the new calendar.**

7. **Click OK.** The changes are saved, and the calendar's name appears in the color you selected.

To include a calendar's events and To Do items in the calendar displayed in the iCal window, select its check box. If you deselect a calendar's check box, its events and To Do items are hidden. You can select its check box to see its events and To Do items again.

Genius

To remove a calendar, select it and press Delete. The calendar, along with all its events and To Do items, is removed from iCal. Most of the time, you're better offer by hiding a calendar because it won't appear in iCal anymore, but you can access its information at any time. When you delete a calendar, all its information gets deleted too.

Creating events in a calendar

You use events to plan periods of time, for example, setting up meetings for you and your team. You can invite others to join the event by sending them an invitation. In addition to time and date, you can include other useful information in iCal events such as file attachments, URLs, and notes. To add an event to a calendar, perform the following steps:

1. **Select the calendar on which you want the event to appear by clicking it.** It becomes the active calendar and is highlighted in the CALENDARS section.

2. **Do one of the following tasks:**

   - On the mini-calendar, click the date you want the event to occur; it becomes highlighted In gray in the calendar window. Select File ⇨ New Event, or press ⌘+N. A new event appears on the calendar with its title selected. By default, the time of the event is the next hour on the calendar.

   - While hovering over the date and time you want the event to occur, open the contextual menu by right-clicking or Ctrl+clicking and select New Event. A new event appears on the calendar with its title selected. By default, the time of the event is the next hour on the calendar.

   - When you are viewing the Calendar in Day or Week view, place the pointer at the approximate time and date of the event, and press the mouse or trackpad button. Drag for the length of time of the event (as you drag, the end time is shown at the bottom of the event) and release the button. A new event appears on the calendar with its title selected.

   - When you are viewing the Calendar in Day or Week view, double-click on the calendar. A new event appears on the calendar with its title selected.

   - When you are viewing the Calendar in Month view, double-click on the calendar. A new event appears on the calendar, and its Edit sheet opens with the event's name ready to edlt. When you use this option, skip steps 4 and 5.

3. **Enter the name of the event and press Return.** The event name is saved, and it appears in the same color of the calendar with which it's associated. If you enable a default alarm (in the iCal Preferences dialog box) for events, that alarm is part of the event automatically. If that's all the information you want to include for the event, you're finished and can skip the remaining steps. But to fully configure an event, read on.

4. **Double-click the event.** Its summary window appears. Here, you see the name, the from and to dates and times, time zone, and alarm information.

5. **Click the Edit button.** The Edit sheet appears, as shown in figure 3.7.

6. **Enter information about the location of the event by clicking the word None next to the location label and entering a description of the event's location.**

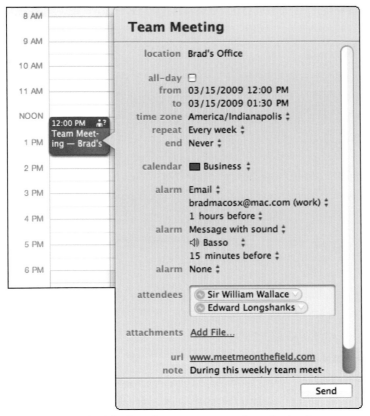

3.7 You can use the Edit sheet for an event to configure its details.

7. **Select the all-day check box if the event is an all-day event.** The duration of the event is marked for the 24-hour period in which it occurs. If it occurs over multiple days, the 24-hour periods are marked for each day. When you select this, time tools disappear because they don't apply.

8. **Use the from and to fields to set start and end dates and times for the event, and choose the time zone for the event on the time zone pop-up menu if it appears.** This associates the event with a specific time zone. As you change the overall time zone for iCal, the event's time information is shifted according to the time zone with which it is associated.

Note These steps assume iCal's time zone support (the Advanced tab of the iCal Preferences dialog box) feature is turned on. If not, just ignore any time zone information you read or see here.

9. **Determine if you want the event to repeat using the repeat pop-up menu.** The options are standard frequencies, such as Every day or Every week, or Custom. If the event repeats, use the end pop-up menu to choose an end date for the repeating event. This becomes the last date the repeating event occurs. Choose Never to repeat the event indefinitely, On date to set the end date, or After to set the end date after a specific date.

10. **Set the end date based on the option you selected in step 9.**

11. **Choose a different calendar on the calendar pop-up menu if you want to change the calendar with which the event is associated.**

12. **Use the alarm pop-up menu to set an alarm for the event.** If you have enabled default alarms for events, you see the default alarm configured already. Your options for the alarm are the following:

    ● None, which has no alarm.

    ● Message, which displays a text message.

    ● Message with sound, which displays a text message and plays a sound.

    ● Email, which causes an email to be sent to an address you select.

    ● Open file, which opens a file of your choice.

    ● Run Script, which causes a script you select to run.

    ● Previous alarms, which provides a list of alarms you used previously. This option appears only after you've selected one of the other options.

    If you select an alarm with sound, the sound pop-up menu appears. If you choose any type of alarm, a pop-up menu to set the alarm time appears. If you select Email, you see a pop-up menu for selecting which email address to send the alarm to. A new alarm pop-up menu also appears so you can set multiple alarms for the event.

13. **Set any additional options based on your choice in step 12.** If a sound is associated with the alarm, select the sound on the sound pop-up menu to change the default sound. If the alarm is sent through email, select the address to which the alarm will be sent on the email add pop-up menu.

Genius

The email addresses that appear on the alert pop-up menus for events or To Do items are those on your vCard in Address Book.

14. **Set the time for the alarm using the lowest pop-up menu in the alarm section.** The times you can choose are all relative to the event start time, such as hours before or minutes after. You also can click a date to set a specific time and date for the alarm. If you selected a relative time for the alarm, enter the number of hours, days, or minutes. If you selected a specific date, set it by entering the date and time the alarm should be issued.

15. **To add more alarms, repeat steps 12 through 14 for each alarm you want to add.**

Genius

To remove an alarm, open its pop-up menu and choose None.

16. **To add other people to the event, click Add Attendees.** A box for address information appears.

17. **Enter the name (if the person is in your Address Book) or email address of the person you want to add.** As you type, iCal tries to match what you type with information you've entered previously and with information in Address Book. When it finds a match, select it or continue typing to complete the attendee information. Press Return, or type a comma and repeat to enter more attendees.

Genius

To select people in your Address Book, select Window ➪ Address Panel. You can drag people from the Addresses window onto the attendees list. You can enter multiple attendees by dragging each onto the attendees field.

Genius

To remove or change an attendee's information, open the pop-up menu that shows his name or email address. Use the resulting pop-up menu to select the appropriate command, such as Remove Attendee to remove the person from the event.

18. **Click Add File to associate a file with the event.** Use the resulting Open dialog box to move to and select the file you want to attach. You can click Add File again to add additional files.

19. **If a URL is associated with the event, enter it in the URL field or copy and paste it there.**

20. **Enter any notes about the event in the note field.**

21. **If you added people to the attendees list, click Send; if the event is only for your calendar, click Done.** After you click Send, an email is created in your default email application and the event is attached to it. The people who receive these invitations can easily add the event to their own calendars by accepting them. After you click Done, changes you made to the event are saved.

You can open an event's Info window at any time by opening its contextual menu and selecting Get Info. If you want to change the event, click Edit. When you're finished, click Done. If you make any changes to an event that has attendees, you see the Update button. If you click this, the attendees receive an updated email.

Check out these tips for managing events you create:

Genius

To close an Info window without sending an update, select a different event or just click the iCal calendar. When you're ready to send the event, open it and click Send.

- You can change the calendar on which an event occurs by opening its contextual menu (Ctrl+click the event) and selecting the event's new calendar.

- You can change the date on which an event occurs by dragging it from one date in the calendar to another.

- As you configure events, icons appear at the top of the event on the calendar to indicate when an alarm has been set, whether the event is a repeating event, if people have been invited, and so on.

- You can email an event to others by opening its contextual menu and selecting Mail Event. The same action happens when you click the Send button for an event. The difference is that you can address the email that is created to anyone. When you use Send, the email is sent only to those people listed as attendees for the event. Your default email application opens, and the event is included as an attachment. The recipient can then drag+click the attachment, which has the extension .ics, onto iCal to add it to her calendar.

- When you use the Send command, as people add the event to their calendars, you see a green check next to their names in the event's Info window. This green check indicates that the attendee has accepted the event by adding it to his calendar. If an attendee hasn't added the event to his calendar, his name is marked with a question mark icon. This tracking doesn't occur when you use the Mail Event command.

You can duplicate an event by opening its contextual menu and selecting Duplicate, selecting Edit ⇨ Duplicate, or by pressing ⌘+D. You can drag the copy onto a different date.

- When you change an aspect of a repeating event, such as an alarm, you're prompted to make the change to all the events or only to the current one. If you choose only the current one, the current event is detached from the series and is no longer connected to the other instances of the same event. This is indicated by (detached event) being appended to the frequency shown in the repeat section for the event.

- Several of the data elements for events have contextual menus on the Info window to enable you to perform actions. For example, if you click the alarm element, you can add more alarms or remove an existing alarm. If you add a URL, you can use its contextual menu to visit that Web site.

Publishing calendars

One important part of managing time is to manage how your time interacts with other people's time. This is especially true in the context of a small business where you need to coordinate your activities with your team members, potential customers, current customers, and partners. Fortunately, iCal is designed to be a collaborative calendar tool. You can publish your calendars, and other iCal users can subscribe to them to see your calendar information in iCal on their computers. You also can share your calendars with Windows users or with Mac users who don't use iCal. Of course, you can subscribe to other people's calendars to add their information to your iCal window.

Being able to view other people's activities makes coordinating with them much easier. For example, if you need to meet with one of your team members, you can check her availability on her calendar in your iCal application before setting up the meeting. This saves the steps of sending emails or making a call to check on availability.

You can publish calendar information in two ways. The method you use depends on the people with whom your want to share your calendar. If everyone you want to share your calendar with uses iCal, you can use iCal's Publish tool to make your calendar easy to add to their iCal calendars. If you want to share your calendar with people who use Windows (or Mac users who don't use iCal), you can provide a URL to your calendar so they can view your calendar using a Web browser.

With your MobileMe account and iCal, publishing calendars for other people to view within their iCal application is simple, as demonstrated in the following steps:

1. **Select the calendar you want to publish.**

2. **Choose Calendar ⇨ Publish.** The Publish sheet appears, as shown in figure 3.8.

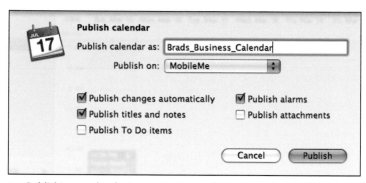

3.8 Publishing a calendar is a great way to share your calendar with other iCal users.

3. **Type the name of the calendar as you want it to appear to someone with whom you share it.** By default, the calendar's shared name is the same as its name in iCal, but you can change this if you want to.

Genius

It's a good idea to remove any spaces in the calendar's name because in the URL for a calendar, spaces are replaced by %20, making the URL cumbersome. If you don't want the words in the name to run together, use underscores instead of spaces.

4. **Select MobileMe from the Publish on pop-up menu.**

5. **Choose from several options for publishing in the Publish sheet:**

   - Publish changes automatically (this keeps your calendar –current automatically)

   - Publish titles and notes

   - Publish To Do items

   - Publish alarms

   - Publish attachments

6. **Click Publish.** When the calendar has been published, you see the confirmation dialog box, which provides the following:

   - The URL someone can use to subscribe to the calendar in iCal

   - The URL to view the calendar on the Web

   - The Visit Page button that takes you to the calendar on the Web

   - The Send Mail button that creates an email message you can send to iCal users to enable them to subscribe to your calendar

   - The OK button that closes the dialog box, as shown in figure 3.9

Calendar Published

Your Calendar "Business" has been published successfully, and can be subscribed at URL:

webcal://ical.me.com/bradmiserenterprises/
Brads_Business_Calendar.ics

or be viewed with a browser at URL:

http://ical.me.com/bradmiserenterprises/
Brads_Business_Calendar

Visit Page   Send Mail   OK

3.9 This dialog box confirms that the calendar has been published successfully and provides the information you or others need to access it.

Caution

One limitation of publishing a calendar via MobileMe is that you can't protect it with a password. Anyone who can access its URL can visit it.

Here are some additional points to consider when publishing your calendars:

- **When a calendar is published, the published icon (which looks like radiating waves) appears next to the calendar's name on the list of calendars.**

- **If you open a published calendar's contextual menu, you see several interesting commands.** These include Unpublish, which removes the calendar from the Web; Send Publish Email, which enables you to send an email announcing the published calendar and its URL; Copy URL to Clipboard, which copies the calendar's URL to the Clipboard so you can paste it into documents; Refresh, which publishes any changes you have made to the calendar; Refresh All, which updates all your published calendars; and Change Location, which enables you to move the calendar to a different site.

- **If you don't set a calendar so that changes are published automatically, you must refresh it to make changes visible to others.**

- **When you sync your calendars via MobileMe, you can view and manage them with a Web browser from the me.com Web site (see Chapter 9).**

- **You can change a published calendar by selecting it and selecting the Get Info command.** Use the tools in the calendar's Info sheet to make changes to the calendar's publishing and other settings.

- People who access your calendar, whether via subscribing to it in iCal or viewing it on the Web, can't make changes to it.

- **To share your calendar with people who don't use iCal, simply send them the URL to your calendar.** The easiest way to do this is to open the calendar's contextual menu and choose Send Publish Email. Your email application opens, and an email message containing the link to the calendar is created. Delete the subscription information, and then complete and send the email. The recipient can click the URL to visit your calendar on the Web; he can bookmark it to make it easy to return to any time he wants.

Genius

If all your team members are also iCal users, each person can publish his own calendar and subscribe to other team members' calendars. This is a great way for everyone involved in your business to know what's happening. iCal allows all team members' calendars to be viewed at the same time within the same window..

When people share their calendars with you through iCal Publishing tools, you can subscribe to those calendars to add them to your iCal window, as shown in figure 3.10:

1. **Open the email message containing the invitation, click the Subscribe link, and click Subscribe.** The Subscribing configuration sheet appears.

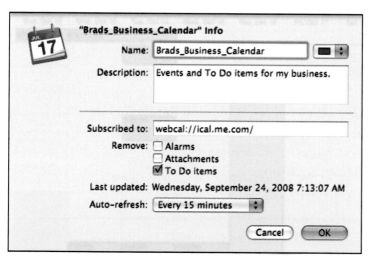

3.10 When you subscribe to a calendar, you can access it within your iCal window.

2. **Edit the title that you want to be used for the shared calendar in iCal.** The title can be the same as or different from the name that the person who is sharing the calendar entered.

3. **Choose a color for the calendar using the Color pop-up menu.**

4. **Edit the description of the calendar in the Description field.**

5. **Select the Remove alarms check box if you don't want the calendar's alarms to have any impact.**

6. **Select the Remove Attachments check box if you don't want the calendar's attachments included in your version.**

7. **Select the Remove To Do items check box if you don't want the calendar's To Do items to show up in your iCal window.** Display the To Do items on a calendar only if you are actually using them with that calendar.

8. **If you want the calendar's information to be refreshed automatically, choose the frequency at which you want the refresh to occur on the Auto-refresh pop-up menu.**

9. **Click OK.** The calendar is added to the SUBSCRIPTIONS section of your iCal window, and you can view it just like your own calendars. You can't make any changes to the calendar. If you try, you see an error message. If you configured the calendar to be refreshed automatically, iCal keeps it current.

Genius

If you don't set a calendar to be refreshed automatically, you can refresh it manually by opening its contextual menu and selecting Refresh.

Synchronizing Safari bookmarks on your Mac

Safari bookmarks enable you to move to locations on the Web easily, and you can set a bookmark for any location you want to return to later. You can include Safari bookmarks in your MobileMe synchronization so you can have the same set of bookmarks available to you no matter which computer you are running Safari on.

Note

In the current version of MobileMe, only Safari bookmarks are supported. If you use a different browser, you can't use MobileMe to keep your bookmarks in sync. You can move bookmarks from Firefox into Safari and then sync, but you have to then move those bookmarks from Safari into Firefox on each computer you use. Also, changes aren't moved automatically. To keep Firefox bookmarks in sync, see the section on syncing Firefox bookmarks later in this chapter.

To set a bookmark in Safari, perform the following steps:

1. **Open Safari.**

2. **Browse the Web until you hit a page that you want to bookmark.**

3. **Do one of the following:**

   - Select Bookmarks ⇨ Add Bookmark.

   - Press ⌘+D.

   - Click the Add Bookmark button (+), which is located just to the left of the Address field in the Safari toolbar.

     The bookmark sheet appears, as shown in figure 3.11.

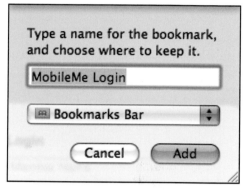

Type a name for the bookmark, and choose where to keep it.

MobileMe Login

📖 Bookmarks Bar

Cancel   Add

4. **Type a name for the bookmark.** The default name is the page's title. You can leave that as the bookmark's name or edit it.

3.11 Setting a bookmark makes any Web site just one click away.

5. **On the pop-up menu, choose one of the following locations to save the bookmark (the default location is the location where you most recently saved a bookmark):**

   - Bookmarks Bar, which puts the bookmark on the left end (the first position) of the Safari's Bookmarks bar that appears just below the Address bar

   - Bookmarks Menu, which makes the bookmark available on the Bookmarks menu

   - A folder that you've created one of Safari's default folders

6. **Click Add.** The sheet closes, and the bookmark is created in the location you selected.

Genius

Choose the location based on how often you'll access the Web site. If you visit the site frequently, place the bookmark on the Bookmarks bar or menu. If it's an occasional site for you, place it in a folder.

As you add bookmarks, you should keep them organized to make using them more efficient. You can use Safari's Bookmarks tools to create and manage folders in which you can store your bookmarks on the Bookmarks bar, the Bookmarks menu, and in the Bookmarks window. Along with any bookmarks you've created, how you have your bookmarks organized is also part of syncing with MobileMe so you have the same bookmarks organized in the same way on each device.

To manage Safari's bookmarks, open the Bookmarks window by clicking the Bookmarks button at the left end of the Bookmarks bar, by selecting Bookmarks ⇨ Show All Bookmarks, or by pressing Option+⌘+B. The Bookmarks window replaces the contents of the page you were browsing, as shown in figure 3.12.

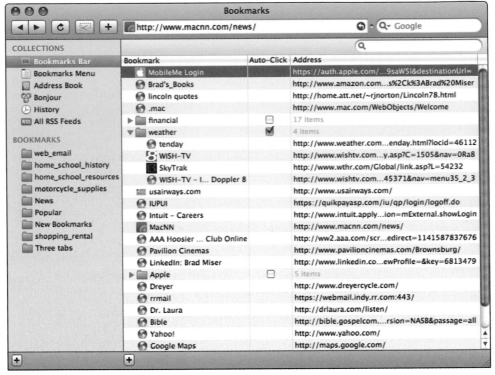

3.12 Safari's Bookmarks page enables you to organize your bookmarks.

In the left pane of the window are two groups of bookmarks: collections and bookmarks.

At the top of the pane is the COLLECTIONS section. Collections are special groups of bookmarks you can work with. The Bookmarks Bar and Bookmarks Menu collections contain the bookmarks in those areas. Under those are the Address Book and Bonjour collections (if they include preferences that are enabled). Below those is the History collection that contains a list of sites you have visited. At the bottom of the Collections section is the All RSS Feeds collection that contains all your RSS feeds.

In the lower part of the left pane is the BOOKMARKS section, which shows folders of bookmarks. Safari includes several folders containing bookmarks by default. You can change these folders or add your own folders and bookmarks.

To view the contents of a collection or folder, select it. The bookmarks it contains are shown in the right pane. For each bookmark, its name and address are shown. If an item in the collection is a folder, you see the folder along with its expansion triangle. Click this triangle to expand the folder's contents to see its bookmarks.

To create a new folder and add bookmarks to it, follow these steps:

1. **Click the Add button (+) located at the bottom of the left pane of the window.** A new untitled folder appears. Name that folder.

2. **Select a location containing bookmarks you want to move into the folder.** For example, if the bookmark is on the Bookmarks menu, select that option in the COLLECTIONS section; the bookmarks it contains appear in the right pane.

3. **Drag the bookmark from its current location onto the new folder; when that folder is highlighted in blue, release the mouse button.** The bookmark is placed into the folder.

4. **Select the folder you created.** The bookmarks you placed in it appear on the list in the right pane.

5. **Click the Add button (+) at the bottom of the right pane to create a folder within the selected folder.** A new, nested folder appears that you should name.

6. **Drag bookmarks onto the nested folder to place them in it; when the folder is highlighted, release the button to place the bookmark in the folder.**

7. **Drag bookmarks and folders up and down in the folder to change the order in which they appear within the parent and nested folders.**

Adding a folder is just one way to organize your bookmarks. Check out the following techniques:

- Add the bookmarks you use most frequently to the Bookmarks bar or Bookmarks menu by dragging them onto the relevant icons. Drag folders of bookmarks onto these icons to add them to the bar or menu. The folders are hierarchical so you can drill down into the bookmarks they contain from either location.

- Organize the contents of the Bookmarks bar or Bookmarks menu just like other locations. For example, if you drag a bookmark to the top of the Bookmarks Menu list, that bookmark appears at the top of the Bookmarks menu. Place the bookmarks you use most frequently at the top of the Bookmarks menu to make selecting them easier and faster.

- Rename a collection, folder, or bookmark by selecting it, opening its contextual menu (Ctrl+click), and selecting Edit Name.

- Change the URL for a bookmark by selecting it, opening the contextual menu, and selecting Edit Address.

- Move to a URL by double-clicking it or opening its contextual menu and choosing Open or Open in New Window.

- If you select the Auto-Click check box for a folder in the Bookmarks Bar collection, all the bookmarks in that folder open, with each bookmark appearing in a separate tab, when you click the folder's button on the Bookmarks bar.

- Delete a collection, folder, or bookmark by selecting it and pressing Delete or by opening its contextual menu and choosing Delete. If you delete a folder or collection, you also delete any bookmarks they contained.

- Search your bookmarks using the Search tool at the top of the Bookmarks pane. After you've searched, you can scope the results by clicking the button with the name of the collection you are searching or All to show the bookmarks in all collections or folders.

Configuring MobileMe synchronization on a Mac

Setting up a Mac to keep its information synchronized via MobileMe moves that Mac's information to and takes information from the MobileMe cloud. You can use that information from many locations and devices, and the information you access on each device is consistent and current. To configure MobileMe synchronization, follow these steps:

1. **Open the MobileMe pane of the System Preferences application.**

2. **Click the Sync tab, as shown in figure 3.13.**

3. **Select the Synchronize with MobileMe check box.**

4. **On the pop-up menu, choose how you want syncs to occur.** Choose Manually to sync manually; choose a time, such as Every Hour, to sync at those times; or choose Automatically to have syncs performed automatically when data in either location changes.

5. **Select the check box next to each kind of information you want to include in the sync.** You can sync these types of information:

   - Bookmarks

   - Calendars

   - Contacts

   - Dashboard widgets

   - Dock items

- Keychains

- Mail accounts

- Mail rules, signatures, and smart mailboxes

- Notes

- Preferences

- Entourage Notes

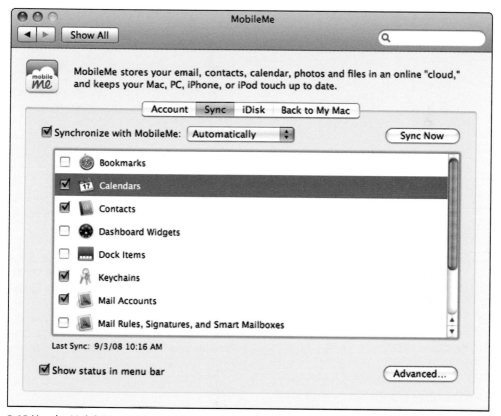

3.13 Use the MobileMe pane's Sync tab to determine how and when information is moved to and from the MobileMe cloud.

6. **Click Sync Now.** The information you selected is copied onto MobileMe. As the process moves ahead, you see the progress indicated in the Status area at the bottom of the list of check boxes. When the process is complete, you see the date of the last sync. Some of the information may already exist on MobileMe because you've previously synced another computer to it. In this case, you see an alert.

79

7. **On the alert's pop-up menu, choose how you want data to be synced.** For example, if you want the data on MobileMe to be merged with the information on the Mac, choose Merge all data. Or you can choose to replace data on MobileMe or on the computer.

8. **Click Sync in the alert box.** The sync process begins. As changes are made to data, you're prompted about what's going to be done.

9. **Click the Sync button to allow the sync to continue.**

10. **Repeat step 9 at each prompt.** When the process is complete, you see the time and date of the last sync at the bottom of the Sync tab.

11. **Repeat these steps for each computer you want to include in the sync.**

After you synchronize the Mac's information, it is available in the MobileMe cloud. There, it can be accessed by the MobileMe Web applications and by other devices you sync with. As changes are made to the information on other devices, the sync process moves them back to your Mac.

Managing MobileMe synchronizations on a Mac

If you rely on synced information, I don't recommend that you choose the Manually setting. If you don't remember to perform the manual sync, you might be missing needed information on another device. However, if you want to run a sync at a specific time, you can start the sync in the following ways:

- Open the MobileMe pane of the System Preferences application, and select Sync Now.

- Open the Synchronization menu on the Finder, and click Sync Now, as shown in figure 3.14.

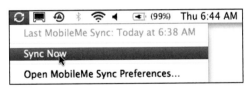

To determine the date and time of the last sync, open the Synchronization menu. You see that information at the top of the menu.

3.14 You can use the Sync menu to manually perform the synchronization process.

Note If you don't see the Synchronization menu, open the Sync pane of the MobileMe System Preferences application and select the Show status in menu bar check box.

You also can see which computers are synced and perform other tasks related to managing syncs. On the Sync tab, click the Advanced button. The Advanced sheet appears, as shown in figure 3.15.

The following computers are being synchronized using this MobileMe account:

Registered Computer	Last Synchronized
Brad Miser's MacBook Air (This Computer)	Today at 6:45 AM
BradsiMac – Troubleshooting	Never Synchronized

Unregister

Reset Sync Data...   Done

3.15 Use the Advanced sheet to see which computers are being synced through MobileMe.

On the Advanced sheet, you see the following:

- **List of synced computers.** At the top of the sheet, you see the list of computers that are part of the sync for the MobileMe account. The computer you are using includes "(This Computer)" next to its name. For each of the other computers, you see the computer's name and the user account that is being synced. You see the time and date of the last sync for all the synced computers.

- **Unregister.** Select a computer and click the Unregister button to remove it from the sync process. If you try to sync that computer again, the process will fail. To return the computer you are currently using to the Sync, repeat the synchronization process configuration steps. To return a different computer to the sync, open the Advanced sheet on that computer and click Reregister This Computer to return it to the sync process.

- **Reset Sync Data.** When you click this button, it is as if the Mac was never synced. A sheet prompts you about what to do with the data being synced. You can choose to replace all the information you are syncing or only specific information. You also can choose the direction of the next sync, such as from the computer to MobileMe or in the opposite direction. This option is useful when you've added information to the Mac, but then decide to replace that information with what is stored on the MobileMe cloud. Or perhaps you've decided that you want to create a new master set of information on the Mac and replace the data in the MobileMe cloud with it.

As MobileMe syncs occur after a reset or when you restart a sync, you may be prompted about what you want to do in the MobileMe Sync Alert dialog box, as shown in figure 3.16. Select an action on the pop-up menu, such as Replace data on computer to determine how synced information is moved or merged.

3.16 When this alert appears, you need to make decisions about how you want data to be synced.

To be more specific and select options for individual kinds of information, click the More Options button. The dialog box expands, and you see each kind of information being synced, as shown in figure 3.17. Choose an option for each kind of data. For example, to replace all the Contacts on the Mac with contact information from the MobileMe cloud, choose Replace data on computer on the Contacts pop-up menu. Repeat this for each kind of data included in the sync.

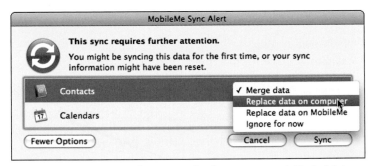

3.17 Use more options to determine what happens to each kind of data you are syncing.

After you configure the options, click Sync to complete the synchronization process.

Syncing Files

MobileMe synchronization works great for data, but it doesn't do anything for files. However, as you learn in Chapter 4, you can configure your online iDisk to be automatically synced to a local version of that iDisk stored on your Mac's hard drive. Then you can store the documents you want to keep in sync on your iDisk. As you make changes to your documents, the updated versions are also stored on the online version of the iDisk. As long as you have each Mac configured to sync the iDisk automatically, each computer will always have the most current version of your files available on its desktop.

Syncing Firefox bookmarks

Even though your Firefox bookmarks are left out of the MobileMe syncing picture, you can still sync them. You just have to use a tool called foxmarks — an add-on to Firefox. Here's how:

1. **Go to www.myfoxmarks.com and create a foxmarks account.**

2. **Select Tools ⇨ Add-ons.** The Add-ons tool appears.

3. **Search for foxmarks.**

4. **Select Foxmarks Bookmark Synchronizer.**

5. **Click Add to Firefox and Install Now.**

6. **Restart Firefox.** The Foxmarks Setup Wizard appears.

7. **Follow the onscreen instructions to sync your Firefox bookmarks.** Log into your fox-marks account, and choose how you want bookmarks to be synced. When the process is finished, you see the Success screen, as shown in figure 3.18. Click Done.

8. **Repeat these steps on each computer on which you want to sync your bookmarks.**

You can manage the synchronization settings for foxmarks by selecting Tools ⇨ Foxmarks. By default, Foxmarks is set to sync automatically, but you can perform manual syncs as well. After you have foxmarks configured on each computer, you have the same set of bookmarks available to you on each computer.

Unfortunately, Firefox bookmarks don't sync to an iPhone, and the Safari Web browser currently doesn't have an equivalent for foxmarks on the iPhone. But you can access you synced bookmarks by using the iPhone's Web browser to move to mobile.foxmarks.com.

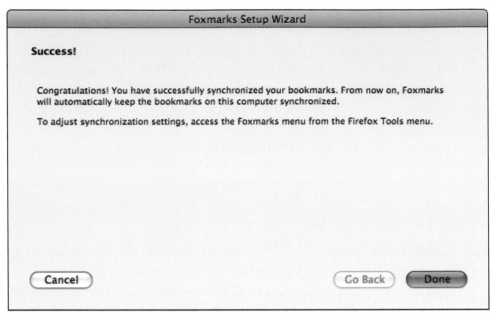

3.18 The Foxmarks Setup Wizard takes just a minute or two to sync your Firefox bookmarks.

Using MobileMe to Synchronize Windows PCs

You can configure a MobileMe email account in an email application, such as Microsoft Outlook on a Windows PC. You can then use that MobileMe account and synchronize it with other devices. You also can synchronize contacts and calendars stored in Outlook to and from the MobileMe cloud. If you use Internet Explorer or Safari, you can synchronize your favorites or bookmarks to and from the MobileMe cloud so you can have a consistent set of bookmarks available to you.

Before synchronizing information via MobileMe, you need to configure the Windows PC to have the appropriate information that you want to sync. In the following sections, you learn how to set up a MobileMe email account. Outlook, create contacts, and set up a calendar in Outlook. You also read how to set bookmarks in Safari.

After information is available on a Windows PC, you can use the MobileMe control panel to determine how and when that information is moved to and from the MobileMe cloud.

Note This section focuses on Microsoft Outlook 2003, Internet Explorer version 7, and Safari version 3. If you use different applications or different version of these applications, the steps may be slightly different. You can synchronize information from Outlook version 2003 and later. You also can synchronize contacts stored in the Window Contacts application.

Configuring MobileMe email accounts in Outlook

Setting up a MobileMe email account in Outlook is similar to setting up other kinds of email accounts, as shown in the following steps:

1. **In Outlook, select Tools ⇨ Email Accounts.** The E-mail Accounts Wizard appears.

2. **Select Add a new email account, and click Next.**

3. **Select IMAP, and click Next.** The Internet E-mail Settings (IMAP) dialog box appears, as shown in figure 3.19.

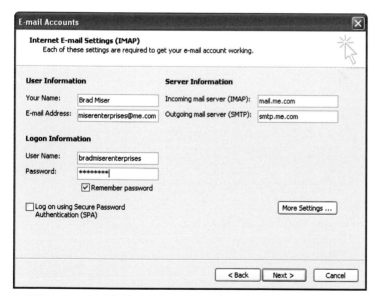

3.19 Enter your MobileMe email account information in the Internet E-mail Settings (IMAP) dialog box.

4. **Enter the name you want recipients to see as the From address on email messages you send in the Your Name field.**

5. **Enter your MobileMe email address in the Email Address field.**

6. **In the Incoming mail server field, enter mail.me.com.**

7. **In the Outgoing mail server field, enter smtp.me.com.**

Note

Based on the email address you entered, your MobileMe member name is entered into the User Name automatically.

8. **Enter your MobileMe pass word in the Password field.**

9. **Click More Settings.** The Internet E-mail Settings dialog box appears.

10. **Click the Outgoing Server tab.**

11. **Select the My outgoing server (SMTP) requires authentication check box.**

Note

Leave the Use same settings as my incoming mail server radio button selected so you don't have to re-enter your account information.

12. **Click the Advanced tab.** The next steps configure Outlook to use encrypted connections, which are more secure. If you don't want to allow this for some reason, skip to step 15.

13. **Select both This server requires an encrypted connection (SSL) check boxes.**

14. **Change the number in the Outgoing server field from 25 to 587, as shown in figure 3.20.**

15. **Click OK.** The dialog box closes, and you return to the Internet E-mail Settings (IMAP) dialog box.

16. **Click Next.**

17. **Click Finish.** The wizard closes, and the MobileMe email account is added to Outlook. Any email currently in the Inbox and other folders on the MobileMe servers appears in Outlook.

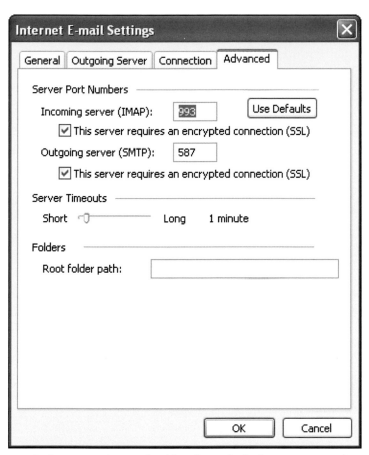

Internet E-mail Settings ☒

General | Outgoing Server | Connection | Advanced

Server Port Numbers

Incoming server (IMAP): `993` [Use Defaults]

☑ This server requires an encrypted connection (SSL)

Outgoing server (SMTP): `587`

☑ This server requires an encrypted connection (SSL)

Server Timeouts

Short ⟜⟝──────── Long   1 minute

Folders

Root folder path: [   ]

[OK] [Cancel]

3.20 For better security, you should configure Outlook to use encrypted connections for your email.

You can use the MobileMe email account as the wizard configured it; however, you should change the default name to make it recognizable on the Mail pane:

1. **In the Mail pane, right-click the mail.mac.com folder.**

2. **On the resulting menu, choose Properties for "mail.mac.com."** The Properties dialog box appears.

3. **Click the Advanced button.** The Personal Folders dialog box appears.

4. **Enter a better name for the account in the Name field.** For example, you might want to call it MobileMe email or something that is more recognizable than the default (mail.mac.com).

5. **Click OK two times in a row to close both dialog boxes.** The MobileMe email folder now has the name you entered in step 4.

You can work with the MobileMe email account by selecting any of the folders under its icon, such as the Inbox to see email you have received. You also can use Outlook's email tools to create new folders to keep your email organized.

Creating contacts in Outlook

Outlook includes a Contact module that you can use to manage contact information. Like other contact manager applications, it uses the concept of an address card, which is a vCard (virtual card). You can create address cards for each of your contacts and capture information, such as phone numbers, addresses, and so on. To use this information in other places, such as on an iPhone, you can sync the contact information via MobileMe.

To create a basic contact in Outlook, follow these steps:

1. **Select File ⇨ New ⇨ Contact.** The Untitled-Contact dialog box appears, and you see the default fields for contacts.

2. **Enter the person's full name in the Full Name field.**

3. **If you are creating a work-related contact, enter the person's title and company in their respective fields.**

4. **On the File as drop-down list, choose how you want the contact's name to be organized in Outlook.** For example, you can choose last, first; by full name; or by other combinations of information, such as company (full name).

5. **Enter the contact's phone numbers in the appropriate fields, such as a cell number in the Mobile field.** You can change the labels for the fields using the field's drop-down list.

6. **To add a physical address for the contact, choose the type of address you are going to add on the drop-down list in the Addresses section, such as Business to enter a business address.**

7. **Enter the address.**

8. **To make the address the default mailing address, select the This is the mailing address check box.**

9. **Repeat steps 6 through 8 to add more addresses.**

10. **Enter the primary email address for the contact in the E-mail field.**

11. **To enter another email address, choose a different label on the E-mail drop-down list and enter the additional address.**

12. **If the contact has a Web site, enter its address in the Web page address field.**

13. **The contact uses IM, enter his IM address in the related field.**

14. **Click the Image button located to the left of the E-mail field.**

15. **Move to the contact's image file, select it, and click OK.**

16. **Enter notes about the contact in the space provided, as shown in figure 3.21.**

17. **Click Save and Close.** The contact is saved in Outlook.

3.21 You can configure basic information for a contact on the General tab.

Creating calendars and events in Outlook

Outlook also contains calendar tools to help you manage your time. You can create calendars for various purposes and then schedule events on them. After you configure the Windows PC to synchronize its information, your calendars are available in the MobileMe cloud.

Creating calendars in Outlook

You can create additional calendars in Outlook to track specific kinds of events, for example, one calendar for business events and one for personal events. Outlook uses the default calendar for all events that require collaboration, such as when you want to invite other people to a meeting. When you create a calendar, it can be used only to track events that are specific to you. Still, these calendars can be useful in specific situations.

To create a calendar in Outlook, follow these steps:

1. **Select Go ⇨ Folder List.** You move to the folder list where you see the various folders being managed by Outlook, including email folders, contacts, and so on.

2. **Right-click the Calendar folder.**

3. **Choose New Folder on the resulting contextual menu.** You see the Create New Folder dialog box.

4. **Enter a name for the calendar in the Name field.**

5. **Click OK.** The new calendar is created and appears under the Calendars folder.

To work with the calendar you created, select it on the folder list. The calendar appears in the right pane of the Outlook window.

Creating events on Outlook calendars

To plan for activities, such as team meetings or meetings with business associates, you can create events on an Outlook calendar. These events include date, time, location, invitees, notes, and other information relating to the event. To create an event, complete the following:

1. **On the folder list, select the calendar on which you want the event to be created; if you are inviting others to the event, select the Calendar entry on the Folder List.** That calendar appears in the right pane of the window.

Note Outlook's collaboration tools, such as meeting invitations, work only with the main calendar. If you want to invite others to an event, you need to select and work with your main calendar instead of another one you have created.

2. **Go to the date the event occurs; one way to do this is by clicking a date in the mini-calendar at the top of the Folder List.**

3. **Drag over the time for the event on the date it occurs.** The block of time you selected is highlighted.

4. **Right-click and choose New Meeting Request if you want to invite others to the event, or choose New Appointment if you are the only one involved in the event.** The new meeting dialog box appears.

5. **If you selected New Meeting Request, enter the email addresses of the invitees (separated by semicolons) in the To field; if you selected New Appointment, skip this step.**

6. **If you are sending invitations to the event and have more than one email account, use the Accounts drop-down list at the top of the window to choose the account from which the invitation will be sent.**

7. **Enter a title of the event in the Subject field.**

8. **Enter a location for the event in the Location field; you can use the drop-down list to select a previous location.**

9. **Use the Label drop-down list to choose a label for the event, such as Business.** With the text comes a color that will be applied to the event.

10. **If you need to adjust the time and date for the event, use the Start time and End time fields.**

11. **Select the Reminder check box and choose the amount of time before the event that you want an alarm to activate on the drop-down list.**

12. **On the Show time as drop-down list, choose how the time should be blocked out on your calendar.** This is important when someone tries to schedule an event with you. If you choose Busy, she sees that you are scheduled at this time. If you choose Free, the meeting does not show up when she views your calendar as she schedules a meeting.

Genius

To change the sound for the meeting reminder, click the speaker icon next to the Reminder drop-down list.

13. **Enter notes or other information for the event in the text area.**

14. **To include attachments with the meeting, drag them onto the text area, as shown in figure 3.22.**

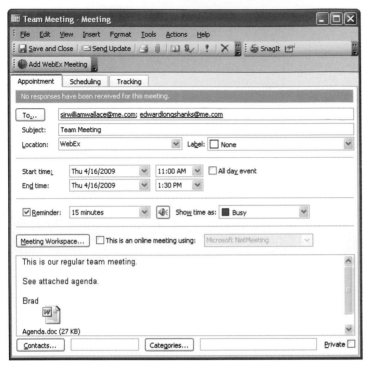

3.22 Along with the basic information, such as time and date, you can associate files with events on Outlook calendars.

15. **If the meeting involves other people, click Send; if it is only for your calendar, click Save and Close.**

After the event has been saved, it appears on your calendar. If you invited others to the meeting, they receive meeting invitations email messages. As people accept or decline your invitation, you see their status by opening the event (double-click it) and selecting the Tracking tab.

Creating and organizing Web bookmarks in Safari on a Windows PC

Apple's Safari Web browser is one of the two browsers fully supported by MobileMe on Windows PCs; Firefox is the other. Like all Web browsers, you can set bookmarks for Web sites to make them easy to access. With MobileMe, you can synchronize the Safari bookmarks on your Windows PC so that you can have the same set of bookmarks on all your devices, including Windows computers, Macs, and iPhones.

Note

You also can synchronize favorites in Internet Explorer. However, because MobileMe isn't fully compatible with Internet Explorer, that browser isn't covered in this book. You can't synchronize Firefox bookmarks through MobileMe, but you can do so with the Foxmarks add-on. See "Syncing Firefox Bookmarks" earlier in this chapter for details.

Safari on a Windows PC is pretty much like Safari on a Mac. For details about setting and organizing bookmarks in Safari, see the section on synchronizing Safari bookmarks on your Mac earlier in this chapter. As you read through that section, keep the following minor differences in mind:

- Instead of the ⌘+D keys to set a bookmark, on a Windows computer you press Ctrl+D.

- To open the Bookmarks window on a Windows PC, press Ctrl+Alt+B.

- Instead of pressing the Return key to save changes to a folder name or other object, press Enter.

Configuring MobileMe synchronization on a Windows PC

After you have configured information and tools on a Windows PC, configure the information to be synchronized by accomplishing these tasks:

1. **Open the MobileMe control panel.**

2. **Select the Sync tab, as shown in figure 3.23.**

3. **Select the Sync with MobileMe check box.**

4. **On the drop-down list, choose how you want syncs to occur.** Choose Manually to sync manually; choose a time, such as Every Hour, to sync at those times; or choose Automatically to have syncs performed automatically when synced data changes.

5. **To include contact information in the sync, select the Contacts check box and choose the application whose information you want to include on the drop-down list.** For example, if you use Outlook for your contact information, select that application on the drop-down list. Options include Yahoo! Address Book and Windows Address Book.

Note

If an application you use for specific information, such as contacts, doesn't appear on the related sync drop-down list, it isn't available for MobileMe synchronization. Your options are to rely on the MobileMe Web applications, move the information to a supported application, or use a different tool to keep the information synchronized.

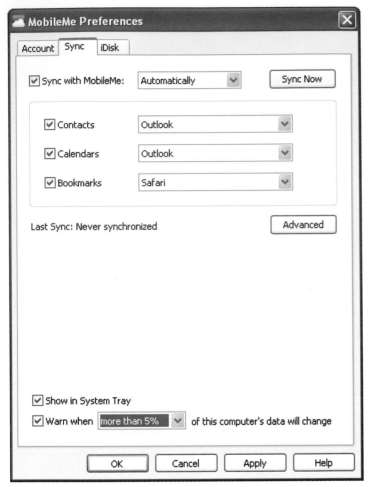

3.23 Use the Sync tab of the MobileMe control panel to determine how and when information on a Windows PC is synced with the MobileMe cloud.

6. **To include calendar information in the sync, select the Calendars check box and choose Outlook; if you use a different application to manage your calendars and that application appears on the list, choose it instead.**

7. **To include bookmarks in the sync, select the Bookmarks check box and choose Safari or Internet Explorer on the drop-down list.**

8. **Select the Show in System Tray check box to include the MobileMe icon in the System Tray.**

9. **Select the What when check box and choose the amount of change that triggers an alarm on the drop-down list to be warned when data on the computer is changed because of the sync.** The options are any, which sends an alarm when any data changes, and more than 5%, more than 25%, or more than 50%, which trigger alarms at those percentages.

10. **Click OK.** The control panel closes and the sync options you selected take effect.

Genius

Set the alarm trigger to a small amount of change, such as any or more than 5%, when you first start syncing information. As you get more comfortable with the sync process and are sure that only changes you want are being made, turn the warning off or set it to a high value, such as more than 50%.

Managing MobileMe synchronizations on a Windows PC

If you configured MobileMe to sync manually, which I don't recommend, you can start a sync in the following ways:

- Right-click the MobileMe icon in the System tray, and select Sync Now.

- Open the Sync tab of the MobileMe control panel, and click Sync Now.

You can determine the date and time of the last sync by opening the Sync pane of the MobileMe control panel. That information is under the sync check boxes.

You also can see which computers are synced and perform other tasks related to managing syncs. On the Sync tab, click the Advanced button. The Advanced Settings dialog box appears, as shown in figure 3.24.

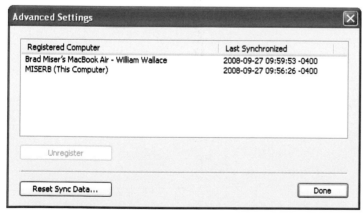

3.24 Use the Advanced Settings dialog box to see which computers are being synced through MobileMe.

On the Advanced sheet, you see the following information and tools:

- **List of synced computers.** At the top of the sheet, you see the list of computers that are part of the sync for the MobileMe account. The computer you are using includes "(This Computer)" next to its name. For each of the other computers, you see the computer's name and the user account that is being synced. You see the time and date of the last sync for all the synced computers.

- **Unregister.** Select a computer and click the Unregister button to remove it from the sync process. If you try to sync that computer again, the process will fail. To return the computer you are currently using to the Sync, repeat the synchronization process configuration steps. To return a different computer to the sync, open the Advanced sheet on that computer and click Reregister This Computer to return it to the sync process.

- **Reset Sync Data.** When you click this button, it is as if the computer was never synced. A sheet appears that prompts you about what you want to do with the data being synced. You can choose to replace all the information you are syncing or only specific types of information. You also can choose the direction of the next sync, such as from the computer to MobileMe or in the opposite direction. This option can be useful when you've added information to the Windows PC, but then decide to replace its information with that stored on the MobileMe cloud. Or, perhaps you've decided you want to create a new master set of information on the Windows PC and replace the data in the MobileMe cloud with it.

As MobileMe syncs occur after a reset, when you restart a sync, you are prompted about what you want to do in the MobileMe Sync Alert dialog box, as shown in figure 3.25. Select an action on the pop-up menu, such as Replace data on computer to determine how synced information is moved or merged.

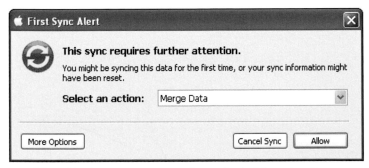

3.25 When this alert appears, you need to make decisions about how you want data to be synced.

To be more specific and select options for individual kinds of information, click the More Options button. The dialog box expands, and you see each kind of information being synced, as shown in figure 3.26. Choose an option for each kind of data. For example, to replace all the Contacts on the computer with contact information from the MobileMe cloud, choose Replace data on computer on the Contacts pop-up menu. Repeat this for each kind of data included in the sync.

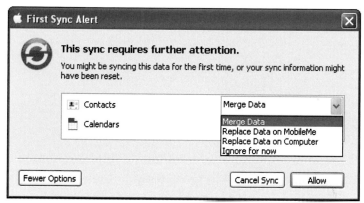

3.26 Use more options to determine what happens to each kind of data you are syncing.

When you've configured the options, click Allow to complete the synchronization process.

When the data on the computer will be changed more than the threshold you set, you see the Sync Alert dialog box, as shown in figure 3.27. In the dialog box, you see the kind of information that will be changed, such as Calendars, and the number of items that will be added, deleted, or changed. To allow the sync, click Allow. To stop the sync so that the data on the computer isn't changed, click Cancel Sync.

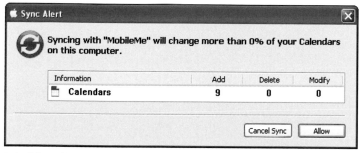

3.27 When data will be changed on the computer above the alert threshold, you see this Sync Alert dialog.

If you cancel a sync, the next time it is attempted, you see the Sync Alert dialog box again. You can clear this by performing one of these actions:

- Allowing the sync, which changes the data on the PC

- Turning off the alert, which also changes the data on the PC the next time the sync runs, but you aren't warned about it

- Undoing the changes on the devices where they were made so that the synced information is no longer different

- Removing that kind of information from the sync

Using MobileMe to Synchronize iPhones

When you configure a MobileMe account on an iPhone, you can choose to synchronize email, contacts, calendars, and bookmarks with the MobileMe cloud, and thus with other devices, such as a Windows PC or Mac. To do this, you move to the account's Synchronization settings screen and enable or disable each syncing for each kind of information, as shown in figure 3.28. Details about how to do this are provided in the section on configuring a MobileMe account on an iPhone in Chapter 2.

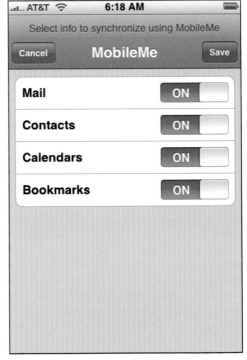

3.28 After you have configured a MobileMe account on an iPhone, you can keep its email, contacts, calendars, and bookmarks in sync with the MobileMe cloud.

How Can I Get the Most Out of MobileMe iDisks?

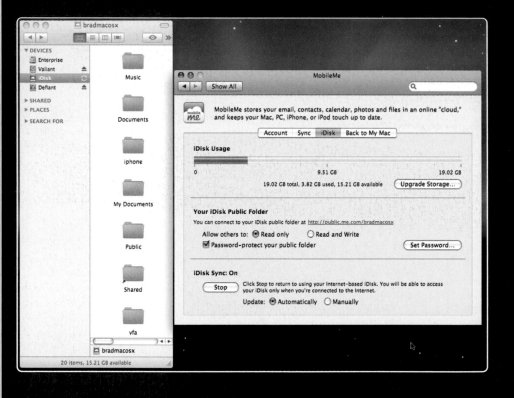

An iDisk is disk space on the MobileMe servers, and it's a great way to store files. An iDisk enables you to easily access the same files from multiple computers, such as from a Mac and a PC. You also can share files on your iDisk and provide a place for your team members to store files they want to share, making collaboration easier. Your iDisk is remote, so it's ideal for protecting critical files. Even if something severe happens to a computer, backed-up files are still available on your iDisk.

Accessing an iDisk from the Mac Desktop

The purpose of an iDisk is the same as any other kind of storage device. Like the internal drive in a Mac, you use an iDisk to store files. And the iDisk is connected to some of the services provided by MobileMe. For example, when you use iWeb to publish a Web site, the files for that site are actually stored in specific folders on your iDisk. Your iDisk is remote, meaning that you access it over the Internet; therefore, it works a bit differently than the disk in a Mac or an external hard drive connected to a Mac. However, the tools you need to work with an iDisk are built into Mac OS X, so you can easily access your iDisk from the Mac desktop.

Configuring synchronization and security options for your iDisk

An iDisk has two basic modes: unsynced or synced.

In the unsynced mode, you access the iDisk online, meaning that any files you move to or from the iDisk move across the Internet immediately. The benefit of this approach is that the iDisk doesn't take up any space on a Mac's hard drive. The downside is that you have to be connected to the Internet to be able to access the disk, so if you are someplace where Internet access isn't available, you can't get to your iDisk. If you want to store files on your iDisk, you have to wait until you can connect to the Internet and then manually move the files to your iDisk.

In the synced mode, a copy of the iDisk resides on your Mac's desktop. You move files to and from this local copy of the iDisk. The files aren't actually moved onto the online iDisk until it is synced with the local version, which can be done manually or automatically. This approach has a couple of benefits. One is that you can access the local version of the iDisk at any time because it is stored on your hard disk. Another is that the speed of the iDisk is faster because you are really just using your Mac's hard drive instead of working over the Internet. (The sync process takes place in the background so it doesn't interfere with your other tasks.) The downside of this approach is that all the files stored on the iDisk have to be stored on your Mac's hard drive too. If you have plenty of disk space, this isn't a problem. But if you have lots of large files on your iDisk and the space on your Mac's hard drive is limited, you might not have enough space to have a local copy.

Each iDisk contains a Public folder, whose name implies its use, which is to make files available to "the public." You can store files in your Public folder and allow other people to access them over the Internet. For example, you might want your team members to be able to access files related to your business. You simply save those files to the iDisk, and your team members can move to the Public folder to get the files using any computer with Internet access. You also can allow others to place files in your iDisk to store them there, such as files your team members change and want to provide to you. You can determine if other people can only read (copy) files from your Public folder or if they can read files from and write files to the Public folder. You also can determine if a password is needed to be able to access your Public folder.

You configure and manage your iDisk from the MobileMe pane of the System Preferences application as demonstrated in the following:

1. **Select Apple menu ⇨ System Preferences.**

2. **Click the MobileMe icon.**

Note

If you don't see the iDisk tab, you aren't logged into a MobileMe account. Enter the member name and password, and click Sign In to log in. The iDisk tab appears.

3. **Click the iDisk tab.** At the top of the pane, you see a gauge showing how much of your iDisk space you are currently using. The green part of the bar, shown in figure 4.1, represents the space being used.

Genius

If the usage gauge shows that your iDisk is full or getting close to being full, move to the iDisk and delete files from it to free up more space. However, make sure you don't delete files that you use on your Web sites. Removing files might have consequences you don't intend. If you can't find files to remove and the disk is full, click the Upgrade Storage button to add more space to your iDisk.

4. **If you want people who access your iDisk to be able to store or change files in your Public folder, select Read and Write; to limit people to only copying files from your iDisk, select Read only.**

Caution

You should protect your Public folder with a password. If you don't require a password, anyone who stumbles across your iDisk can access it. Because URLs to an iDisk have a pattern, you can move to any person's iDisk by simply knowing his member name. So people you don't know can at least copy files from your iDisk. Or if you allow write access, they can store files there too. That's not a good idea for many reasons.

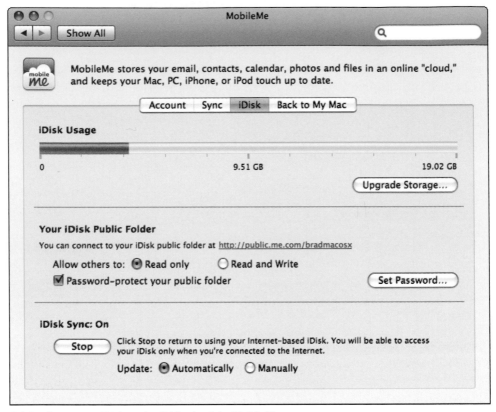

4.1 Configure your iDisk on the iDisk tab of the MobileMe pane.

5. **Select the Password-protect your public folder check box to put a password on your Public folder.** The Password sheet appears, as shown in figure 4.2.

6. **Enter the password for the folder in the Password field.** Passwords must be between 6 and 8 characters long and can't be the same as the password for your MobileMe account.

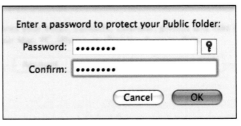

4.2 You should always set a password for your Public folder so you can control access to it.

7. **Confirm the password by entering it again in the Confirm field, and click OK.**

8. **To use your iDisk in the synced mode, click the Start button.** A copy of your iDisk is made on your Mac's hard disk.

9. **If you want the sync process to happen automatically, click the Automatically radio button. If you want to manually sync the iDisk, click the Manually radio button.** Your iDisk is ready to use.

Note

An iDisk is a very useful thing, and you may find that the amount of space you have isn't sufficient. See Chapter 2 for information about increasing the size of your iDisk.

Working with your iDisk on the Mac desktop

Working with an iDisk is similar to using the hard disk in your Mac. You can open it in any of the following ways:

- Open a Finder window, and click iDisk in the DEVICES section of the Sidebar.
- On the Finder's menu bar, choose Go ⇨ iDisk ⇨ My iDisk.
- Press Shift+⌘+I.

When you open the iDisk, you see its contents in the resulting Finder window, as shown in figure 4.3. These include a set of default folders similar to those in your Home folder, including Documents, Movies, and Music. Like your Home folder, you can create new folders, move files around, create new files, and so on. In this respect, using an iDisk is just like using your Mac's hard drive.

If you use the iDisk in the unsynced mode, files you move to or from the iDisk are moved across the Internet. This can take some time, so don't expect the kind of response you get from your hard drive. If files are larger than a MB or two, you see the Copy dialog box on the screen for a while; copying works in the background so you can just ignore the window. When the copy process is complete, the Copy dialog box closes.

If you use the iDisk in the synced mode, you see the Sync button next to its icon on the Sidebar. You also see the time and date of the last synchronization at the bottom of the window. To manually sync the disk, click the Sync button. Files on the local version are copied to the online version and vice versa until the two versions are duplicates of each other. If you selected the Automatic option, Mac OS X takes care of this for you. However, you can manually sync the disks at any time. Suppose you've just completed an important file and want to make it available to your team members immediately: Click the Sync button and the file is moved to the online iDisk right away.

Sync button

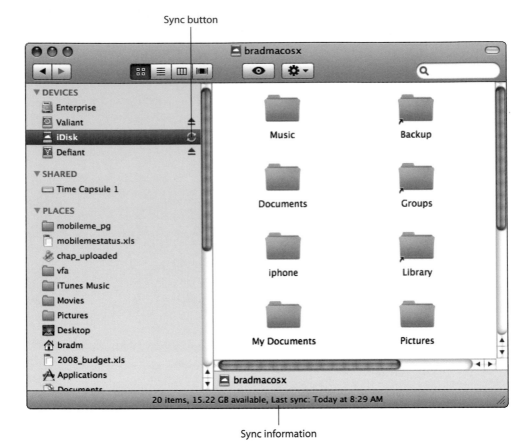

Sync information

4.3 Your iDisk folders function much the same way your hard drive folders do.

Note The first time you sync an iDisk can take a long time, especially when large amounts of data are on the disk. Subsequent syncs are much faster because only files that have been changed are involved.

Working with other people's iDisks on the Mac desktop

Although you access your own iDisk via the iDisk icon on the Sidebar, you can almost as easily access other people's iDisk from your desktop.

If you know the associated member name and password, you can mount any iDisk on your desktop, regardless of the iDisk that is mounted when you log into a MobileMe account on the Account pane of the System Preferences application. You can access that iDisk just as if it is from the account your Mac is logged into. Here's how:

1. **Select Go ➪ iDisk ➪ Other User's iDisk.** You're prompted to enter the other user's member name and password, as shown in figure 4.4.

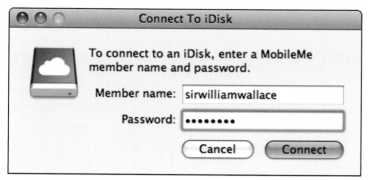

4.4 You can mount any iDisk on your Mac as long as you know the associated member name and password.

2. **Enter the member name and password.**

3. **Click Connect.** The iDisk is mounted on your desktop, as shown in figure 4.5.

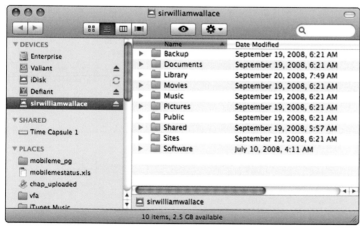

4.5 Here, you can see that this Mac has access to iDisks from two different accounts.

Note One difference between mounting an iDisk using the Go menu and logging into an account on the MobileMe pane is that iDisks you mount from the Go menu can't be synced; you always work with the online version of the iDisk. (The exception to this is when you use the Go menu to access your own iDisk, in which case you are using the mounted version, which is a local copy if you are using the synced mode.)

To create a disk space that is common to your team so that everyone can easily access files stored there, consider creating a dedicated Individual account or a Family Member account (see Chapter 2) for this purpose. After the account is created, provide the associated member name and password to each of your team members. All of you can then have the same iDisk mounted on your desktops to make sharing files simple.

Caution With an account's member name and password, someone can access that account via the me.com Web site to manage it. You need to be sure you trust the people with whom you share this information.

The Public folder on an iDisk is ideal for sharing files among a group of people because anyone provided the folder's password can access that folder over the Internet. For example, you can create a project folder within an iDisk's Public folder. Your team members can access that folder just by opening it on their desktop. Of course, if you want people to be able to add or change files there, you need to enable the Write permission for the Public folder, as described previously.

Note You don't need to have a MobileMe account to access a Public folder on someone's iDisk. All you need is the member name associated with the iDisk and password for it (if required).

You can mount just the Public folder for any MobileMe member on your desktop by performing the following steps:

1. **Select Go ⇨ iDisk ⇨ Other User's Public Folder.** You're prompted to enter the other user's member name, as shown in figure 4.6.

2. **Enter the member name for the person whose public folder you want to access.**

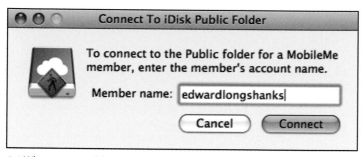

4.6 When you provide a member name, you move to a user's Public folder.

3. **Click Connect.** If the Public folder requires a password, you're prompted to enter it; if not, the Public folder mounts on your desktop and you can use it, so you can skip the rest of these steps.

4. **Enter the password in the Password field.**

5. **If you are going to be using the Public folder regularly, select the Remember this password in my keychain check box so you don't have to enter it each time.**

6. **Click OK.**

When the public folder is mounted, it appears in the DEVICES section on the Sidebar just like other disks you have mounted. The name of the disk has "-Public" appended to it so you can tell you are accessing only the Public folder on that iDisk.

Note

When you access a Public folder, you see that "public" is entered as the user name automatically. This is the user name associated with all public folders on all iDisks.

If the public folder provides Read-only access, you can copy files from the folder. If it has Write permission, you also can store and change files there.

Genius

If you have a Family Pack account, you can create a Family Member account that is specifically for sharing files outside your team. Create the account with a member name that is easy for people to relate to your business, such as mycompanyfiles. Copy the files you want to share to the Public folder on that account's iDisk. To share those files, all you have to do is provide the URL http://public.me.com/mycompanyfiles to the people you want to share with. They can access those files by using a Web browser.

Accessing a Public Folder via the Web

Earlier, you learned that your Public folder is available on the Web. On a Mac, the Public folder is accessible via the URL shown on the iDisk tab of the MobileMe pane of the System Preferences application. On a Windows PC, it is accessible through the MobileMe control panel. To access a MobileMe iDisk's Public folder on the Web, enter its address in a Web browser, which is public.me.com/*membername*, where *membername* is the MobileMe member name. You move to the folder's Web page. If a password is required, the Name and Password sheet appears. Enter public in the Name field and the folder's password in the Password field. Click Log In. The contents of the Public folder are shown. You can download files by clicking their links. If enabled, you can upload files by clicking the Upload button and then selecting the files you want to add to the Public folder.

Accessing an iDisk from the Windows Desktop

You can use an iDisk from the Windows desktop like you use other hard drives, such as the one installed in a PC. However, because the iDisk is a virtual disk space that you access over the Internet, it behaves a bit differently. You configure how the iDisk works on the PC and then map it as a network drive for easy desktop access. Once mounted, you can use the iDisk like other storage devices you have.

Note

Some Virtual Private Network (VPN) software can interface with your ability to mount an iDisk on a Windows PC. If you are unable to mount a disk, make sure you aren't connected to a network through a VPN and try again. This often solves a connection problem.

Managing an iDisk using the MobileMe control panel

You can use the iDisk tab of the MobileMe control panel to get information about your iDisk and to configure the security of the iDisk's Public folder.

Each iDisk contains a Public folder, whose name implies its use, which is to make files available to "the public." You can store files in your Public folder and allow other people to access them over the Internet. For example, you might want your team members to be able to access files related to your business. When you store those files in the Public folder, your team members can access them from any computer with an Internet connection. You simply save those files to the iDisk, and your team members can move to it to get the files. You also can allow others to place files in your iDisk to store them there, such as files your team members change and want to provide to you. You can determine if other people can only read (copy) files from your Public folder or if they can read files from and write files to the Public folder. You also can determine if a password is needed to be able to access your Public folder.

To configure your iDisk, perform the following steps:

1. **Open the MobileMe control panel.**

Note
If you don't see the iDisk tab, you aren't logged into a MobileMe account. Enter the member name and password, and click Sign In to log in. The iDisk tab appears.

2. **Click the iDisk tab.** At the top of the pane, you see a gauge showing how much of your iDisk space you are currently using. The blue part of the bar, shown in figure 4.7, represents the space being used. Above the gauge, you see the exact amount of total disk space, the amount you are using, and the amount that is free.

Genius
If the usage gauge shows that your iDisk is full or getting close to being full, move to the iDisk and delete files from it to free up more space. However, make sure you don't delete files that you use on your Web sites. Removing files might have consequences you don't intend. If you can't find files to remove and the disk is full, click the Upgrade Storage button to add more space to your iDisk.

3. **If you want people who access your iDisk to be able to store or change files in your Public folder, select Read and Write; to limit people to only copying files from your iDisk, select Read only.**

MobileMe Preferences ☒

| Account | Sync | iDisk |

iDisk Usage

Total: 2.56 GB
Used: 0.09 MB
Available: 2.56 GB

0   1.28 GB   2.56 GB

Open MobileMe iDisk...   Upgrade Storage...

Your iDisk Public Folder

You can connect to your iDisk public folder at:
http://idisk.me.com/sirwilliamwallace-Public

Allow others to: ⊙ Read only   ○ Read and Write

☑ Password-protect your public folder   Set Password...

OK   Cancel   Apply   Help

4.7 The iDisk tab of the MobileMe control panel provides information about and controls for your iDisk.

Caution

You should protect your Public folder with a password. If you don't require a password, anyone who stumbles across your iDisk can access it. Because URLs to an iDisk have a pattern, you can move to any person's iDisk by simply knowing her member name. So people you don't know can at least copy files from your iDisk. Or if you allow write access, they can store files there too. That's not a good idea for many reasons.

4. **Select the Password-protect your public folder check box to put a password on your Public folder.** The Password sheet appears, as shown in figure 4.8.

5. **Enter the password for the folder in the Password field.** Passwords must be between 6 and 8 characters long and can't be the same as the password for your MobileMe account.

6. **Confirm the password by entering it again in the Confirm field, and click OK.**

7. **Click OK.** Your changes take effect.

Set Password

Enter a password to protect your Public folder:

Password: ••••••

Confirm: ••••••

Cancel   OK

4.8 You should always set a password for your Public folder so you can control access to it.

Note

If you click the Open MobileMe iDisk button, you move to the .me Web site where you can use the iDisk Web application, which is covered later in this chapter.

Mapping an iDisk as a network drive

You can map your iDisk as a network drive to make it directly accessible from the Windows desktop. Here's how:

1. **Open an Explorer window on the desktop.**

2. **Select Tools ⇨ Map Network Drive.** The Map Network Drive dialog box appears, as shown in figure 4.9.

3. **On the Drive drop-down list, choose the letter with which your iDisk should be labeled.**

4. **In the Folder field, enter http://idisk.me.com/*membername*, where *membername* is the member name of the account whose iDisk you want to map.**

5. **Select the Reconnect at logon check box if you want to reconnect to the drive each time you log into Windows.**

6. **Click the different user name link.** The Connect As dialog box appears, as shown in figure 4.10.

7. **Enter the member name and password for the MobileMe account.**

8. **Click OK.** The dialog box closes, and you return to the Map Network Drive dialog box.

9. **Click Finish.** Windows connects to the iDisk and mounts it on the desktop.

4.9 When you map an iDisk as a network drive, you can access it from the Windows desktop.

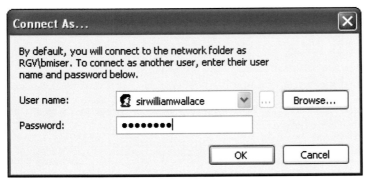

4.10 Enter the member name and password for the iDisk you want to map to in the Connect As dialog box.

Working with your iDisk on the Windows desktop

Using an iDisk on the Windows desktop is similar to using other kinds of disks, except that it is accessed over the Internet. When you open the My Computer folder, you see the iDisk. When mounted, the iDisk is named with the name of the MobileMe account followed by "on 'idisk.me.com'" and its type is shown as a Network Drive, as shown in figure 4.11 (which shows the window in Details view). When you open the iDisk, you see its default folders, which include Backup, Documents, Library, Movies, Pictures, and so on. You can add folders and files to the iDisk as you can to other disks you work with.

4.11 After an iDisk is mounted on your Windows desktop, you can access it like other disks you use.

Caution Remember that the Public folder on an iDisk is designed to be shared. If you place folders there, people can access them by connecting to your Public folder. You should configure your Public folder to be password-protected so only trustworthy people can access it.

Working with iDisk Public folders on the Windows desktop

The Public folder on the iDisk is useful for sharing files with other people. Depending on the permissions configured for another user's Public folder, you can either copy files from (with Read permission) or copy files to and change files in (with Write permission) the Public folder of an iDisk.

As an example, suppose you are doing a project for your business on which your team members are collaborating. You can store files for that project in an iDisk Public folder. Everyone who needs access to those files can get to them by simply opening that Public folder.

You can access a Public folder from the Windows desktop in a couple of ways. If you access it only occasionally, you can enter its URL in an Explorer window. If you access it regularly, you can map it to your computer.

To move to a Public folder from a Windows Explorer window, perform the following steps:

1. **Open an Explorer window.**

2. **In the Address bar, type http://public.me.com/*membername*, where *membername* is the MobileMe member name of the user whose Public folder you want to access and press the Enter key.** Your default Web browser opens and moves to the Public folder. If the Public folder is secured with a password, you're prompted to enter the user name and password. If not, you move into the Public folder and can skip the rest of these steps.

3. **Enter public as the user name.**

4. **Enter the password you were provided by the person whose Public folder you are accessing and click OK.** The Public folder of the iDisk opens in the Web browser.

When the Public folder is open in the Web browser, you can work with its folders and files. If you have only Read permission, you can copy files from the iDisk to your computer. If you have Read and Write permission, you can click the Upload button to add files to the folder and you can click the New Folder button to create a new folder there.

Note   You don't need to have a MobileMe account to access a Public folder on someone's iDisk. All you need is the member name associated with the iDisk and password for it (if required).

If you are going to be using a Public folder regularly, map it to your computer as a network drive:

1. **Open an Explorer window on the desktop.**

2. **Select Tools ⇨ Map Network Drive.** The Map Network Drive dialog box appears.

3. **On the Drive drop-down list, choose the letter with which your iDisk should be labeled.**

4. **In the Folder field, enter http://public.me.com/*membername*/, where *membername* is the member name of the account whose Public folder you want to map.**

5. **Select the Reconnect at logon check box if you want to reconnect to the folder each time you log into Windows.**

6. **Click the different user name link.** The Connect As dialog box appears.

7. **Enter** public **as the member name.**

8. **Enter the Public folder's password.**

9. **Click OK.** The dialog box closes, and you return to the Map Network Drive dialog box.

10. **Click Finish.** Windows connects to the Public folder and mounts it on the desktop, as shown in figure 4.12.

4.12 In this My Computer window, you can see that an iDisk has been mounted (the disk whose name includes "on 'idisk.me.com'") along with another user's Public folder (the disk whose name contains "'public.me.com'").

Note At the time this book was written, Windows didn't read the size of iDisks correctly. So you should ignore the information shown in the Total Size column when viewing the My Computer folder.

If you have Read access to the folder, you can copy files from it to your desktop. If you have Read and Write permission, you can create folders on it, add files to it, and change files that are stored on it.

Genius

If you have a Family Pack account, you can create a Family Member account that is specifically for sharing files outside your team. Create the account with a member name that is easy for people to relate to your business, such as mycompanyfiles. Copy the files you want to share to the Public folder on that account's iDisk. To share those files, all you have to do is provide the URL http://public.me.com/mycompany-files to the people you want to share it with. They can then get to those files using a Web browser.

Keeping an iDisk in sync with a Windows PC

Like with any other network drive, to use an iDisk you must have a connection to the network to which the drive is connected. In this case that network is the Internet. If you use a mobile computer, you may want to use that computer without an Internet connection at times. When you do, the files you work with can become out of sync with files on your iDisk. You can resync these files in two ways.

Manually copying files to your iDisk

The least expensive approach is to manually copy files to and from your iDisk before and after you disconnect from the Internet. Create a folder on your computer's internal hard drive and copy the files you'll need from the iDisk to that folder. You can then use those files even when you aren't connected to the Internet, such as when you are using a laptop on an airplane. When you have an Internet connection again, simply copy the files you've changed from the computer's hard drive onto the iDisk.

The benefits to this approach are that it's easy and doesn't cost anything. The downsides are that it requires effort and you must copy all the files you need to your computer's drive before disconnecting from the Internet. And then you must copy all the changed files to the iDisk after you reconnect to the Internet. This is time consuming, and unless you are disciplined about it, files can become out of sync. Then you must figure out which version you want or how to merge multiple versions together.

Using a cloning application

A more complicated approach at least initially, is to obtain and use a file synchronization application called a cloning application. You can configure a cloning application to automatically sync the files on your iDisk with a folder on your computer's hard drive. As you change files in either location, the application ensures that the changes are reflected in both places. For example, when you change files on your hard drive, the changed files are moved from the hard drive onto the iDisk.

The benefit of a cloning application is that it does the work for you. And you are less likely to lose files you need when you aren't connected to the Internet. Also, you won't have to deal with files that aren't in sync between your hard drive and iDisk.

The cons to this software are its cost and the time it takes to install, configure, and maintain it.

Of the different cloning applications available, I recommend FolderClone, which is produced by Salty Brine software. To learn more about it, go to www.folderclone.com. You can download and try the application at no cost by clicking the Try Now button.

FolderClone should be configured to create a mirror of your iDisk, or a subset of folders on it, on your computer's hard drive. Then you set a schedule and direction for synchronization, such as from your computer's hard drive to your iDisk or in both directions. After that's done, the application handles copying the appropriate files for you automatically. That way, your iDisk is always in sync with files on your computer's hard drive. You also can start the synchronization manually, for example, when you've been using the computer while it isn't connected to the Internet and want to move changed files from the computer to your iDisk.

Note

An iDisk is a very useful thing, and you may find that the amount of space you have isn't sufficient. See Chapter 2 for information about increasing the size of your iDisk.

Using the iDisk Web Application

Your .me Web site includes the iDisk Web application that you can use to access your iDisk through any computer with an Internet connection and either Safari or Firefox. Like accessing an iDisk from the desktop, you can move files to and from the iDisk, organize the files it contains, create folders, and so on.

Accessing your iDisk through a Web browser is useful when you aren't using one of your own computers, or when you haven't mounted an iDisk on your desktop.

Exploring the iDisk Web application

To check out your iDisk via the Web, perform the following steps:

1. **Go to me.com.** You're prompted to enter your member name and password.
2. **Enter your member name and password, and click Log In.** You move into your .me Web site.

3. **Select the iDisk icon.** You move into the iDisk Web application and see your iDisk, as shown in figure 4.13. Along the left side of the window, you see the Sidebar where you can store folders. By default, you see your Home folder, which is the entire iDisk, and the iDisk's Public folder. After you've published a Web site with either iWeb or HomePage, the Sidebar has two sections. One section is the IDISK, which contains iDisk folders. The other section is SITES, which contains folders related to iWeb and HomePage Web sites. If you haven't created a Web site with iWeb or HomePage tools, you see only the two default folders and any folders you've added to the Sidebar.

Sidebar   iDisk icon

Info button

4.13 Using the iDisk Web application is a great way to access your iDisk from any computer with Safari or Firefox and an Internet connection.

4. **Select the Info button to see how much disk space you are using.** At the bottom of the Sidebar, you see a gauge that shows this information. The blue shaded area shows the amount of space you are using, and the exact amount is shown in text under the gauge.

Genius   If you click the right-facing arrow button under the disk usage gauge, you move to the Storage section of the Account application, where you can set the proportion of disk space your iDisk uses or upgrade the size of your iDisk; see Chapter 2 for details.

120

5. **Select a folder's icon on the Sidebar to view the contents of that folder.** Along with their icons, folders have a right-facing arrow at the edge of the pane. The contents of that folder appear in the pane to the right of the Sidebar. For example, when you select the Home folder, you see all the folders on your iDisk in the pane immediately to the right of the Sidebar.

6. **To view the contents of a folder within the one you selected in the previous step, select it.** Its contents appear in a pane to the right of the one showing the folder you selected. The folder whose contents you are viewing in the pane to its right is always highlighted in a darker gray. Its parent folder is highlighted in a lighter gray in the column to the left. By looking at the "path" the highlight follows, you can always see the path you are browsing.

Genius

You can change the width of the columns in the iDisk window by dragging the line that separates them to the left or to the right.

You can continue moving up and down within the iDisk by selecting the folders whose contents you want to see. The panes within the iDisk window adjust accordingly so you always see the contents of the currently selected folder in the pane to the farthest right side of the window.

When you select a file, you see its information in the far right pane. This information includes its icon, name, file type, size, and the date and time it was last modified, as shown in figure 4.14. You also see the Download button.

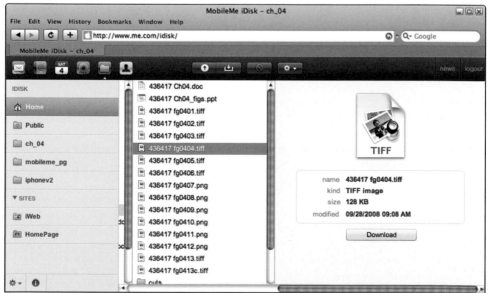

4.14 When you select a file on your iDisk, you can see information about it and the Download button.

Uploading files to an iDisk

You can use the Web application to upload files onto your iDisk. Here's how:

1. **Select the folder to which you want to upload the files.**

2. **Click the Upload button, which is the one with the upward-pointing arrow in the iDisk toolbar.** You see the Uploads dialog box.

3. **Click the Choose button.** You see the select files dialog box.

4. **Go to and select the file you want to upload.**

Genius

On the Mac, you can hold the ⌘ key down to select multiple files to upload. However, the equivalent key on Windows PCs, typically the Ctrl key, doesn't allow you to select multiple files. As MobileMe software evolves, I hope this will be corrected.

5. **If you are using a Mac, click Select; if you are using a Windows PC, click Open.** The file you select begins to upload, and you see the Uploads dialog box. This dialog box shows each file being uploaded. When the upload is complete, you see a check mark next to each file you've uploaded, as shown in figure 4.15.

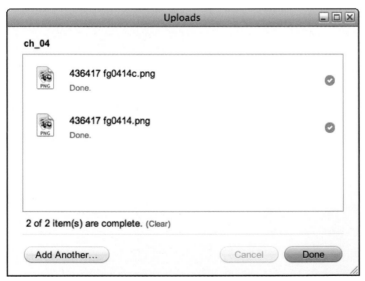

4.15 Use the Uploads dialog box to monitor the progress of files you are uploading to your iDisk.

6. **Click the Add Another button to upload more files, and repeat steps 4 and 5.**

7. **Click Done when you're finished uploading files.** The dialog box closes, and you see that the files you uploaded are now available on your iDisk.

Genius

You can use the Add Another button to upload more files while files you selected previously are still being uploaded.

Downloading files from an iDisk

You can download files from an iDisk to your computer by taking the following actions:

1. **Go to and select the file you want to download.**

Note

If you select multiple files (⌘+click each file on a Mac, or Ctrl+click each file on a Windows PC) and the click the Download button, the files you selected are compressed and saved as a single ZIP file. You can then download the ZIP file to your computer and expand it to work with the files you downloaded.

2. **Click the Download button under the file's icon, or select the Download button on the toolbar.** (Its icon has a downward-facing arrow point to an inbox.) If you are using a Windows PC or using Firefox on a Mac, go to step 3. If you are using Safari on a Mac, the file is downloaded to your default downloads location, and you can skip the rest of these steps.

3. **Select the Save option.** If you are using Firefox, the file is downloaded to your default downloads folder, and you can skip the rest of these steps. If you are using Safari on a Windows PC, you see the Save As dialog box.

4. **Choose the location to which you want to download the file, and click Save.** The file is downloaded to your computer.

Working with the iDisk Web application

You can accomplish a number of tasks with the iDisk Web application:

- **Create folders.** To add folders to an iDisk, select the folder in which you want to create a new folder. Select the Action button on the toolbar (the icon with the gear). Select the New Folder command. A new, untitled folder is created within the folder you selected. Select the new folder, and press the Return key (Mac), press the Enter key (Windows), or select the Action button and choose Rename. The folder's name is highlighted. Type the folder's new name.

- **Delete folders or files.** To remove folders or files from an iDisk, select the folder or file you want to delete and select the Delete button on the toolbar (the red circle with a slash through it). You're prompted about deleting the selected items. Click OK. The items you selected are deleted from the iDisk.

123

● **Move folders or files.** To change the location of folders or files, drag the folder or file from its current location to where you want it. For example, you can place a file within a folder by dragging its icon onto the folder, just as you do on a computer's desktop.

● **Add folders to the Sidebar.** You can place folders you use frequently on the Sidebar for quick access. Select the folder you want to place on the Sidebar, and click the Action button located at the bottom of the Sidebar, as shown in figure 4.16. Select the Add *"folder-name"* to Sidebar command, where *foldername* is the name of the folder you selected. The folder is added to the Sidebar. (You can't add files to the Sidebar.)

4.16 Adding folders to the Sidebar makes them easy to access.

● **Remove folders from the Sidebar.** If you no longer want a folder on the Sidebar, select it and click the Action button located at the bottom of the Sidebar. Select the Remove *"foldername"* from Sidebar command, where *foldername* is the name of the folder you selected. The folder is removed from the Sidebar. It remains on the iDisk.

Using an iDisk for Backups

Because data on your iDisk is stored securely and remotely, it is an ideal location to back up important data. If you lose a computer or even hard drives stored in the same area (such as from theft or a flood), you can always retrieve your data from your iDisk to any computer. You can back up data to your iDisk manually by copying it there. Or you can set it as the save location in a backup application. For Macs, use Apple's Backup, which stores backup data in the Backup folder on your iDisk by default.

Of course, the default 20GB of drive space isn't sufficient to back up lots of information, especially if you are using your iDisk for other things, such as your business documents. However, you can probably still back up your most critical files there and still have some working space. You also can upgrade your iDisk space to have more room for backed-up data.

Genius

You can't change the order in which folders are shown on the Sidebar by dragging them up or down. You have to add the folders in the order you want them to appear (the folder you add first appears toward the top of the Sidebar).

- **Compress files and folders.** You can conserve space on an iDisk by compressing files and folders. The resulting ZIP file consumes less space than the uncompressed version. And you have to compress files to be able to download multiple files at the same time. To compress a folder or a group of files, select the folder or files you want to compress. Select the Action button on the toolbar (the icon with the gear). Select the Compress command. The items you selected are compressed into a single ZIP with the name of a single item (such as folder or file) that you compressed or Archive.zip. You can rename the compressed file just like you rename a folder. If you want to save space on the iDisk, delete the files you compressed and store just the compressed file on the iDisk.

- **Hide some of the default folders.** On the iDisk, you can hide some of the folders that you might not use. Select the Action button on the toolbar (the icon with the gear). Select the Preferences command. Select the Show simple folder layout check box, and click Save. Some folders that you don't use directly in iDisk (for example, Backups) or that you don't use at all (Software on a Windows PC) are hidden. Deselect the check box to show those folders again.

⦿ **Share files via the Public folder.** Remember that you can share files with other people using the Public folder. Move the folders and files you want to share into the Public folder. Then configure your Public folder's security, and provide the information others need to access it. (Information about configuring and accessing the Public folder is provided earlier in this chapter.)

Genius

You can use iDisk to uncompress any ZIP file. Upload the file onto the iDisk. Select the ZIP file you want to decompress, and click the Action button located at the bottom of the Sidebar. Select the Decompress command. The ZIP file is expanded, and you see a folder named with the ZIP file's name. This zipped file contains the files that were compressed.

How Can I Take Advantage of MobileMe Chat Features?

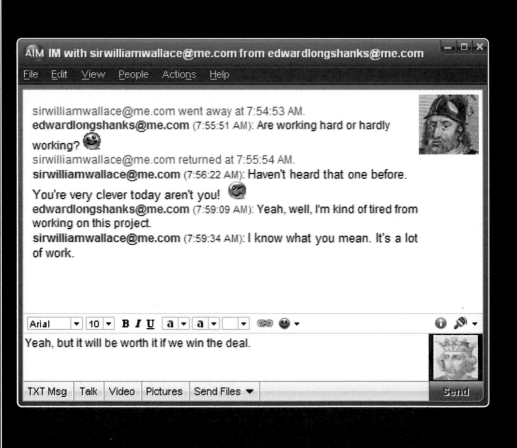

Effective communication is vital to having and growing a small business. This can be especially challenging when your team members aren't physically located in the same space. Fortunately, using MobileMe, your team members can use text, voice, and video chatting to communicate effectively with each other, business partners, customers, and potential customers. These techniques offer benefits over face-to-face or phone communication, not the least of which is being extremely inexpensive; communicating using chatting costs you nothing beyond the cost of MobileMe accounts and the associated hardware and software (which you probably already have or can get for free).

Understanding How MobileMe Can Help You Communicate

MobileMe offers the "pipeline" over which you can text, audio, and video chat. When you obtain a MobileMe account, you also get an iChat account and an AOL Instant Messenger (AIM) account. You can use these accounts to communicate using both Macs and Windows PCs. The software and hardware you use on each platform is different, but the end result is similar: You can communicate effectively without needing to be co-located and without any cost impact.

On Macs, you can use the Mac OS X iChat application to chat with other Mac users and with Windows users who have the AIM application (and required hardware to audio or video chat). All Mac models, except the Mac Pro, include built-in microphones and iSight cameras, so you can audio and video chat at no additional cost. (If you use a Mac Pro, you must purchase a microphone and camera to be able to audio or video chat. Or, you can use one of Apple's LED Cinema Displays that feature a built-in iSight camera.)

On Windows PCs, you can use the free AIM application to text chat. If your Windows PC has a microphone and a Web cam, you can audio and video chat with other AIM users of Windows computers or Mac users who have iChat.

The rest of this chapter is divided into two major sections, one for Mac users and one for Windows users. Information about communicating with people using the other platform (such as Mac users communicating with Windows users) is provided when there is a significant difference.

Communicating Using a Mac

Mac OS X includes the iChat application that you can use to text chat; if you have a current Mac model (other than a Mac Pro), you also have an iSight camera and microphone, so you can use iChat to audio and video chat as well. (If you use a Mac Pro, you need to purchase and install a camera and microphone to be able to audio and video chat.) In addition to chatting, iChat offers a number of other useful features, such as sharing documents online, controlling other Macs, and being able to make presentations over the Internet.

Configuring iChat

Before you start chatting, you need to do some basic configuration to prepare iChat. There are two basic paths. One is to start iChat and have the Assistant walk you through the configuration steps. The other is manual configuration; even if you used the Assistant, you should work through a manual configuration so you can tweak iChat to make it work as well as possible for you.

Configuring iChat with the Assistant

To get started, launch iChat and use the following steps to configure it through the Assistant, which starts with the Welcome screen:

1. **Review the information in the Welcome screen.**

2. **Click Continue.** The Set up a new iChat Account window appears. Because you already have a MobileMe account configured for the current Mac user account, the account information is configured automatically.

3. **If you use Jabber Instant Messaging, select the check box, enter your Jabber account name and password, and click Continue; if not, just click Continue.** The Set up Bonjour Messaging window opens.

4. **If other Macs are on a local network with which you can communicate, select the Use Bonjour messaging check box.** This enables you to chat with others on your local network because all Bonjour devices are found automatically. If you use a wireless network in a public place, you might want to leave this option turned off.

5. **Click Continue.** The Set up iChat AV window appears. During this step, iChat shows you the image that is being captured by the built-in iSight camera or external camera (Mac Pro). Just under the image is a volume level indicator that displays the relative volume of the audio input from the Mac microphone.

6. **Click Continue.** The Conclusion screen appears.

7. **Click Done.** The basic configuration of iChat is complete, and you move into the chatting windows. You can start setting up buddies for chatting (see the section on creating and managing buddies in iChat later in this section), or move into the next section to learn how to configure iChat manually.

Configuring iChat with preferences

iChat offers a number of preferences that you can use to configure the way it works. You don't have to set all these preferences at once, and you should plan on adjusting them over time to tweak the way iChat works. To access iChat preferences, select iChat ⇨ Preferences. The Preferences window has a number of tabs that are summarized in the following sections.

Note

You'll find a number of preferences that aren't described here, but that might be useful to you. As you explore the preferences, watch for those that might meet your style. I've included only the ones that are most widely used.

The aptly named General tab of the iChat Preferences dialog box, shown in figure 5.1, enables you to configure some general behaviors.

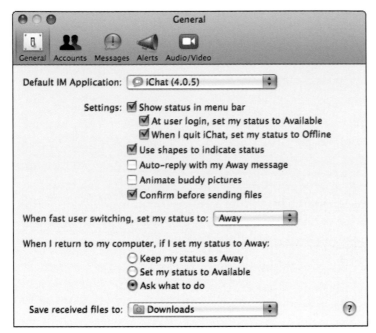

General

General Accounts Messages Alerts Audio/Video

Default IM Application: iChat (4.0.5)

Settings: ☑ Show status in menu bar
☑ At user login, set my status to Available
☑ When I quit iChat, set my status to Offline
☑ Use shapes to indicate status
☐ Auto-reply with my Away message
☐ Animate buddy pictures
☑ Confirm before sending files

When fast user switching, set my status to: Away

When I return to my computer, if I set my status to Away:
○ Keep my status as Away
○ Set my status to Available
● Ask what to do

Save received files to: Downloads

5.1 The General tab enables you to set status preferences, such as what happens to your chat status when you start using your Mac after a period of inactivity.

Here are some of the more useful settings:

- **Show status in menu bar.** This is useful because it places an iChat menu on your menu. From there, you can easily change your chat status, see which of your buddies is available, and move to your buddy lists. Use the two sub-check boxes to automatically configure your status when you log in and when you quit iChat.

- **Confirm before sending files.** You can exchange files with others through chats. It's a good idea to enable this setting so you don't send any files that you don't intend to.

- **When fast user switching, set my status to.** Use this pop-up menu to automatically set your status when someone else logs into your Mac. In most cases, you want to set your status to Away or Offline so people don't try to talk with you when you aren't using your computer.

- **When I return to my computer, if I set my status to Away.** Use these radio buttons to set an iChat status when you return to your user account. The Ask what to do option is useful because your computer prompts you about your status. If you select Set my status to Available, you immediately become available for chatting when you log into your Mac.

- **Save received files to.** Use this pop-up menu to select the folder into which files are stored when you receive them through iChat.

You can create and use multiple kinds of accounts within iChat, including any on this list:

- MobileMe
- AIM (AOL Instant Messenger)
- Jabber
- Google Talk

To configure iChat user accounts, open the Accounts tab of the Preferences window, shown in figure 5.2.

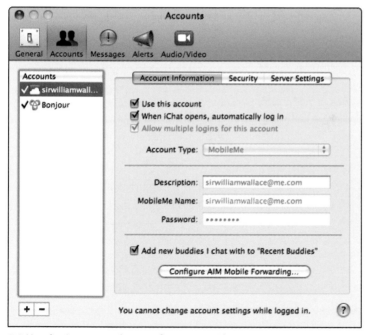

5.2 Use the Accounts tab to configure your iChat accounts.

Some of the more useful tools and settings are described in this list:

- **Accounts list.** In the left pane, you see the accounts that are currently configured. To add a new account, click the Add button (+) at the bottom of the Accounts list, and follow the onscreen instructions in the Account Setup sheet to configure the account. Once configured, you can use the account to chat.

- **Use this account.** Select an account you want to use for chatting, and select this check box. You can have any of the configured accounts active so you can use them at the same time.

- **When iChat opens, automatically log in.** Select this check box if you want to log into the account as soon as you open iChat.

Note

You have to be online to be able to set a number of these preferences. If a preference that you want to set is disabled, check your chat status.

- **Add new buddies I chat with to "Recent Buddies."** When you select this check box, anyone with whom you chat is added to your recent list, making it easier to chat with him again.

- **Security sub-tab.** Use this sub-tab to control the security of your chats. You can block people from being able to see that you are idle. You also can set the privacy level, which determines who can see when you are online. For example, if you select the Allow people in my Buddy List radio button, only people who are on your buddy list can see your status. I recommend that you do limit this, or you might get chat requests from people that you don't have any interest in communicating with.

The Messages pane, shown in figure 5.3, enables you to set various formatting options for your messages.

Following are some useful controls on the Messages tab:

- **Pop-up menus.** Use these menus to set the colors for your text balloons and the text that appears within them. Select the Reformat incoming messages check box and use the pop-up menus next to it to configure how messages that you receive are formatted (if you leave this option deselected, then messages are formatted according to the sender's preferences).

- **Set Font buttons.** Use these buttons to select the font for your chats (sending and receiving).

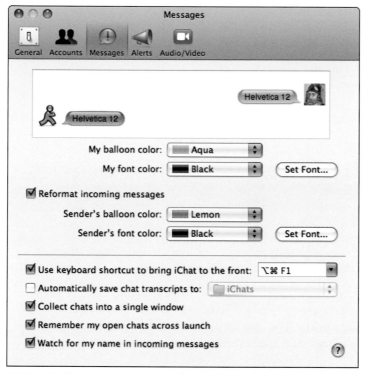

5.3 Use the Messages preferences to format how your text chats appear and to set options, such as automatic transcripts.

- **Use keyboard shortcut to bring iChat to the front.** Select this check box and choose the keyboard shortcut on the pop-up menu to be able to bring iChat to the front quickly.

- **Remember my open chats across launch.** When you select this check box, iChat remembers the state of your on-going chats, even after you quit the application. When you start it up again, you return to where you left off.

Note

When you chat, iChat displays an icon to represent you, and you see icons that represent the people with whom you chat. Your default icon is the image associated with your user account.

Use the Alerts pane to set the alerts and notifications that iChat uses to get your attention. Select the event for which you want to configure an alert on the Event pop-up menu, and then select the specific alert using the check boxes and pop-up menus to configure it. You can choose from the following events: a sound playing, the iChat icon on the Dock bouncing, an AppleScript running, or an announcement being displayed. You can be alerted about many different events, including when you log in and log out. You can have a unique alert for each event, or you can use the same alert for multiple events. You also can set alerts to repeat until you acknowledge them by selecting the Repeat check box.

You can use these preferences to prepare for audio and video chats. Following are the important settings:

- **Image preview.** In this pane, you see the current image that is being received from your Mac's iSight camera. If you can see yourself well, then people with whom you chat also can see you. If not, you may need to adjust lighting, your position relative to your Mac's camera, or other conditions.

- **Audio meter.** Just under the image preview is an audio meter that provides a graphic representation of the volume level being received. You can use the built-in microphone or another audio input device, such as a Bluetooth headset.

- **Play repeated ring sound when invited to a conference.** When this check box is selected and you are invited to an audio chat or videoconference, you hear a ringing sound until you respond to the request.

Creating and managing buddies in iChat

The people with whom you chat are called buddies, and in order to chat with someone, you must configure them as buddies. You can create two kinds of buddies. One type is the people whom your Mac can see on a local network through Bonjour. The other type, and the one you are likely to deal with more often, is people who are configured in your Address Book and have a MobileMe email address, a Jabber account, or an AIM screen name.

By default, when you open iChat, you see two windows: One is titled Bonjour List, and the other is labeled AIM Buddy List, as shown in figure 5.4. The people shown on the Bonjour list are found automatically when your Mac searches your local network for Bonjour users. You add people with whom you want to chat on the AIM Buddy List. You can chat with people on either list in the same way. Because using the AIM Buddy List is the more common way, I focus on it for the rest of this chapter, but you can do anything with the Bonjour list that you can with the AIM Buddy List.

You can add people to your buddy list in several ways. You can create a buddy in iChat, or you can add someone who is in your Address Book as a buddy.

5.4 The AIM Buddy List shows the people with whom you can chat, along with their current status.

Creating a buddy in iChat

To create a new buddy in iChat, do the following:

1. **Click the Add button (+) located in the lower-left corner of the AIM Buddy List window.**

2. **Select Add Buddy.** The Add Buddy sheet appears.

3. **Choose the type of account the buddy uses on the pop-up menu on the right side of the sheet.** If the buddy uses a MobileMe account, select MobileMe; @me.com is filled in for you.

4. **Enter the buddy's account name.** For MobileMe accounts, this is the same as the MobileMe email address. Don't overwrite the @me.com that was added automatically, or the buddy won't work.

5. **Enter the buddy's first name in the First Name field.**

6. **Enter the buddy's last name in the Last Name field, as shown in figure 5.5.**

7. **Click Add.** The buddy is added to your buddy list. If the buddy is online, he appears in the Buddies section along with status information, such as if he is idle, away, and so on. If the buddy is not online, he appears in the Offline section.

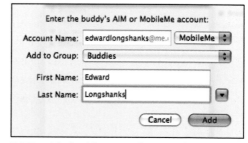

5.5 To add a buddy to your list, complete the information on this sheet.

Caution   iChat doesn't check the account information you enter to make sure it's correct. If the account information for a buddy is wrong, the buddy's status is always Offline. So make sure you are using the correct information. If the person uses a MobileMe account, you can send email to his MobileMe email address because it is the same as his iChat account. If he receives the email, then you know you have the iChat information set up correctly.

Adding someone from your Address Book as a buddy

To add someone who is already in your Address Book as a buddy, use the following steps:

1. **Click the Add button (+) located in the lower-left corner of the AIM Buddy List window.**

2. **Select Add Buddy.** The Add Buddy sheet appears.

3. **Click the Expand button (the downward-pointing triangle next to the Last Name field).** The lower pane of the sheet expands, and you see a mini-Address Book viewer.

Genius   Use the pop-up menu in the column heading to the right of the Name field to select AIM to view AIM, or Email to view email account information, for the people shown on the sheet.

4. **Search or browse for the person you want to add as a buddy.**

5. **Select the name of the person you want to add.**

6. **If the person has more than one email address or AIM account, click the account you want to associate with the person for chatting.**

Caution   If the person you select doesn't have a valid account, the Add button remains disabled. You must either enter account information at the top of the sheet or update the person's information in the Address Book before you can add her as a buddy.

7. **Click Add.** The buddy is added to your buddy list. If the buddy is online, she appears in the Buddies section. If not, she appears in the Offline section.

Organizing buddies in groups

Organizing buddies in groups make them easier to manage. To create a group and place buddies in it, do the following:

1. **Click the Add button (+) located in the lower-left corner of the AIM Buddy List window, as shown in figure 5.6.**

2. **Select Add Group.** The group name sheet appears.

3. **Enter the name of the group and click Add.** The group you created appears on the AIM Buddy List.

4. **Drag buddies from their current locations into the group.**

Working with the AIM Buddy List in iChat

At the top of the AIM Buddy List window, you see your information, including your name, status, video icon (if your Mac has a working iSight camera), and the image associated with your name.

The dot next to and text below your name indicate your status. A green dot means you are available, and those who have permission to see your status know that you are available. Text also is associated with each status, and you can have multiple text labels for the same status; the default is Available when you are online, but you can make it anything you want, such as the song you are currently listening to in iTunes as shown at the top of figure 5.7. A red dot means you are online, but unavailable; like the Available status, you can associate different text messages with the Unavailable status; the default is Away. When no dot is shown, you are Offline, meaning you aren't signed into chatting services. When a gray dot with an empty circle appears, it means that you are online, but can't be seen by anyone (the Invisible status).

5.6 Buddies on the AIM Buddy List are organized in groups.

5.7 Information about your status and the image that people you chat with see in their windows appear at the top of the AIM Buddy List.

139

Genius

When you create a buddy, you can place her into a group by choosing that group on the Add to Group menu on the new buddy sheet.

Genius

To change your status manually, open the pop-up menu immediately below your name at the top of the AIM Buddy List window and choose the status you want to set. To create a custom status message, select Custom Available or Custom Away. Then type your status name in the text box, and press Return. Your status message is saved and can be seen by others who have permission to view your status.

Next to your account image is a box indicating the status of your A/V capabilities. For example, if you are using a Mac with a working iSight camera, you see the video camera icon. If you are capable of audio chatting, but not video chatting, you see a telephone receiver.

Note

The same A/V icons apply to buddies. If a buddy's icon has the video camera icon, you can video chat with that buddy. If a buddy's icon has the text icon (the letter *A*), you can only text chat with that buddy.

At the far right of the top section, you see the image for your account. This image appears next to your name on other people's AIM Buddy Lists and next to your comments in a text chat. The default image is the one associated with your card in the Address Book application. You can change the image associated with your account by clicking the image to open the image menu and choosing one of the following options:

- Click an image to use it.
- Click Edit Picture to open the Buddy Picture dialog box. Using this tool, you can capture an image using your iSight camera or drag an image onto the image well and edit it. When you click Set, the image you configured is used as your iChat icon.
- Click Clear Recent Pictures to remove the images from the menu.

In the AIM Buddy List window, buddies are organized by groups. The default groups are Buddies, which contains your buddies who are online, and Offline, which contains your buddies who have Offline as their status. Other default groups are available that you may or may not find useful.

The section on organizing buddies in groups explained how to create groups and add buddies to them. You can remove a group you don't use by opening its contextual menu, choosing Delete Group, and clicking Delete in the warning sheet.

Note The Offline group contains all your buddies who are currently offline. These buddies are disabled, and you can't even try to chat with any of them. The Offline group can't be deleted.

Use the expansion triangles to expand or collapse the groups you see. When a group is collapsed, you see the number of buddies in that group. When expanded, you see each buddy in the group.

When expanded, you see status information next to each buddy in a group along with the buddy's name and image. If you see a green dot, the buddy is online and available for chatting; you also see the buddy's status message below his name. If you see a red dot, the buddy is online, but not available for chatting; you also see his current Away status message under his name. If you see an orange triangle, the buddy is online, but idle, meaning he isn't doing anything on his computer.

Note You might see different status symbols for people using other applications. For example, when the status of a buddy using AIM on a Windows computer is Away, you see a red square instead of a red circle.

As buddies change status, you hear alerts as you have configured them on the Alerts tab of the iChat Preferences dialog box.

You can change the information for a buddy, including name and image, by selecting the buddy you want to change, opening the contextual menu, and selecting Show Info. In the resulting Info window, you can change any of the buddy's information, such as the image you see for the buddy. As long as you don't change account information, you can still chat with the buddy.

Note When someone using the AIM application on a Windows computer adds you as a buddy, you are prompted to log into AOL Instant Messenger. Enter your MobileMe email address as the Login ID, enter your MobileMe account password as the Password, select the Remember this password in my keychain check box, and click Login. With these settings, you have to do this only once.

Using iChat to text chat

Text messaging/chatting (a.k.a. instant messaging) is a preferred way of communicating for many people. Text chats are easy to do, fast, and convenient. Using iChat, you start your own text chats or answer someone's request to text chat with you. You also can chat with more than one person at the same time.

Starting a text chat

You can start a text chat with others by following these steps:

1. **Select the buddy with whom you want to chat, as shown in figure 5.8.** If the person is on the Offline list, he isn't available for chatting, and so you'll need to communicate in some other way. Even if the person is online, make sure his status indicator shows that he's available for chatting before you initiate a chat session — look for the green dot.

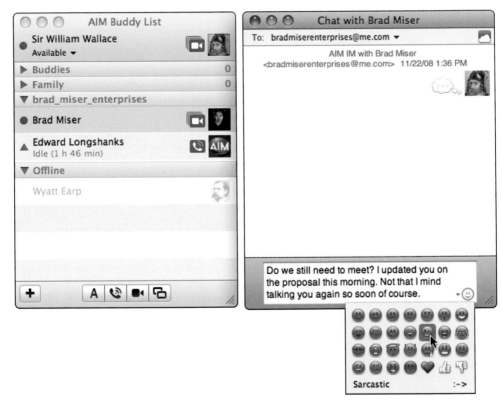

5.8 Here, William is starting a text chat with Brad.

2. **Click the Text Chat button, which is the A located at the bottom of the window.** An empty Instant Message window appears. The name of the window is "Chat with *buddy*" where *buddy* is the name associated with the person with whom you are chatting.

142

3. **Type your message in the text bar at the bottom of the window.**

Genius

You can use the pop-up menu (marked with a smiley icon) at the end of the text bar to add emoticons to what you type. On the resulting menu, you see the various emoticons that are available. Click one to add it. When you hover over an emoticon, you see what it means, and the text equivalent at the bottom of the menu.

4. **When you are ready to send what you typed, press Return.** You see the message you typed near your name on the right side near the top of the window, and it is sent to the person with whom you are chatting. Your message appears in a text bubble in that user's iChat or other text-messaging application. When the user accepts your request and then types and sends a reply, you receive it.

   When you receive a reply to your message, you see the person's picture along with the text he sent, as shown in figure 5.9. The responder's text appears on the left side of the window and is formatted according to the settings on the Messages pane of the iChat Preferences dialog box.

 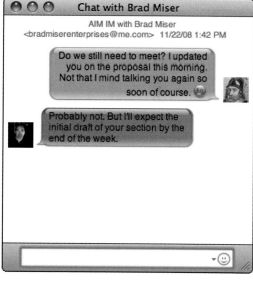

5.9 When the person responds to your request, you see his text message in the window as the next block in a conversation.

5. **Type your response in the text box at the bottom of the window.**

6. **Press Return.** Your response is sent to the buddy.

7. **Continue chatting.** You don't have to wait for a response before sending another message, but it's usually less confusing if you do.

8. **When you are finished chatting, close the chat window.**

Genius

You can also start a chat by double-clicking a buddy's name.

Responding to a text chat invitation

You can respond to text chat invitations that you receive to start a text conversation. When a person wants to chat with you, a box appears on your screen with the name of the person who sent it as its title and the text he sent. Respond to the request by following these steps:

1. **Click the initial text chat window, as shown in figure 5.10.** It expands to a chat window that includes the text bar and the following buttons:

   - **Block.** Click this button to decline the chat and block future requests from the sender. Skip the rest of these steps.

   - **Decline.** Click this button to decline the chat. Nothing is sent back to the person who is trying to chat with you. Skip the rest of these steps.

   - **Accept.** Click this button to accept the chat. The window expands to become a text chat window with the sender's information at the top, his initial text in the center pane, and the text bar at the bottom. Continue with these steps.

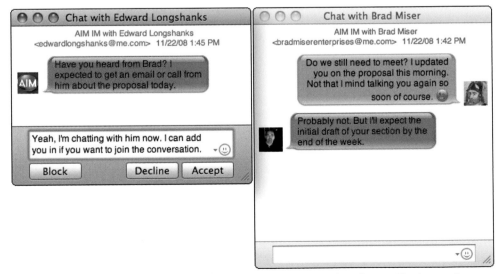

5.10 When someone sends you a chat request, you can accept or decline the specific chat session or block the person requesting the chat.

144

Genius

You can type a response and then click the Accept button to send it.

2. **Type your response in the text bar.**

3. **Press Return.** Your text is sent.

4. **Continue the chat.**

Genius

Open the text chat pane's contextual menu to see a pop-up menu containing various formatting commands, such as Show as Boxes, which changes the text balloons to text boxes organized on top of each other instead of on each side of the window.

When someone leaves a chat, you see a status message saying so at the bottom of the window.

Chatting with more than one person

You can include more than two people in a text chat in a couple of ways. You can invite multiple people to the same chat, or you can use a chat room. Invite people to the same chat when everyone you want to chat with is a buddy. Use a chat room when you want to chat with people who aren't configured as buddies.

To invite multiple people to a chat, perform the following steps:

1. **Select each buddy with whom you want to chat by holding down the ⌘ key while you click the buddy on your list.**

2. **Click the Text Chat button.** You see the text chat window, with each buddy that is included in the chat shown at the top of the window.

3. **Type your message.**

4. **Press Return.** The message is sent to each buddy.

   As a buddy responds, his message appears in your window. Everyone who joins the chat sees the messages from each participant as he comes in, as shown in figure 5.11. You see each buddy's image next to his text as it comes in.

5. **Continue chatting as you normally do.** Each participant sees all the messages being typed by the other participants. The messages you send continue to be along the right side of the screen while all the other messages appear along the left side of the screen. As buddies leave the chat, you see status updates in the text window.

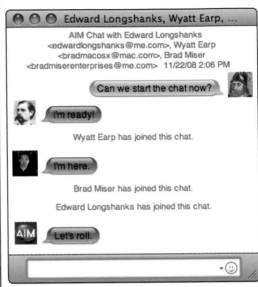

5.11 You can text chat with multiple people at the same time.

Note

Over time, you may see more categories appear in the AIM Buddy List window, such as Recent Buddies, which shows you that people with whom you've recently chatted are online. Like other groups, you can expand or collapse these groups to see the people they contain.

You also can have a chat with multiple people by using a chat room. To start a chat room, perform the following steps:

1. **Select File ⇨ Go to Chat Room.** The Go To Chat Room dialog box appears. If you've previously created a chat room, you see it on the list. Along with its name, you see the account that created the room and whether it is set to be autojoined.

2. **Start a chat room by doing one of the following:**

   - Choose an existing chat room on the menu at the top of the dialog box.

   - Type a name for a new chat room, and click the Add button (+) in the lower-left corner of the window.

Caution

Don't include any spaces or special characters in the name of the chat room. For best results, use a one-word name.

3. **With the room you want to use selected, click Go.** You see an empty chat window named Chatting in *roomname*, where *roomname* is the name of the chat room you selected; the Participants drawer appears on the side of the window. This is what you use to manage the people chatting in the room.

4. **Click the Add button (+) in the lower-right corner of the Participants drawer.** A menu appears showing each of your AIM buddies along with the Other option.

5. **Invite people to chat by doing one of the following:**

   - Select a buddy.

   - Select Other, enter the email address of the person you want to invite to the chat room, and click OK.

   The invitation sheet appears.

Caution You can use the Other option to invite someone who isn't a buddy to a chat. However, that person must have and be using an instant messaging application to be able to participate in the chat.

6. **Enter the text you want to send to the person whom you are inviting, and click Invite.** The first time you do this, the text is a default message; if you change it, your updated message appears each time you invite someone. You can use that text or change it for each invitation.

   The person you invited receives an invitation. If he is a buddy, it appears in the normal text chat window, except that each time a person joins the room, he sees that person on his Participants list.

7. **Repeat Steps 5 and 6 until you've invited everyone to the chat room, as shown in figure 5.12.**

8. **Chat by typing your messages and reading messages other people type.** Any messages sent to the chat room are seen by all the participants. If someone leaves the chat, he disappears from the Participants list and you see a status message in the text window.

Note You can have multiple text chats going on with one person in each conversation at the same time; depending on your preference settings, each chat appears in a separate window or they all appear in the same window. The difference between this and a group chat is that the people with whom you are chatting can see only the messages you type in their text chat window.

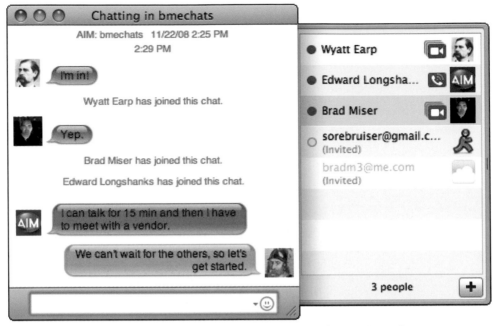

5.12 When you use a chat room, you see a list of all the invitees on the Participants list.

Using iChat to audioconference

An iChat audio chat is pretty much like a combination of a text chat and talking on the telephone. Starting an audio chat isn't any harder than starting a text chat, either, as you can see in the following steps:

1. **Select the buddy with whom you want to chat.** The person must be online and should have an Available status (green dot). Her icon also must be either the video camera or the telephone receiver. If it's just the letter *A,* the buddy is unable to have an audio chat.

Genius

To start an audio chat with multiple buddies, hold down the ⌘ key while you select each buddy.

2. **Click the Audio Chat button (the telephone receiver) at the bottom of the AIM Buddy List window.** The Audio Chat with *buddy* window appears, where *buddy* is the person you selected.

   The person you invited to the chat hears and sees an alert (assuming her alerts are configured). When your chat request is accepted, the Audio chat window collapses. If your request is declined, you see a message saying so at the bottom of the window.

3. **When the buddy accepts the request, start chatting.**

4. **As you chat, you can use the following controls to manage your chat session, as shown in figure 5.13:**

5.13 Chatting with audio is as easy as it should be.

- **Audio meter.** Use the Audio meter to gauge your own volume. As you speak, the green part of the bar should move to at least the halfway point. If not, you need to increase your volume by moving closer to the microphone or using the Input level control on the Sound pane of the System Preferences application.

- **Add buddies.** Click the Add button (+) located in the lower-left corner of the window to add more people to the audio chat. Just like text chats, you can add multiple people to an audio chat. Each person in the conversation has his own audio window with its own controls. You can have up to ten people in the same audio chat.

- **Mute.** Click the Mute button (the microphone) to mute your end of the conversation. Click it again to unmute your sound so that the other people In the chat can hear you again.

- **Volume slider.** Drag to the right to increase the volume, or drag to the left to decrease it.

Note

If you are listening to iTunes when you start an audio or video chat, it automatically pauses. It starts playing again when the chat ends.

If a participant leaves the chat, the others see a status message update.

5. **When you're finished, close the chat window.**

When someone wants to audio chat with you, you see a window with the person's name as its title and the Audio icon. Click the window, and then click one of the following buttons:

- **Text Reply.** This declines the audio invitation and starts a text chat.

- **Decline.** This declines the audio invitation. The person who sent it to you sees a status message stating that you declined.

- **Accept.** This accepts the invitation and starts the chat.

Caution

To be able to participate in audio or video chats with more than two people involved, the participants must be using a chat application that is capable of this functionality. iChat is capable of audio chats with up to ten people and video chats with up to four people, but the current freeware version of AIM for Windows is limited to two people for each kind of chat so you can't include AIM users in multi-party audio or video chats.

Using iChat to videoconference

Using iChat to videoconference is amazingly cool. And it is as simple to use as the other types of chatting. However, a video chat requires lots of bandwidth, so it's more sensitive to the Internet connection of each person involved in the chat. And you can only video chat with someone who is using iChat or the most current version of Instant Messenger for Windows (assuming he has a working camera for his computer, of course).

To video chat, do the following:

1. **Select the buddy with whom you want to chat.** The buddy must be available, and her icon must be the video camera. If it is the telephone receiver or the letter A, you need to chat using some other technique.

2. **Click the Video Chat button (the video camera) at the bottom of the AIM Buddy List window.** The video chat window opens, and you see the green "on" light next to your iSight camera. You see a preview of the view that others see of you and a message that iChat is waiting for a response.

   The buddy whom you invited hears or sees alerts. When the buddy accepts your chat invitation, you see her image in the larger part of the chat window. The smaller, inset preview window shows you what the other person sees in her chat window, as shown in figure 5.14.

3. **Talk to and see the other person.**

4. **As you chat, you can manage your chat session in the following ways:**

   - **Move the preview window.** Drag the preview window within the larger chat window so it's where you want it to be on the screen. This affects only your view.

   - **Add buddies.** Click the Add button (+) to add more people to the video chat. As you add people, the chat window remains the same size, and each person appears in his own window. You can have up to four people in the same video chat.

   - **Mute.** To mute your end of the conversation, click the Mute button (the microphone); click it again to unmute it.

- **Fill Screen.** To make the chat window fill the desktop, click the Fill Screen button (two diagonal arrows). To see the toolbar while in full screen mode, move the pointer. The toolbar appears on the screen, and you can use its controls, which are similar to the ones in the standard video chat window.

- **Resize Screen.** Drag the Resize handle located in the lower-right corner of the window to increase or decrease the size of the chat window.

- **Effects.** When you click the Effects button, you see the Video Effects palette. You can browse the available effects and click one to apply it to your image. The preview updates, and other participants see you as the effect changes you.

5. **When you're finished, close the window.** Other participants see that you have left. If others leave, you see that information in your window.

5.14 You can videoconference with up to three other people.

As you read earlier, the downside of videoconferencing is that it requires lots of bandwidth. If the participants are using a cable, DSL, or faster connection, you shouldn't have any trouble. Any slower connection methods probably won't work. Sometimes, problems are from only one side, such as when some participants can hear and see the others fine, but can't be seen. Any problems you experience with video chats are most likely tied to the connections speed of the recipients.

Applying Backgrounds During a Video Chat

The standard effects you can apply to a video chat are kind of cool. You also can apply backgrounds to video chats that make it appear as if you are someplace you aren't. A background can be a static image or a video. iChat includes some backgrounds by default, but you can use your own images as backgrounds as well.

To add a default background, do the following:

1. **Start a video chat.** While you are waiting for the chat to start, you can use the following steps to set the background.
2. **Click the Effects button.**
3. **Scroll to the right in the Video Effects palette until you see the images and video that are provided by default.**
4. **Click the image or video that you want to apply as a background.**
5. **Move out of the camera view at the prompt.**
6. **When the prompt disappears, move back into the picture.** It will look as if you are actually in front of the background. The effect isn't perfect, but it is pretty amazing.

To add your own images or video as backgrounds, do the following:

1. **Select Video ⇨ Show Video Effects.** The Video Effects palette appears.
2. **Scroll in the palette until you see the User Backdrop categories.**
3. **Drag an image file or video clip into one of the User Backdrop wells.**
4. **Click the image or video that you want to apply as a background.**
5. **Use the previous steps to start a video chat and apply the background you added.**

If you are having difficulties during a conference, select Video ➪ Connection Doctor. The Connection Doctor window appears, as shown in figure 5.15. Use the Show menu to select Statistics to see the quality of the connection for each participant, Capabilities to check what each participant is capable of, and Error Log to see any errors that have occurred. If the problem is related to a participant's bandwidth, that participant must find a faster way to connect to be able to conference successfully.

Connection Doctor	
Show:	Statistics
Chat Duration:	00 : 00 : 24
Local	
Framerate (fps):	14.1
Bitrate (kbps):	477.2
Wyatt Earp	
Framerate (fps):	15.0
Bitrate (kbps):	1,869.9
Audio Quality:	97%
Video Quality:	98%

5.15 Use the Connection Doctor to troubleshoot video chats.

Using iChat to give a presentation

In some cases, you might want to just share a document with someone else. You can do this with iChat Theater. This is ideal for making remote presentations. You can show the presentation and provide narration. You can use the same steps to share other kinds of documents, as well. Here's how to do your own remote presentations:

1. **Select File ➪ Share a File With iChat Theater.** You see the Share with iChat Theater dialog box.

Caution

Sharing a document works only with other iChat users.

2. **Move to and select the document (such as a presentation) that you want to share.**

3. **Click Share.** The document is prepared, and you see a message stating that iChat Theater is ready to begin.

4. **Select the buddy with whom you want to share a document.**

5. **Start a video chat.**

   When the buddy accepts your invitation, you see the Video Chat window. You also see a window showing the document you are sharing. In the lower-left corner of the window, you see a preview window showing the buddy with whom you're chatting, as shown in figure 5.16.

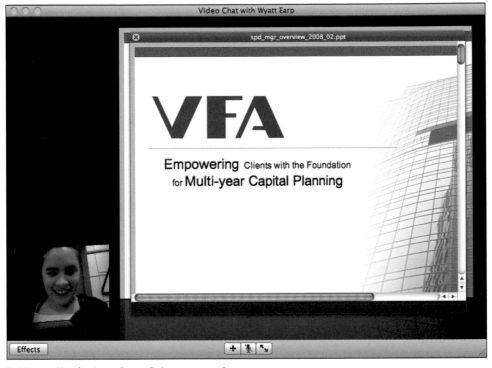

5.16 Here, I'm sharing a PowerPoint presentation.

Genius

If you want to see a preview window showing yourself, select Video ⇨ Show Local Video. A second preview window appears, and you see the image that your audience is seeing in their preview window.

6. **Move through the document, and speak to deliver your message to the audience.** If you share a Keynote presentation, you can use the Keynote controls to present the document.

7. **When you're finished, close the Video Chat window.**

Controlling a Mac over the Internet with iChat

You can share your desktop with people you chat with. When you do this, the person with whom you share it can control your computer. He sees your desktop on his screen and can manipulate your computer using his keyboard and mouse (or trackpad). Using a similar process, you can share someone else's desktop to control her computer from afar.

Sharing screens is useful for many things, such as collaborating on documents. But it can be even more helpful when you need to get help from someone or when you want to help someone. You

can share your desktop with a buddy, and he can watch exactly how and where you are getting into trouble, which is usually the biggest challenge when remote troubleshooting. He also can take control of your Mac to help you fix problems. Likewise, you can share your Mac knowledge with your team members to help them with problems or teach a team member how to do something.

Caution

Sharing screens works only with other iChat users.

Accessing a Mac being shared with you

You can share someone else's desktop to take control of his computer. Here's how:

1. **Start the sharing session in one of the following two ways:**

   - Select the buddy whose desktop you want to share. Click the Share Desktop button (the two boxes overlapping each other). Select Ask to Share *buddy*'s screen, where *buddy* is the name of the buddy you selected. When your request is accepted, you see a message that the sharing feature is starting, and two windows appear on your screen, as shown in figure 5.17.

5.17 When you share someone else's desktop, you can control his computer.

- When you receive a request to share your screen, click Accept. You see a starting sharing message, and two windows appear on your screen, again as shown in figure 5.17.

One window is the buddy's desktop, which is the larger window by default. The other, smaller window is a preview of your desktop, which is labeled "My Computer."

Genius

You can move the preview window around the screen if it blocks the part of the shared desktop that you want to see.

2. **You can work with the buddy's computer just as if you were sitting in front of it.** For example, you can make changes to documents or use commands on menus. An audio chat is started automatically so you can communicate with the other person.

3. **To move back to your desktop, click the My Computer window.** The two windows flip-flop so that your desktop is now the larger window and you can control your Mac.

Genius

It's a good idea to explain what you are doing as you are doing it, so the person whose computer you are controlling knows what's going on. Remember, all he can see is his computer doing things without him making the commands.

4. **Perform the tasks you need to do on your Mac.**

5. **Click back in the other computer's window to control it again.**

6. **When you're finished sharing, click the Close button on the My Computer window.** The sharing session ends.

Sharing your Mac with someone else

To share your desktop with someone else, perform the following steps:

1. **Select the buddy with whom you want to share your desktop.**

2. **Click the Share Desktop button (the two overlapping boxes).** If the Share Desktop button doesn't become active when you select a buddy, the buddy is not capable of sharing your desktop.

Caution

When you share your screen, you are sharing control of your Mac, so you want to make sure you know with whom you are sharing it. Someone who shares your screen can do anything remotely that you can do directly.

3. **Select Share My Screen with *buddy*, where *buddy* is the name of the buddy you selected.** iChat sends a screen-sharing request to the buddy you selected, and you see the Screen Sharing window.

When the buddy accepts your invitation, you see the screen-sharing startup message. You also see the Sharing status indicator at the top of the iChat menu on the menu bar.

The buddy with whom you are sharing your screen can now use your Mac. She also can talk to you because, when you share the desktop, you also have an audio chat session going. Expect to see your Mac do things without any help from you.

Going further with iChat

iChat is a powerful application that includes lots of features and capabilities that I don't have space to cover here. Here is a brief description of some of them:

- By default, when your Mac goes to sleep or when the screen saver activates, your status is changed to Away automatically.

- You can have multiple chats of various types going on with different people at the same time. Each chat appears in its own independent chat window, unless you select the Collect chats into a single window check box on the Messages pane of the iChat Preferences dialog box, in which case the chats appear in one window.

- Use your status settings to prevent unwanted interruptions. For example, if you are online, but busy with something, open your status menu and choose Away or one of the other unavailable statuses. You also can select the Offline status to prevent any invitations.

- To check whether a document can be shared with iChat Theater, select it on the desktop and select File ➪ Quick Look. If the document appears onscreen and looks good to you, you can share it in iChat Theater. If not, you won't be able to share it.

- To change how a buddy appears to you, open the buddy's contextual menu on the buddy list and choose Show Profile. You see the Info window, which has three panes. The Profile pane shows you the person's profile, including his chat name account, capabilities, photo, and notes. On the Actions pane, you can configure actions that are specific to that buddy, such as sounds that play when that person logs in. Use the Address Card pane to associate a card in the Address Book or to enter additional information for the buddy.

- To block someone with whom you don't want to chat, select the buddy and select Buddies ➪ Block *buddy* where *buddy* is the name of the person whom you want to block. You won't receive invitations from people you block.

- Use the View menu to show or hide various elements, such as buddy pictures or video status.

● Use the Video menu to configure and control various video and audio settings. For example, select Video ➪ Record Chat to record a chat session. Use the Enabled commands at the bottom of the menu to enable or disable the microphone, camera, and screen-sharing feature during chats.

Communicating Using a Windows PC

You can use many applications to text, audio, and video chat on a Windows PC. However, not all of these are compatible with MobileMe chatting, specifically with the Mac's iChat videoconferencing. Because the AOL Instant Messenger (AIM) application is compatible with MobileMe chat addresses and also can videoconference with iChat, it is discussed in this section. Your team members who use Windows PCs can use this application to keep in touch with your other team members who use Macs (or Windows PCs for that matter).

Installing and configuring AIM

AOL Instant Messenger can be installed by performing the following steps:

1. **Use a Web browser to go to www.aim.com.**

2. **Click the Download button.**

3. **Save the AIM Installer application to your computer.**

4. **Launch the Installer application.**

5. **Follow the onscreen instructions to install the AIM application.**

6. **When the installation is complete, click Launch.** The AIM application opens.

Logging into AIM

Like other messaging applications, you must have an account to use the AIM application. However, MobileMe accounts are compatible with AIM, so if you have a MobileMe account, you also have an AIM account. To log into AIM, perform the following steps:

1. **In the AIM window, enter your MobileMe email address in the screen name field.**

2. **If you want AIM to remember this information, select the Remember Me check box.**

3. **Enter your MobileMe account's password in the Password field.**

Note When you sign into AIM, a Web browser window pointing to the AIM Dashboard might open. If it does, you can just close it.

4. **To save the password so you don't have to enter it to log in, select the Save Password check box.**

5. **To have AIM automatically sign in, select the Auto Sign In check box.**

6. **Click Sign In, as shown in figure 5.18.** You are logged in, and the AIM window transforms into message mode.

Creating and managing buddies in AIM

In order to be able chat with other people, you need to set up a buddy for each person with whom you want to chat. You also can organize your buddies into groups to make working with many buddies easier. It's a good idea to create a group for your business so you easily add all your team members into it. Create a group by performing the following steps:

1. **Click the Buddy List Setup button (+/-) in the center of the AIM window, and select Add Group (or press Ctrl+G).** The New Group window appears.

2. **Enter the name of the group, and click Save, as shown in figure 5.19.** The group is created, and you can use it to organize your buddies.

5.18 Using your MobileMe account information, signing into AIM is simple.

5.19 Use groups to organize your buddies within the AIM application.

Here's how to configure a buddy:

1. **Click the Buddy List Setup button (+/-) in the center of the AIM window, and select Add Buddy (or press Ctrl+D).** The New Buddy window appears.

2. **On the Buddy Group menu, choose the group you created for your team members.**

3. **Enter the buddy's screen name in the Screen Name field.** If the buddy is a MobileMe member, the screen name should be the MobileMe email address, such as *membername*@me.com, where *membername* is the person's MobileMe member name.

4. **Enter a nickname for the buddy in the Nickname field.** This can be just about anything you want, and it's just a simpler way to identify the person within AIM. You are the only one who sees the nickname.

5. **If you want to be able to send text messages to the buddy via a cell phone, enter the buddy's cell phone number in the Mobile Number field.**

6. **Enter the buddy's email address in the E-mail address field.** This should be the same as the screen name you entered in Step 2.

7. **Enter any notes about the buddy in the Notes field.**

8. **Click Save, as shown in figure 5.20.**

5.20 Create a buddy for each person with whom you want to chat.

9. **Repeat Steps 1 through 8 for each member of your team.** As you create buddies, the counter at the end of the group name in the center pane of the AIM window increases by 1; the counter is formatted as X/Y, where X is the number of buddies in the group that are online and Y is the number of buddies in the group. If the buddy you created is not currently online, he appears in the Offline group instead of your buddy group.

Genius

If you or your team members have an iPhone, you can use the AIM iPhone application to text chat. This is good because you aren't limited by the texting limits of your iPhone account. So you can text as much as you want with no additional cost to you. To download this application, use the App Store within the iTunes Store.

Working with the Buddy List window in AIM

The Buddy List window is your launch point for most AIM activities, such as starting chats. You should use your profile and status information in the Buddy List window to determine how and when people can interact with you and to control some aspects of the interaction. You also can use the Settings tool to configure several aspects of how AIM works. Following are some pointers to get you started.

You should choose a buddy icon to represent you in chats and in other people's status windows. Here's how:

1. **Select Edit ⇨ Settings.** The Settings dialog box appears.

2. **Click the Expressions tab.**

3. **Click the Browse link under the current buddy icon at the far right of the dialog box.** The default buddy icon is the AIM icon.

4. **In the resulting Select a Buddy Icon dialog box, move to the image you want to use, select it, and click Open.**

5. **Click OK in the dialog box reminding you that you shouldn't use a copyrighted image for purposes that violate its copyright.** The image you selected replaces the current buddy icon.

6. **Click Save.** The image you selected appears next to your name at the top of the AIM window and in the windows of people who have you as a buddy.

In your section of the Buddy List window, which is labeled with your AIM screen name, you see your current message and your status on the menu, along with two buttons, as shown in figure 5.21.

- To set your status, use the menu under your name. When you're available to chat, choose Available.

- To configure the status text your buddies see when you are in the Available state, choose Available as your status and type the status text in the box above the menu.

- To choose the status text when you are away, open the menu, select Away Messages, and then select the message you want to use.

Change state

Set me invisible

5.21 Use the status information area to control how other people can interact with you.

Following are some ways you can use this section:

- To create your own away message, open the menu and choose New Away Message. Enter a title for the message at the top of the resulting dialog box and the actual message in the lower part of the dialog box. To save the new message with your other away messages, select the Save with my away messages check box. Click Set Away. Your status changes to Away, and the message you created is displayed. The new message also is added to the menu.

- To change your state from Available to Away or from Away to Available, click the Change state button.

- To hide from your buddies, click the Set me invisible button. You appear to be offline to buddies, you can chat if you want to and you can see activity that is happening online. To become visible again, click the same button.

In the center part of the window, you see your buddies and their current status states. Buddies are organized in groups, and the number of buddies in each group is shown next to the group name. To see the buddies in a group, click its expansion triangle. To hide the buddies, click the triangle again.

When a buddy is offline (or has set his status to invisible), he appears in the Offline group, meaning that the buddy is not available for chats.

When a buddy is online, you see him in the appropriate group along with an indication of his status. If a buddy is active, you don't see an icon next to his name. If a buddy is idle, you see the paper icon. If the buddy is Away, you see the paper icon and the buddy's Away message. If a buddy's computer has been idle for a long time, you see the icon with "zz" in it.

At the bottom of the buddy list are buttons you use to start chats and perform other actions.

By default, the AIM Buddy List window is always on top, which means it can get in the way. If you don't want this, select View ⇨ Buddy List Window Always On Top to disable this feature.

Genius

By default, AIM launches your default Web browser and moves to the AIM Dashboard home page whenever you log in. To stop this annoying behavior, select Edit ⇨ Settings. In the Settings window, click Sign In/Sign Out. In the section labeled When I sign in, display the following, click None. Click Save. From then on, you won't be bothered by the AIM Dashboard each time you sign into AIM.

Using AIM to text message

You can use the AIM application to have text chats with other people. You can start a chat, respond to chat requests, and have text chats with multiple people.

Starting a text chat

To start a text chat, do the following:

1. **Select the buddy with whom you want to chat.** Of course, that buddy should be in an available state.

2. **Click the IM button.** The IM window appears. In the top pane of the window, you see the icon for the buddy you selected; this is the history area for the chat. Each status change or message is tracked in this part of the window. The lower pane is the message pane where you type and format your messages; along the right side of this pane, you see your icon.

3. **In the lower pane of the window, type the message you want to send.**

4. **Use the formatting tools at the top of the message pane to format the message if you want to.** Most text chats are quick and to the point, so it usually doesn't make sense to format your messages, and the recipient might or might not be able to be see your formatting, depending on the application he is using.

5. **Use the Emoticon menu (the yellow face) to add emoticons to the message.**

6. **Click Send, or press Enter.** An invitation and your text is sent to the buddy you selected. Your text moves to the history pane and is time stamped to show when you sent it. If the buddy accepts and responds to you invitation, you see the response in the history pane.

7. **Reply to the messages to keep the conversation going, as shown in figure 5.22.**

8. **Close the chat window when you're finished.**

Genius

To clear the history pane, open the Edit menu and choose Clear History.

Responding to a text chat request

When someone requests a chat with you, the IM window opens on the desktop and you see the most recent messages in the history pane. To reply to the message, type your reply in the message pane and press Enter. To ignore the request, just close the IM window.

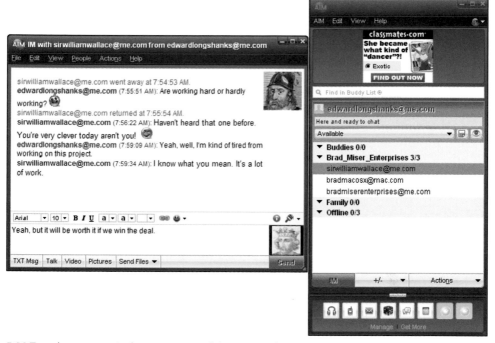

5.22 Text chats appear in the upper pane of the AIM window.

Genius

If you want each IM session to start out empty, open the General IM tab of the Settings dialog box and deselect the Keep IM conversation text after IM is closed check box. Each time you close the IM window, the text chats are deleted.

Starting a text chat with multiple people

You can start a text chat with more than one person by performing the following steps:

1. **Select the buddies with whom you want to chat.**

2. **Click the IM button.** The Chat Invitation window appears. At the top of the window, you see the screen names of each buddy you selected. In the Chat Room area, you see the default name for the chat room you'll create when you start the chat.

3. **If you want to, change the name of the chat room by editing the text in the Chat Room box, as shown in figure 5.23.**

AIM Chat Invitation from edwardlongshanks@me.com ✕

Screen Names to Invite (separated by commas):

bradmacosx@mac.com,bradmiserenterprises@me.com,sirwilliam
wallace@me.com

Chat Room: | BME Chat |

Send | Cancel

5.23 When you invite multiple buddies to chat, you create a chat room.

4. **Click Send.** The Chat Room window appears; the name of the window is Chat room '*room-name*' where *roomname* is the name of the room you entered in Step 3 (or the default name if you didn't enter a name). Each buddy you invited receives an invitation to the chat. As people respond to your request, you see status information in the upper-left pane of the window. Each participant's screen name appears in a different color. In the right pane of the window, you see the screen name of each person in the chat.

5. **Type your message to the group, and press Enter.** The message is sent to each participant.

Genius

You can add more people to a chat room by entering screen names in the box at the top right pane of the window and clicking Add.

6. **Read messages other people add to the chat in the upper-left pane of the window.** You also see status information, such as when someone leaves the chat (in which case, her name disappears from the right pane of the window).

7. **Continue the conversation by reading messages other people post and responding to messages you read, as shown in figure 5.24.**

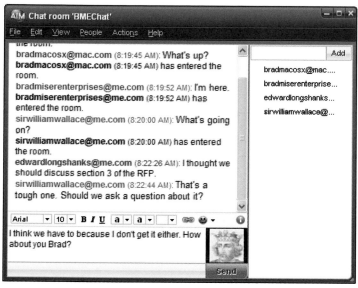

AIM Chat room 'BMEChat'

File   Edit   View   People   Actions   Help

bradmacosx@mac.com (8:19:45 AM): What's up?
bradmacosx@mac.com (8:19:45 AM) has entered the room.
bradmiserenterprises@me.com (8:19:52 AM): I'm here.
bradmiserenterprises@me.com (8:19:52 AM) has entered the room.
sirwilliamwallace@me.com (8:20:00 AM): What's going on?
sirwilliamwallace@me.com (8:20:00 AM) has entered the room.
edwardlongshanks@me.com (8:22:26 AM): I thought we should discuss section 3 of the RFP.
sirwilliamwallace@me.com (8:22:44 AM): That's a tough one. Should we ask a question about it?

Add

bradmacosx@mac....
bradmiserenterprise...
edwardlongshanks...
sirwilliamwallace@...

Arial   ▼   10   ▼   **B** *I* U   a ▼   a ▼   ▼   ⊜   😊 ▼

I think we have to because I don't get it either. How about you Brad?

Send

5.24 A chat room enables you to text chat with multiple people at the same time.

Note

The AIM Settings dialog box has many options you can set to configure how AIM works for you. It's worth your time to open that tool (by selecting Edit ⇨ Settings) and explore the options you have to personalize AIM to your preferences.

Using AIM to audioconference

To be able to audioconference, your PC must have a microphone installed and working. If the computer doesn't have a microphone installed, you can add one via a USB headset or other audio input. Or, if you want to be able to videoconference, you can install a Web cam because most of them include a headset that also works for audio-only chats.

To get started, install and configure the external audio input device or configure an internal one so it can receive your voice as audio input.

When you are ready to audioconference, perform the following steps:

1. **Select the buddy with whom you want to audioconference.**

2. **Open the Actions menu, and select Talk.** The IM window appears in the background, while in the foreground you see the Talk with '*buddyname*' window, where *buddyname* is the

buddy you selected. An audio chat invitation is sent to that buddy. When the buddy accepts your request, the talk window contains a volume bar for you at the bottom of the window and one for the buddy at the top of the window, as shown in figure 5.25.

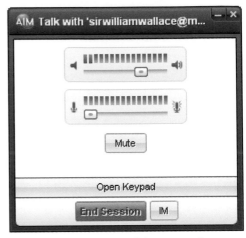

3. **Speak to the buddy, and listen to what the buddy says.**

4. **To control the volume of the buddy's voice, use the slider under the volume bar at the top of the window.** In the bar, you see a graphical representation of the volume level when the buddy speaks; it fills with green as the buddy talks.

5.25 Control the volume of chats using the volume bars in the Talk window.

5. **To control the volume level of your input, use the slider under the volume bar at the bottom of the window.** Ideally, when you speak at a normal level, the bar should fill with green to between 1/2 and 3/4 of its length.

6. **To mute your side of the conversation, click the Mute button; click the UnMute button to resume the conversation.**

7. **To end the conversation, click End Session.**

Caution Whether you can audioconference with more than one person depends upon the application each person uses. To try it, select the buddies with whom you want to audioconference, open the Actions menu, and choose Talk. In the resulting Talk window, you only see the screen names of the buddies who use applications that support AIM's version of multiple person audioconferences. In most cases, each person must be using the same application, such as AIM, to be able to participate in a multiparty chat.

Using AIM to videoconference

To be able to videoconference, your Windows PC needs to be equipped with a Web cam that is compatible with your version of Windows and the AIM application. Because AIM is such a popular chat application, most Web cams are compatible with it. To prepare for a videoconference, perform the following steps:

1. **Connect the Web cam to a USB port.**

2. **Connect the headset to the microphone and headphone ports, if necessary.**

3. **Start up AIM, or restart it if it is already running.**

Fixing Web Cam Issues

Getting videoconferencing to work in AIM can be a challenge. Give it a try using the nearby steps. If you are fortunate, everything will work fine on your first attempt. However, it isn't unusual to have problems getting AIM to recognize your camera, or sometimes it reports that the camera is already in use by another application even if AIM is the only application running.

If AIM fails to recognize your camera, open the My Computer folder and double-click the USB Digital Camera device. If you see an image, you know the camera is connected and is recognized by Windows, so the problem is with AIM. If not, you know the problem is between the camera and Windows.

The most common solution, and the first one to try, is to visit the support area of the camera manufacturer's Web site and download and install the latest driver for the camera. This usually fixes most issues.

To videoconference, perform the following steps:

1. **Select the buddy with whom you want to videoconference.**

2. **Open the Actions menu, and choose Video.** You see the Video Invitation window. The screen name of the buddy you selected is shown at the top of the window. You see a status message about your camera at the bottom of the window.

Note When I was writing this, AIM was reporting that it couldn't find my camera, but I was able to send the invitation and complete videoconferences anyway. So don't let such a message stop you from trying to videoconference.

3. **Click Send.** An invitation is sent to the buddy you selected. The IM window opens in the background, and you see the Video with '*buddyname*' window, where *buddyname* is the name of the buddy you want to videoconference with. If the buddy accepts your invitation, you see the buddy's image in the Video window along with a smaller image showing your preview. If your buddy rejects your invitation, you see a status message in the Video window.

4. **Talk to and see the buddy.** While you're in a videoconference, you can do the following, as indicated in figure 5.26:

- Click Open Volume Controls. The two volume bars appear. Use the upper bar to gauge and control the buddy's volume level. Use the lower bar to gauge and control your volume level. Click Close Volume Controls to hide the volume bars.

- Click Mute to mute your end of the videoconference.

- Drag the preview window around the Video with window to move it out of the way.

- Resize the video window by dragging its Resize handle. Don't be surprised if video quality degrades when you make the window larger.

- Open the Actions menu to show or hide your preview and display the video in full screen.

Better Conferencing

iChat and AIM are good for conferencing among your team members and for limited purposes. However, both of these methods have severe limitations, the most significant of which is that participants must have the applications installed on their computers and have the appropriate accounts. They also are limited in the number of participants and types of conferences allowed, based on the specific applications being used; for example, you can't have multiple people in the same audio chat unless they are all using the same application. A better solution, especially for conferencing with customers or potential customers, is a Web-based conferencing solution. My favorite is WebEx, located at www.webex.com. WebEx is supported on all computer platforms and browsers, and WebEx conferences can include audio, video, text chatting, document collaboration, application sharing, presentations, and so on. The number of participants is not limited, and joining a WebEx conference is simple. Participants don't need specific hardware, software, or an account; they just need a Web browser and a phone. Scheduling and inviting people to conferences are easy for you. The only downside to a service like WebEx is its cost, but if you need to communicate with customers or business partners, this cost can be well worth it, and you can choose from a variety of plans to keep your costs as low as possible. Most services, including WebEx, offer free trials, so you can try before you buy.

5.26 An AIM videoconference is an effective way to communicate with someone who is remote.

5. **To end the videoconference, click End Session.** The Video with window closes, and the conference terminates.

Caution

Whether you can videoconference with more than one person depends upon the application each person uses. To try it, select the buddies with whom you want to videoconference, open the Actions menu, and choose Video. In the resulting Talk window, you see only the screen names of the buddies who use applications that support AIM's version of multiple person videoconferences. In most cases, each person must be using the same application, such as AIM, to be able to participate in a multi-party videoconference.

How Can I Use MobileMe to Publish a Company Web Site?

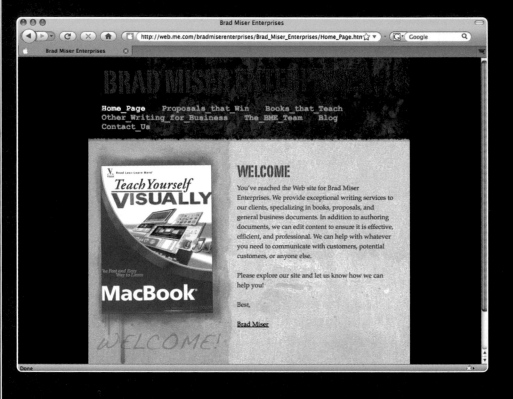

All businesses need a Web site. At the least, people should be able to use your site to easily get information about your business and to contact you, especially for marketing your products or services. You might also want to provide help resources or sell directly from your site. You can use MobileMe to easily and inexpensively publish your business's Web site. You can create and publish your site via MobileMe in a couple of ways using iWeb or any other Web application. You can choose to publish it under a MobileMe URL or one for your personal domain.

Understanding MobileMe Web Site Options

As part of your MobileMe account, you have access to a Web server so you can quickly and easily publish your own Web sites. Because access to this service is included as part of your MobileMe account, you can have one or more sites published to the Web at no additional charge.

To use MobileMe to publish a site, two steps are required and one step is optional:

1. **Create your Web site.**

2. **Publish the site via MobileMe.**

3. **Register and configure a personal domain (this step is optional).**

To accomplish steps 1 and 2, you have two basic options. You can use iWeb to create and publish your site, or you can create your sites in another application and use your MobileMe iDisk to publish it.

Apple's iWeb application is a template-based tool that you can use to build Web sites by choosing a template for each page on your site and linking the pages together with the application's tools. You also can add HTML snippets and other features to your pages.

One benefit of iWeb is that it is very fast and easy to create a site that looks pretty good, even if you aren't artistically or graphically inclined. Another benefit of iWeb is that MobileMe is integrated so you can publish sites to the Web just by clicking a button; also, updating your Web sites is very simple. Lastly (and perhaps most importantly for someone running a business), iWeb requires less effort to maintain and update a site than some other tools do.

While iWeb makes it easy to publish professional Web sites, the application does have some downsides. First, iWeb is Mac only, so you can't use it if you have only Windows computers. Second, if you are an expert Web designer, you may find iWeb (or any other template-based Web tool for that matter) limiting to your creativity. Third, iWeb isn't really intended for sites that are for transactions; although you can create some basic pages to sell products or services, you should use a different tool if selling products or services is the primary purpose of your site.

The good news is that you can use MobileMe to publish a Web site you've created in any tool; you use your application of choice to create your sites and then use your iDisk to publish them. Publishing and updating Web sites that are created in something other than iWeb is slightly more complicated than using iWeb, but it still isn't difficult.

Any Web site you publish under MobileMe (using iWeb or something else) has the default URL http://web.me.com/*membername*, where *membername* is your MobileMe member name. This URL works fine, but it may not be easily recognizable as being for your business. Also, the domain (web.me.com) isn't associated with your business, and it adds length to the URL someone has to type to visit your site. Fortunately, you can publish your Web site under a domain you have registered so it's both easier to type and to associate with your business (such as bradmiserenterprises.com instead of web.me.com/bradmiserenterprises).

If you have a Mac with the iLife suite installed, want to get a site up as easily and quickly as possible, and don't expect a large amount of traffic, give iWeb a shot; you'll find detailed instructions in the next section. If you prefer another application (or maybe you don't have a Mac), skip to the subsequent section to learn how to use MobileMe to publish sites you create in a different tool.

In either case, see the last section in the chapter to learn how to publish your site under a custom domain.

Note
When you publish a site via MobileMe, your account has a limit to data that can be transferred on a monthly basis. If you have a large site and it is visited frequently, you might not have enough transfer allowance (see Chapter 2 for the limits). Also, if you plan to have many transactions on your site, you should consider a hosting service that is more geared toward retail transactions.

Using iWeb to Create and Publish a Web Site

iWeb, part of the iLife suite, has been installed on every new Mac for the past several years, so unless your Mac is very old, you have the application already. (If you are using an older version, you should consider upgrading to the latest version because each new version gets more powerful.) You can use iWeb to create and publish your Web sites. As your business changes, you can easily keep your Web sites up-to-date with iWeb's editing tools.

Creating an iWeb Web site

Even with iWeb, building a Web site that effectively represents your business is not a trivial exercise. The process takes time, creativity, and effort. A significant amount of trial and error is involved, because you probably won't get things right the first time on each page. The fastest way to get started is to implement your site in stages, starting with the core pages for your business and adding to them as you have time to do so.

Also, creating a Web site is not a one-time activity. You should be prepared to maintain and update your site as your business changes and grows. Little is more discouraging for customers and potential customers than to visit a company's Web site that is clearly outdated and hasn't been updated for a long time.

Creating a site map

Because iWeb makes it so easy to create a Web site, you may be tempted to fire up the application and start building pages right away. That can work, but it isn't the ideal way to start. You should design the overall organization and content for your site by creating a site map for it. The site map defines each of the pages you are going to include in the site and shows how those pages relate to one another. You can use almost any drawing tool to create a simple site map. It doesn't need to be fancy. At the most basic, you simply show a title/box for each page and show how those pages are connected. A sample site map is shown in figure 6.1.

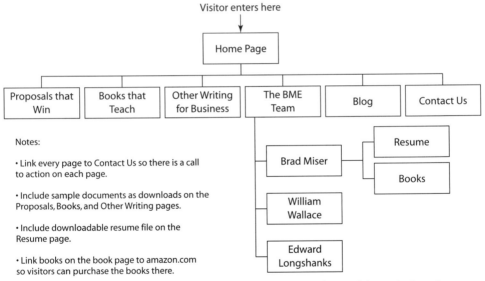

6.1 A site map makes the process of building a Web site easier and faster while producing a better experience for the visitor.

As you design your site, keep the following questions in mind:

- **What information do I want to include on my site?** If your company produces products, you probably want to have detailed information about those products to enable potential customers to get the information they need to make a decision to buy them. You also want to make it as easy as possible for customers to purchase products, such as links that take them directly to Web sites that sell your products. You definitely want to provide contact information for your company; all company Web sites should have a Contact Us page so visitors can visit that page to get in touch with you. You also should include information about your company, such as the key team members so visitors know who they are doing business with.

- **What is the most important information provided on my site?** This information should appear closer to the Home page for your site so that visitors are more likely to visit it.

- **What is a logical flow for the pages on my site?** Put yourself in the role of a "typical" visitor to your site and decide how the various pages should flow together to make the most sense for those visitors. This should drive the basic layout of your site.

Generally, it's better to start with a simple site and add to it over time. This gets you up and running faster and is likely to produce a better Web site in the long run because you'll learn so much when you first create the site; this experience helps you expand the site more effectively than trying to "do it all" from the start. Design a basic set of pages, get the site up and running, add to your design, add those pages to the site, and repeat until your site is what you want it to be.

Building and organizing a Web site layout

With your site map done, it's time to set up the Web site by creating the individual pages and setting the basic navigation through the site.

Each time you add a page to a Web site, you choose a theme and then choose the template for the page from those that are available for the theme you select. Themes consist of colors, designs, and basic layouts for the templates for that theme. Templates are designed with placeholders for specific kinds of content organized in different layouts. You then customize the content for each template to create the page that is included in the published site.

The templates for each theme are named to indicate the kind of content they are designed to contain or purpose they are intended to serve, such as Welcome, About Me, Photos, and so on. Templates are just starting points for your pages, and you can change them in any way you see fit.

Most Web sites have nested pages, which means some pages are "underneath" others (refer to figure 6.1). Unfortunately, you can't show this directly in the iWeb window because all the pages in a site are at the same level. However, you can nest pages within the Web site by configuring the navigation menu that appears at the top of each Web page. By default, this menu contains links to all the other pages in a site. To nest a page, you exclude its link from the navigation menu and only include links from and to the page above it so that the visitor moves up and down the site map as you have laid it out.

Your goal at this stage of the process should to be add all the pages to your site, give them appropriate titles, and set up the basic navigation flow through the site. After this is accomplished, you work with each page individually to complete its content and design.

Following are the steps you should use to implement your site map in iWeb:

1. **Launch iWeb.** The iWeb window opens, and you are prompted to select the theme and template for the first page in the site, as shown in figure 6.2. Themes appear in the left pane of the window, while the right pane contains the templates in the selected theme. You can use the themes available by using the menu at the top of the sheet. When you select a theme, the templates available in that theme appear in the right pane of the sheet.

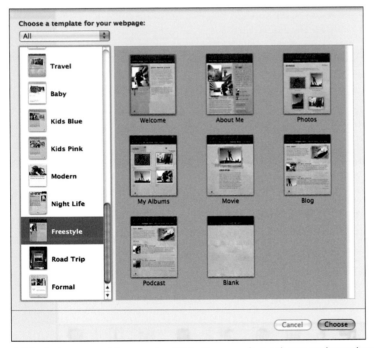

6.2 Each time you add a page to a Web site, you select a theme and template for that page.

2. **Select the template you want to use, and click Choose.** A new page is created from that template and appears in the left pane of the iWeb window. It is nested under the initial Web site (you can add more sites later) to show that it is part of that site.

3. **With the page you added selected, open the View menu and choose Show Inspector or press Option+⌘+I.** The Inspector appears; this important tool lets you configure many different aspects of your Web site and the pages it contains. You should get very familiar with the Inspector because using it effectively makes you much more efficient with iWeb.

4. **Click the Site Inspector tab, which is the leftmost tab in the Inspector.**

5. **Click the Site sub-tab.**

6. **Enter a name for your Web site in the Site Name field.** Using your business's name is an obvious choice, but you can name your site something else if you prefer. This name identifies the site within iWeb and appears in a URL when you publish more than one site. Avoid empty spaces between words; use an underscore instead. As you change the name, the site name shown in the left pane changes.

7. **Enter a contact email address in the Contact Email field, as shown in figure 6.3.** This should be the primary email address for your business.

6.3 The Site Inspector tab shows key information for your site.

Note

At the bottom of the Site Inspector tab, you see iDisk Storage information, the most important of which is how much space your site requires and how much iDisk space you have available. As you build your site, check this to ensure that you aren't exceeding your available space.

8. **Select the first page you added to your site on the left pane, and click the Page Inspector tab, which is the second tab from the left in the Inspector window.** The Page Inspector tools appear.

9. **Click the Page sub-tab.**

10. **Enter the name of the page in the Page Name field, as shown in figure 6.4.** This is the name that appears in the title bar of the Web browser when the page is visited. You should use the page name shown for the top page on your site map. Again, avoid spaces in the name; replace them with underscores.

Genius

You can also change a page's name directly by editing it on the page list in the left pane of the iWeb window.

11. Choose how the navigation bar is configured on the page with the following options:

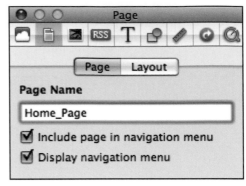

6.4 Use the Page Inspector tab to name a page and determine how it impacts the navigation menu.

- Select the Include page in navigation menu check box if you want the page to be included in the navigation menu that appears at the top of each page; this menu contains links consisting of each page's name. You want this check box to be selected for each of the pages at the top level of your site, but want it unselected for nested pages.

- Select the Display navigation menu check box to show the navigation menu on the page. You typically want this menu to appear on the pages at the top level of your site, but not on nested pages.

Genius

To include a Home page that appears "above" all the other pages, deselect the Display navigation menu check box and instead include links to the first level of pages on the Home page. However, in most cases, you can leave the check box selected even though the result is a Home page that is on the same level as the pages below it.

12. Choose File ➪ New Page, or press ⌘+N. The theme/template sheet appears.

13. Select a theme and template for the next page on your site map, and click Choose. You can choose different themes for different pages on your site, or you can use the same theme for all of them; that's just one of the design choices you'll make. The template you selected is added to the site and appears with the name of the template you selected.

14. Select the new page, and use the Page Inspector tab to name the page and configure its navigation bar options.

Genius

To have the most control over the content and layout of a page, choose the Blank template, which includes only the navigation menu and some very basic elements, such as background colors and title placeholders.

15. **Repeat Steps 12 through 14 until you've added and configured all the pages included in your site map, as shown in figure 6.5.** (Compare this figure to the site map shown in figure 6.1 to see how a site map can be converted into a basic site structure in iWeb.)

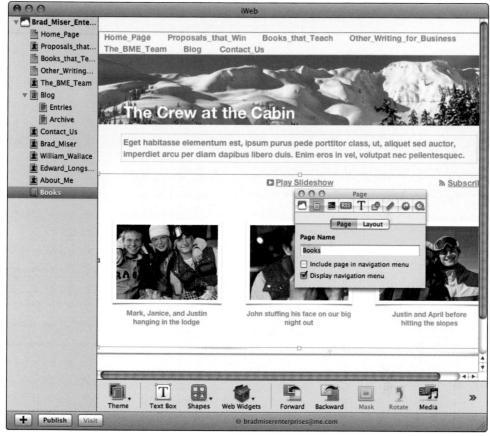

6.5 This Web site now includes the pages shown in the left pane of the iWeb window.

After you have the basic structure of your site in place, you work with each page individually to add the appropriate content and to design or refine its layout.

Designing pages

To complete your site, you work with each page it contains to add your content and to change the design of the pages to be what you want them to be; the sum total of the pages becomes your site. The templates you've used for each page provide a basic structure for those pages along with placeholders for various kinds of content. To design a page, perform the following general steps:

1. **Select the page you want to work on.** The page fills the right part of the window.

Note The page currently selected (and being displayed in the right part of the iWeb window) is highlighted in the page list pane and also on the navigation menu at the top of the page (assuming it's included on the menu, of course).

2. **Select any template elements you don't want to have on the page, and press Delete.** The selected elements are removed.

3. **Replace template content placeholders with your content.** For example, select and type over text blocks to replace template text with your text or replace template graphics with your graphics.

4. **Add new content to the page using iWeb content tools.**

5. **Refine the design of the page until it is what you want it to be.**

Of course, these steps aren't really as linear as they are presented here. You usually do them more or less simultaneously because they have an impact on each other. For example, when you remove template elements, you probably need to replace those elements with your own content.

As you design pages, you use the Inspector to configure various elements on a page. In general, the Inspector works with content as it does with entire pages; you select the set of tools you want to use and then use those tools to work with the appropriate content. An overview of the toolset provided on the Inspector is provided in the following list (from left to right on the Inspector toolbar):

- **Site Inspector.** As you've seen, you use this tab to work with the site as a whole. In addition to naming the site, you can use the Password sub-tab to set a password for a site so that a visitor has to enter the password to be able to view the site.

- **Page Inspector.** You've seen one sub-tab on this tab as well (Page). The Layout sub-tab provides tools you use to work with the general layout of a page, including top and bottom padding, content width, content height, header and footer height, page background, and browser background, as shown in figure 6.6.

- **Photos Inspector.** On this tab, the Photos sub-tab provides control over photos on a page, such as the download size of photos, whether visitors can subscribe to the photos on a page, and how comments are configured. You can use the Slideshow sub-tab to configure slideshows for the images on a page.

● **Blog & Podcast Inspector.** On the Blog sub-tab, you configure a blog page, including the number of excerpts that are shown, the length of those excerpts, whether comments or attachments are allowed, and if the blog can be searched. On the Podcast sub-tab, you configure the identification information for a podcast, such as name and email, parental advisory, and whether the podcast is available in the iTunes Store; you configure this information for the entire series of a podcast as well as each episode in that series.

● **Text Inspector.** This tab contains three sub-tabs. The Text sub-tab contains text formatting tools. The Wrap sub-tab controls how text wraps on a page. You use the List sub-tab to format bulleted and numbered lists on a page.

● **Graphic Inspector.** Use these tools to configure graphics on a page, as shown In figure 6.7. For example, you can determine if and how a graphic is framed, and you can configure drop shadows. You also can control reflections and the opacity of graphics.

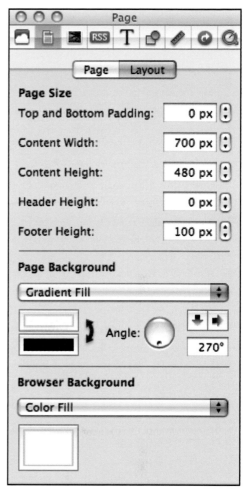

6.6 Use the Layout sub-tab to configure a page's height and width, footer, and background.

● **Metrics Inspector.** With this toolset, you can get information about files on a page. You also can control an object's size, position on the page, and rotation.

● **Link Inspector.** The Hyperlink sub-tab enables you to configure objects with links to within your site as well as to pages external to your site. The Format sub-tab enables you to control format of links, such as how links are displayed, what happens when the visitor points to a link, the format for a site the visitor has used, and the format of disabled links.

● **QuickTime Inspector.** This tab contains tools you use to configure QuickTime content on a page, including the locations where the content starts and stops playing, its poster frame, autoplay, looping, and where the movie controller is displayed.

Each of these Inspector tools becomes active when you have selected the content or element on which those tools work. For example, the Graphic Inspector becomes active when you have selected a graphic element on a page.

Replacing template placeholders with content

Templates include placeholders for many different kinds of elements, including text, graphics, photos, and so on. You can (and should) replace a template's placeholder content with your own content. You also can delete placeholders when you don't want to use that particular element on a page.

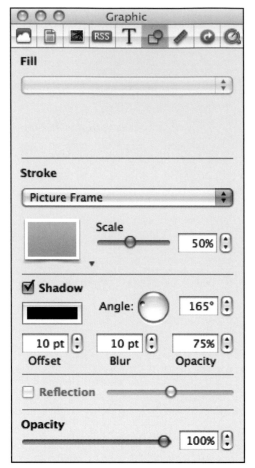

6.7 The Graphics Inspector enables you to configure graphics on a page, such as adding a drop shadow.

Genius

You can delete a text placeholder by selecting it and pressing the Delete key. You can resize a text placeholder by selecting it and dragging its resize handles.

Following are some examples showing how to replace various kinds of template elements. These examples aren't all-inclusive; however, after you've learned how to replace several different kinds of placeholder elements, you can use a similar approach to replace any kind of placeholder content.

Most templates include various kinds of text placeholders. Replace the text content in these place-holders using the following steps:

1. **Select the page you want to work with.**

2. **Double-click the text you want to replace.** It becomes highlighted, indicating the text can be edited.

3. **Type the new text, or copy and paste it.**

4. **Use the Text Inspector tools to format the text, as shown in figure 6.8.**

6.8 This template includes a heading that I changed to "William Wallace," and I used the Text Inspector's text formatting tools to center and spread the text on the page.

Genius   You can format text using the commands on the Format menu, including the Font command to open the Fonts panel along with formatting commands, such as Bold, Italic, Bigger, and so on.

Obviously, graphic elements are critical to any Web page. Templates include several types of graphic elements, including general graphics, photos, and so on. Graphic elements have a mask that determines which part of the image is displayed on the page. You can control the size of the mask and the size of the image, and you can determine which part of the image appears within a mask.

You can replace and format graphic elements by following these steps:

1. **Prepare the graphic you want to use.** You do this outside of iWeb, such as by using iPhoto.

2. **Select the page containing the graphic element you want to replace.**

3. **Drag the graphic you want to use onto the placeholder.** The graphic replaces the content in the placeholder, and the Edit Mask tool appears. The lines around the image represent its mask, anything inside the mask is shown on the page, and part of the image outside the mask is hidden.

4. **Click the Edit Mask button.** The image appears at full size on the screen.

5. **Adjust the size and the part of the image that appears on the screen by performing the following actions:**

   ● Drag the slider to the right to increase the size of the image or to the left to decrease it.

   ● Drag the image inside the mask until the part of the image you want to be visible on the page is shown.

   ● Resize the mask by dragging its Resize handles.

6. **Use the tools on the Graphic Inspector to configure the image, such as to add and format a frame or drop shadow, as shown in figure 6.9.**

7. **When you're finished, click the Edit Mask button.** Everything outside the mask is hidden, and you see the image as it will appear on the page.

Many page templates are designed to include photos; in this context, a photo can be any image file. To replace photos on a template, perform the following steps:

1. **Prepare the photos you want to use on a page outside of iWeb.** iPhoto is ideal for this because you can use iWeb's Media Browser to easily add those photos to a page.

2. **Select the photo placeholder.** The Photo Grid tools appear.

3. **Select the number of photos you want to appear in the grid using the Columns menu.** The number you select determines how many images appear in the placeholder. These images can be linked to any number of images placed in the photo album you display in the placeholder.

6.9 Use the Edit Mask tool to control the size and the part of the image that appears on the page, and use the Graphic Inspector to format the image.

4. **Choose the album style you want to use by clicking the Album style menu and selecting a style.** The style determines the borders appearing around each image in the placeholder.

5. **Drag the Spacing slider to the left to decrease the space between the images or to the right to increase it.**

6. **Use the Photos per page tool to select the number of photos that appear on a page when the photo album is viewed.** Your options are limited to multiples of the value you selected in step 3. For example, if you selected 3 on the Columns menu, you can have 3, 6, 9, 12, and so on images per page.

7. **Use the Caption lines tool to select how many lines of caption can appear for each image, as shown in figure 6.10.** If you don't want any captions, select 0.

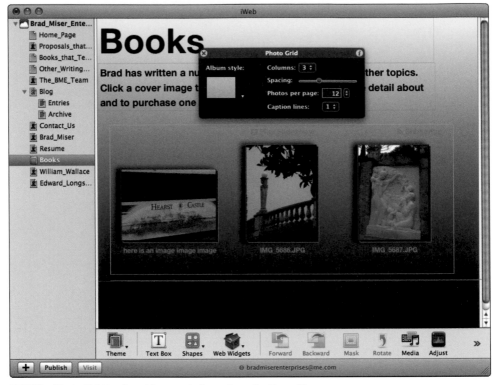

6.10 The Photo Grid tool enables you to format a collection of images on a page.

8. **Click the Media button on the iWeb button at the bottom of the window.** The Media Browser appears.

9. **Click the Photos tab.** You see the iPhoto tools.

10. **Select the source of the photos you want to use on the Web page, such as a photo album.** The photos in that source appear at the bottom of the browser.

Genius

You can drag a photo album onto a Web page to place all the images it contains there.

11. **Drag the images you want to use from the browser onto the Web page, as shown in figure 6.11.** As you drag images into the image placeholder, the images contained there shift around to allow you to place the images wherever you want. When an image is in position, drop it.

6.11 Use the Media Browser to move images from iPhoto onto a Web page.

12. **If you have captions on the images, edit them by double-clicking the text and typing over it.**

13. **To see an image on the detail page, double-click it.** The image zooms to full size, and you see viewing controls. If the image is from an album, you can click Play Slideshow to see all the images in the album. Return to the album view by clicking Back to Album.

14. **To delete an image, select it and press Delete.** The image you selected is removed from the page. (If the image was part of an album, it is replaced by the next image in the album.)

Genius

Most placeholder elements have help text that appears when you point to the placeholder. This can sometimes be useful when you aren't sure what the purpose of a specific placeholder is.

15. **Open the Photos Inspector tab of the Inspector.** One way to do this is to click the "i" button located in the upper-right corner of the Photo Grid dialog box.

16. **Use the Photo Inspector to configure the images.** On the Photos sub-tab, choose a photo download speed, whether visitors can subscribe to the photos, and if comments or attachments are allowed. On the Slideshow tab, configure the slide show for the images by choosing transitions, appearance, and so on.

Adding new elements to a page

In addition to the placeholders that are part of templates you use, you can add many kinds of elements to your pages. These include text, images, links, Web widgets, audio, and so on. Some examples of these tasks show you how to customize your Web pages.

To add more text to a page, perform the following steps:

1. **Click the Text Box tool on the iWeb toolbar at the bottom of the window.** A text box appears on the screen in the center of the page. If a graphic or other element is already there, the new text box can be hard to see; look for the flashing cursor to identify it.

Genius If an image or other element is on top of the text box making it hard to select so you can work with it, select the image or other element and click the Backward button in the iWeb toolbar. This moves the selected element back; continue doing this until the element is behind the text box.

2. **Type the text in the box.**

3. **Drag the handles of the text box to resize it.**

4. **Use the Text Inspector to format the text.**

5. **Drag the text box to move it where you want it to be located.**

The Web is the Web because content is linked together. You can add links to elements on a Web page. Those links can point to areas within your Web site or to any URL. You can add links to text, images, or any other element of the page.

To add a link to another location on your Web site, perform the following steps:

1. **Select the text to which you want to attach a link.** You can select an entire text box or just part of the text it contains.

2. **Open the Link Inspector.**

3. **Click the Hyperlink sub-tab.**

4. **Select the Enable as a hyperlink check box.**

5. **On the Link To menu, choose One of My Pages.**

6. **On the Page menu, choose the page to which the link should point, as shown in figure 6.12.** The text you selected becomes linked to the page you selected.

6.12 The text selected on the current page is being linked to another page on the site.

7. **Click the Format sub-tab.**

8. **Choose the color for the linked text when it is Normal (meaning the user is not pointing to it and hasn't clicked it), when the user points to it (Rollover), when it has been clicked (Visited), and when it is disabled by clicking the color box next to each status.**

9. **For each status, click the Underline button if you want the link's text to be underlined while it is in that status, as shown in figure 6.13.**

10. **Click the Hyperlink sub-tab.**

11. **Select the Make hyperlinks active check box.** The Make hyperlinks active check box on the Links Inspector determines whether links on your site work or if they can be edited. When the check box is selected, links are active so you can click them to see the result. When you need to edit links, deselect this check box.

12. **Move back to the Web page, and click the text you linked.** You should move to the location you wanted; if not, use the Link Inspector to change the location to which the link points.

6.13 Use the Format sub-tab to determine how a text link appears in various status states, such as when a user points to it.

13. **When the link works correctly, deselect the Make hyperlinks active check box.** Leaving this check box unselected makes working with links easier because you can edit them.

You also can link elements on your Web pages to other Web sites. Here's how:

Genius

You can't attach links to some objects on a page. For example, if you added images to an album, you can't create a link to those images. Instead, create another object, such as a shape, and format that object so it is invisible (no fill, no line, and so on). Place that object in front of the object to which you want to link, and set the link to the invisible object. The visitor can't see the linked object, and it appears that the link is connected to the image.

1. **Using a Web browser, move to the URL to which you want to create a link.**

2. **Copy the URL.**

3. **In iWeb, select the image, text, or other element that you want to link to the external site.**

4. **Open the Hyperlink sub-tab of the Link Inspector.**

5. **Select the Enable as a hyperlink check box.**

6. **On the Link To menu, choose An External Page.**

7. **Paste the URL in the URL box.**

8. **To have a new window open when the visitor clicks the link, select the Open link in new window check box, as shown in figure 6.14.** In most cases, you should select this check box so your site remains open. If you leave it unselected, the visitor moves away from your site when she clicks the link.

9. **Test the new link by making hyperlinks active and clicking it.**

6.14 The book cover is now linked to the book's page on Amazon.com.

Genius You can change the theme for a page by selecting it and choosing a new theme on the Theme menu locations on the iWeb toolbar at the bottom of the screen.

iWeb includes a Web Widgets tool that you can use to add the following content to your page:

- **HTML snippet.** If you know HTML, you can use this widget to add a section of HTML code to your Web page, or you can copy and paste a segment of HTML code into the snippet from another source. One thing to keep in mind here is that the code you add to the page must be able to stand on its own; if you copy the code from another source, you need to make sure you get all the code required to make the snippet work.

● **Google AdSense Ad.** These ads are provided through Google. Basically, when you add this element to a Web page, Google places ads on your site with the goal to be for you to get paid by the advertisers. You can control how the ads appear, but Google determines which ads appear on your site. Because you are using the site for your business, you need to keep a close eye on the ads that are being placed on your site.

● **Google Map.** No doubt, you've visited Web sites where you can generate a map related to the site. Using the Google Map widget, you can place maps on your site.

● **MobileMe Gallery.** If you have photos or movies posted in your MobileMe Gallery, you can use this widget to display that content on a page.

Each of these widgets works a bit differently, but an example using the Google Map widget should give you a good idea of how you can use these widgets on your pages:

1. **Select the page on which you want to place a map.**

2. **Open the Web Widgets menu on the iWeb toolbar, and choose Google Map.** A Google map is added to the page along with the Google Map dialog box.

3. **Replace the address in the Address box with the address you want to show using the Google map.**

4. **Click Apply.** The map shows the address you entered.

5. **To enable visitors to zoom on the map, select the Zoom controls check box.**

6. **To show the "bubble" that contains the address and direction links, select the Address bubble check box.**

7. **Resize the map, and place it on the page as you want it to appear, as shown in figure 6.15.**

Genius

You can't format the map box itself. To apply formatting to it, create an object with the Shapes tool that is the same size as the map. Put that object behind the map using the Backward button, and then apply formatting to it.

One of the most important additions you can make to a Web page is to provide a way for people to contact you. A convenient way to do this is to let visitors email you. You can provide this functionality in two ways: You can add an email button to a page, or you can create a link that generates an email.

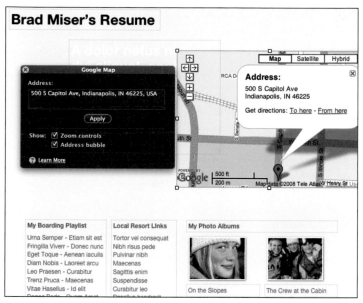

6.15 Adding a Google map to your Web site makes it easy for visitors to find a location.

To add an email button to a page, do the following:

1. **Select the page to which you want to add the button.**

2. **Choose Insert ➪ Button ➪ Email Me.** The email button appears on the page.

3. **Drag the button to its final location on the page.**

Note

You can't format the button at all, so you have to live with its size and appearance. To have more control, create an email link as described nearby.

To create a link a visitor can click to email you, perform the following steps:

1. **Select the page to which you want to add the link.**

2. **Create the object that you want to use as the link.** This can be a graphic or text.

3. **With the object selected, open the Hyperlink sub-tab of the Link Inspector.**

4. **Select the Enable as a hyperlink check box.**

5. **On the Link To menu, choose An Email Message.**

6. **Enter the address to which you want email messages to be sent in the To box.**

7. **Enter the default subject for messages in the Subject box, as shown in figure 6.16.**

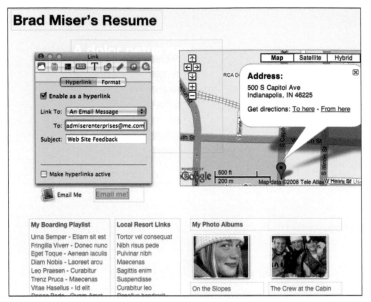

6.16 You can add an email link to a page by inserting the Email button (shown on the left) or by creating an email link associated with text or a graphic.

Preparing to publish a Web site

In the preceding sections, you've seen how you can add content to the pages in your site and how you can add pages. Following are some additional tips to help you get the most out of iWeb's amazing tools:

- Don't be limited by the placeholders on a page. You can resize and reformat placeholders, delete them, and so on.

- You can change the theme for a page by selecting it and choosing a new theme on the Theme menu locations on the iWeb toolbar at the bottom of the screen.

- The Shapes tool enables you to add a variety of shapes to pages. You can then format and size those shapes to add graphical elements to a page.

- You can use the Rotate tool to rotate objects on a page.

- The Adjust tool provides a palette of controls you can use to adjust images, such as photos, as shown in figure 6.17. For example, you can change the brightness, contrast, and saturation.

- Change the order of pages by moving them up or down on the list. This changes the order in which their links appear in the Navigation menu.

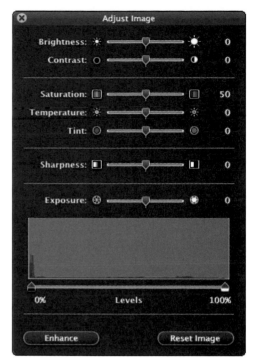

- To password protect a site, select the site and open the Password sub-tab of the Site Inspector. Select the Make my published site private check box. Then enter the username and password for your site in their respective boxes. When you publish the site, no one can see its content without first providing the username and password you set. Sites you protect with a username and password have a key in their icons.

- You can create and manage multiple Web sites with iWeb by choosing File ⇨ New Site. A new site appears on the list in the left pane of the window. You can then add pages to the new site. Each site is identified by the URL http://web.me.com/*membername*/*sitename* where *membername* is your MobileMe member name and *sitename* is the name of the site in iWeb.

6.17 Use the Adjust Image palette to make improvements to photos and other images on your site.

Genius

Take some time to explore the menus in iWeb. You'll find a number of commands and tools that I didn't have room to show you.

As you design and add content to pages and your site, you should continually review each page's layout and your site as a whole to make sure visitors to your site have the experience you intend. When you've completed your site's design, you're ready to publish it.

Publishing an iWeb Web site via MobileMe

After all the work you do to prepare a site, publishing it is a bit anticlimactic because iWeb makes it so easy. Before you send your site out into the world, make sure your MobileMe account is shown at the bottom of the iWeb window and that the green status indicator appears next to it. If this isn't the case, you need to log into your MobileMe account before you can publish the page; see Chapter 2 for help.

Follow these steps to publish your site:

1. **Click the Publish button.**

2. **Click Continue in the copyright warning dialog box (assuming you aren't publishing someone else's content, of course).** iWeb logs into your account and starts the publish process.

3. **Click OK in the message explaining that publishing continues in the background.** Depending on the size of content in your site, this can take a few moments to several minutes. A clock icon appears next to each site's icon to give you a general idea of the progress. When the process is complete, you see a dialog box telling you so, as shown in figure 6.18.

6.18 When you see this message, your sites are on the Web.

4. **Click one of the following buttons:**
   - Click Announce to create an email message with a link to your site.
   - Click Visit Site Now to open your site in a Web browser.
   - Click OK to close the dialog box without taking any other action.

After your site is published, you should visit it with different browsers to see how it appears in those browsers, as shown in figure 6.19.

Genius

When you move to http://web.me.com/*membername*, where *membername* is your MobileMe member name, you move to your default Web site. To determine which of your sites is the default, drag the site you want to be the default to the top of the left pane in the iWeb window. That site becomes the default site the next time you use the Publish command.

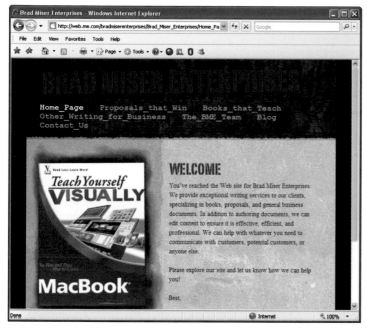

6.19 Test your Web site by viewing it in different browsers on both Macs and Windows PCs.

Updating an iWeb Web site

One of the great things about iWeb is that it makes it very easy to keep a Web site updated, which is critical to keeping your site effective for your business.

To make changes to your site, open iWeb and use its tools to make the needed updates. As you change a page, its icon changes from blue, indicating that the page is published, to orange, indicating that there are changes to the page that haven't been published. When you're ready to update your site, click the Publish button and the site is updated.

Note

In its earliest incarnations, MobileMe was .Mac. Part of .Mac was HomePage, a Web-based application to create Web sites. HomePage still exists, but is hidden unless you previously used it to publish a Web site (in which case, you can access HomePage using the iDisk application on your .me Web site). iWeb is a much better tool, so you have little reason to use HomePage for new sites, but you can still use it to maintain sites published with it initially.

Using Other Web Site Applications to Create and Publish a Web Site

If you don't want to or can't use iWeb to create a Web site, you can still use MobileMe to publish a site you create to the Web. You just need to follow two general steps to accomplish this task: Create a Web site, and publish your Web site using MobileMe.

Creating a Web site

You can use any application capable of creating a Web site to build a site you want to publish via MobileMe. This application can be a dedicated Web creation tool or simply an application that enables you to save content as a Web page, such as Microsoft Word. These are the general steps to create a Web site:

1. **Build a site map defining the overall structure and content of your site.** See the section on creating a site map earlier in this chapter for more information.

2. **Use the application you select to create the content for and organization of your site according to your site map.**

3. **Save the files for your Web site.** Most applications create a group of files for a Web site that include the home page file (named index.html) and a folder containing the rest of the files for the site. Your site must at least have the index.html file to be recognized by MobileMe when you publish it.

Publishing a Web site via MobileMe

After you've created the Web site, you need to store the files for that site on your iDisk in a folder for that site that is within the Web folder, which is itself within the Sites folder on your iDisk.

Preparing your iDisk for a Web site

The Web folder isn't on your iDisk by default. If it doesn't exist, you need to cause MobileMe to create it before you can publish a Web site.

Note

For more details about working with your iDisk, see Chapter 4.

To ensure that you have the Web folder on your iDisk, perform the following steps:

1. **Log into your MobileMe account, and select the iDisk button on the MobileMe toolbar.** The Contents of your iDisk appear.

2. **Select the Home folder.**

3. **Look for the Web folder, as shown in figure 6.20.** If you see this folder, you are ready to publish a Web site; if you've published a Web site using iWeb, you see the Site folder that contains the index.html file along with folders for each site you've published. In this case, you can skip the rest of these steps. If you don't see a Web folder, as shown in figure 6.21, continue with these steps.

4. **Click the Gallery button (the flower) to move into the Gallery.**

5. **Click the Add (+) button at the bottom-left corner of the screen.**

6. **In the resulting sheet, enter a name for the new album and click Create.** It doesn't matter what name you use, and you don't need to change any of the other settings on the sheet. The album is created and selected. The Upload arrow appears in the right part of the window.

7. **Click the Upload arrow.** The Uploads dialog box appears.

8. **Click Choose.**

9. **Move to and select an image file, and click Open.** Again, it doesn't matter which file you choose, but the file you select it uploaded to the Gallery.

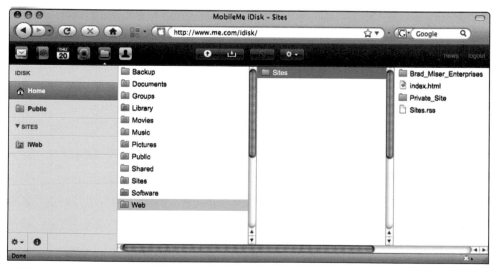

6.20 Here you see a Web folder that contains two Web sites.

6.21 This iDisk doesn't contain a Web folder; one needs to be created by MobileMe before a site can be published under this account.

10. **When the process is complete, click Done.** You move back to the Gallery and see the file you created.

11. **Move back to your iDisk.** You see the Web folder.

Note

You can delete the album you created by moving back to the Gallery, selecting the album, pressing the Delete key, and clicking OK in the resulting dialog box. The album and any files you uploaded are removed, but the Web folder remains.

Creating site folders on your iDisk

The next step is to prepare a folder on your iDisk where your Web site is stored for publishing if necessary. You have two options.

If the site you are publishing is going to be the only site you publish, you don't need to create a specific folder for it because you will place its files within the Site folder within the Web folder. In this case, the URL to your Web site will be http://web.me.com/*membername*, where *membername* is the member name of your MobileMe account.

Genius You can create folders and upload files for a Web site using the MobileMe iDisk application, but it is usually much easier and faster to mount your iDisk on your desktop and work with it directly from there.

If you are publishing multiple Web sites, perhaps one that you've created with iWeb and one that you've created with another application, you need to create a folder within the Sites folder for the Web site you created with a different application. The name of the folder will be included in the URL to the Web site, as In http://web.me.com/*membername*/*foldername*, where *membername* is the member name of your MobileMe account and *foldername* is the name of the folder you create. You should keep this In mind when you name the folder; don't use any spaces in the folder name and keep its name short and obvious.

Note See Chapter 4 for help creating and naming folders on and uploading files to an iDisk.

Uploading the Web site's files

When you are ready to publish a Web site, you upload its main file (named index.html) and associated folders to the appropriate location on your iDisk.

If the Web site is the only one you are publishing, upload its files so its index file and associated folder are directly within the Sites folder. If you are publishing more than one site, upload the index file and associated folder within the folder you created for it within the Sites folder.

Caution The main file for a Web site must be named index.html. If the application you use doesn't automatically name its main file with this name (the Microsoft Office applications don't), you need to rename that file before you upload it to your iDisk.

After the files are uploaded to the appropriate folder, the Web site is published.

Testing the Web site

After the files and folders have been uploaded to your iDisk, use different Web browsers on Macs and on Windows PCs to view the site, as shown in figure 6.22. The URL you use depends on how you configured the site:

● If you published only one site and placed the index file directly within the site's folder, use http://web.me.com/*membername*, where *membername* is the member name of your MobileMe account, to move to the Web site.

● If you published more than one site, use http://web.me.com/*membername*/*foldername*, where *membername* is the member name of your MobileMe account and *foldername* is the name of the folder in which you placed the site's files to move to it.

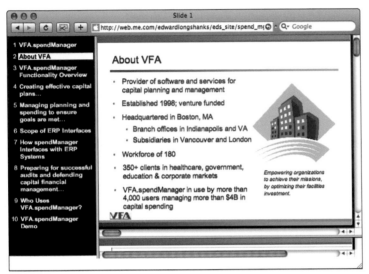

6.22 This site is a Microsoft PowerPoint presentation saved as a Web site on a Windows PC being viewed in Firefox on a Mac.

Updating the Web site

As time passes, you should review and revise your Web sites to ensure that they continue to be effective for your business. To make changes to your Web site, use the application with which you created it to update it. Then repeat the upload process to move the revised files to your iDisk. As soon as the changed files are uploaded, the Web site reflects the changes you made.

Publishing a MobileMe Web Site under a Personal Domain

By now, you know that a Web site you publish through MobileMe has a URL that starts with web.me.com. Because the next part of the URL reflects your MobileMe member name and is, I hope, related to your business name, your MobileMe URL is fairly recognizable as belonging to your company. However, the best URLs are easy to type (short) and are even easier to recognize. For example, even if you don't know Apple's Web site URL, you would probably guess that it's apple.com (and you'd be right, of course).

You can create a personal domain for your Web site and configure MobileMe to work with that. So, instead of moving to your Web site with http://web.me.com/*membername*, where *membername* is your MobileMe member name, someone can move to your Web site with http://www.*yourbusinessname*.com, where *yourbusinessname* is the name of your business.

To do this, you perform two steps: Register your domain, and configure MobileMe to work with your personal domain.

Registering for a personal domain

In order to register for a personal domain, you need to use a third-party domain registration service. Many of these services are available, and each has its own set of fees and additional services. Because you really just want to be able to use the personal domain to move to your MobileMe Web site, you probably won't be interested in the other services, so the cost of the registration is likely to be the most important factor.

The exact steps you perform to register a personal domain depend on the specific service that you use. However, these are the general steps:

1. **Use a Web browser to search for "domain registration."** You see many Web sites offering this service.

2. **Explore the Web sites until you find the combination of cost and service that works for you.**

3. **Click the appropriate link to start the registration process, and follow the onscreen instructions to complete it.**

No matter which service you use, you must perform a couple of steps.

Note Although I can't recommend specific registration services above others, I have used www.aplus.net to register domains. The service works well, is easy to set up, and costs only $9.99 per year, and slightly less if you commit to more than one year.

One step is to select the personal domain you want to use (which is the whole point of the exercise, after all). Because each domain on the Web must be unique, you can't use one that already exists. At some point during the process, you're prompted to try the domain you want to use to see if it is available, as shown in figure 6.23.

6.23 As part of registering for a personal domain, you must search to see if someone else is already using it.

Genius

Consider also registering variations of the top-level of your domain (.com, .net, and so on). You can configure MobileMe to work with only one of these, but it is good to prevent anyone else from using the variants so that people looking for your company aren't routed to a different organization. To have all these addresses actually move to your Web site, you need to host it with a different service because MobileMe limits you to one domain name.

If your domain is available, you're good to go. If not, you need to try variations until you come up with something that works for you. You can make changes to the domain name or to the top-level domain. Your Web site is for a business, so you ideally want your top-level domain to be .com (short for company) because that is what most people assume when they are typing a company's Web site address.

Note

CNAME (canonical name) is a required link between your domain and the hosting service, in this case, web.me.com. If the CNAME isn't configured correctly, people who try to visit your personal domain won't get there, so configuring it correctly is a critical part of the process.

The second required step when you configure the domain is to set the CNAME for your domain to be web.me.com. If this isn't done correctly, the process fails and your personal domain won't work. If setting the CNAME isn't part of the onscreen instructions for the service you select (it probably will be), then search the service's help for the information you need to configure it. This is a common activity, so help for it should be easy to find.

Caution

When you configure the CNAME, pay particular attention to whether an ending period is required. In some cases, the CNAME you configure is web.me.com., and that includes the ending period.

After you've completed the registration process, you may have to wait up to 48 hours for it to take effect.

Configuring MobileMe to use a personal domain

With your personal domain registered, you can configure MobileMe to use it:

1. **Move to the Accounts application by logging into your MobileMe account, clicking the Accounts button, and entering your password.**

2. **Click the Personal Domain option.**

3. **Click Add Domain.**

4. **Enter your personal domain in both fields, as shown in figure 6.24.**

5. **Click Continue.** Your account is updated to use your personal domain.

6. **Click Done.** In the personal domain window, you see the domain you entered.

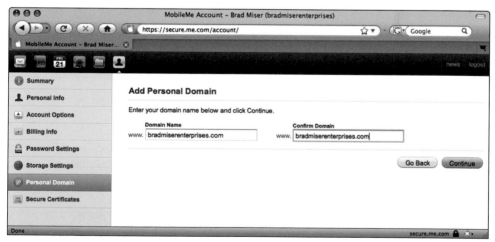

6.24 To link your personal domain to your MobileMe Web site, enter it on the Add Personal Domain screen.

Periodically visit your personal domain's URL to check to see if it is working. After the required time passes, you move to your MobileMe Web site (sometimes it takes effect sooner than 48 hours).

How Do I Use the MobileMe Email Web Application?

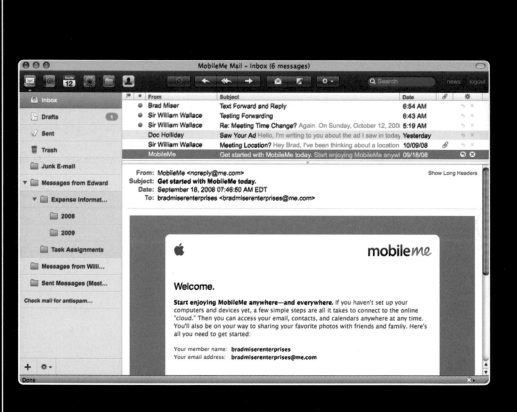

Email is an important way to communicate, especially with team members, current customers, potential customers, and business partners. In addition to an email account, MobileMe includes an email Web application that you can use through either Safari or Firefox. This application provides all the features you probably expect and includes a few that you might not look for, but will find very useful. You can access your MobileMe email via this application, and you can add other email accounts to it. Another helpful feature allows you to set up email aliases so you can use different addresses for various purposes.

Exploring the MobileMe Email Web Application

Like the other MobileMe Web applications, you access the email application by logging into your MobileMe account at the me.com Web site:

1. **Go to me.com.**

2. **Enter your member name and password.**

3. **Click Log In.** You move into your MobileMe account.

4. **Select the Mail button on the toolbar (the envelope).** You see the Mail application, as shown in figure 7.1.

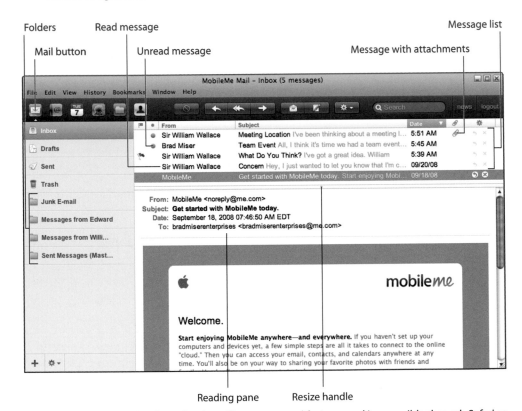

7.1 The MobileMe email Web application offers many good features and is accessible through Safari or Firefox.

The Mail application has three panes. The vertical pane on the left side of the window contains the folder list showing folders in which messages are stored. The top pane in the right part of the window is the message list that shows all the email messages in the folder selected on the folder list. The reading pane, which is the bottom pane on the right side of the window, shows the contents of the message selected on the message list. Above the message list is the Mail toolbar. At the bottom of the folder list are two buttons: Add Folder (+) and the Folder Action menu (the gear icon).

For each message in the message list, you see the following information in the columns from left to right: flagged or unflagged, read or unread status, who sent the message, the message's subject and preview, the date it was received or the time if it was received on the current date, attachment icon, and message action buttons (Quick Reply and Delete). The column by which the message list is currently sorted is highlighted and the sort order (ascending or descending) is shown by the upward- or downward-facing arrow.

Genius

To change the relative height of the message list versus the reading pane, drag the Resize handle up or down. This handle is the small dot in the center of the bar separating the two panes; drag it up to increase the window space used by the reading pane or drag it down to increase the space used by the message list.

The Mail application has several folders by default, including Inbox, Drafts, Sent, and Trash. You can create additional folders as you need them.

You can configure some general aspects of how the application works by performing these steps:

1. **Open the Action menu (the gear icon) on the toolbar, and choose Preferences.** The Preferences dialog box appears.

2. **Select the General tab.** The General preference settings appear, as shown in figure 7.2.

3. **If you prefer to perform all email actions, including creating a new message, in one window, select the 2 panes radio button.** If you leave the default 3 panes option selected, a separate window appears when you create a new message. (The rest of this chapter assumes you are using the 3 panes option.)

4. **If you want to see all your folders and the folders they contain as soon as you log in, select the Show all folders at login check box.** If you create nested folders (folders within other folders) and this option is enabled, you see all the folders on your folder list when you log in. If you don't select this option, you have to expand folders to see nested folders.

Genius

Many of the application's most useful commands have keyboard shortcuts. When you open a menu, these shortcuts are shown next to the command. For example, to open the Preferences dialog box, press ⌘+ on a Mac or Ctrl+ on a Windows PC.

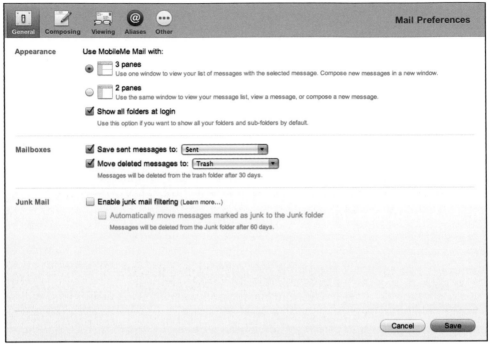

7.2 Use the General preferences to determine if you use the three-pane or two-pane window, among other options.

5. **Select the Save sent messages to check box, and choose the save location on the menu to save sent messages.** The default location for messages you send is the Sent folder, but you can choose a different folder. If you deselect this check box, messages you send are not saved. Not saving sent messages saves some disk space, but you don't have any record of these messages. Tracking sent messages is important for business purposes.

6. **To determine if and where deleted messages are saved, select the Move deleted messages to check box and choose the location where you want messages you delete to be saved on the menu.** If you deselect this check box, messages are removed from your account as soon as you delete them. If this option is selected, messages you delete are stored in the selected folder unless you empty it or until 30 days pass, whichever occurs first.

7. **Click Save to save your changes.** The dialog box closes, and your preference settings take effect immediately.

Note

The Junk mail tools are on the General tab. These are covered later in this chapter.

Reading Email

Email exists to be read, and the MobileMe Web email application offers all the reading tools you need. Before you start reading email, take a few moments to configure the application so that you can read email the way you want to. After you've configured the application, you can read and manage your messages, work with attachments, and so on.

Setting viewing preferences

To set your viewing preferences, follow these steps:

1. **Open the Action menu (the gear icon) on the toolbar, and choose Preferences.** The Preferences dialog box appears.

2. **Select the Viewing tab.** The Viewing preference settings appear, as shown in figure 7.3.

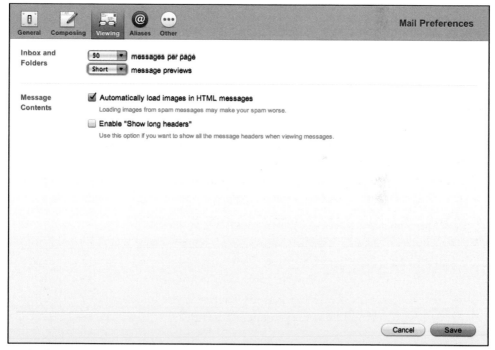

7.3 On the Viewing tab, you can determine how many messages appear on each page in folders and the length of previews.

3. **Use the messages per page menu to determine how many messages appear on each page of the folder you are working with.** Options include 50, 75, 100, 125, 150, or 200.

When the number of messages in a folder exceeds this value, you must move to the next pages of the folder to view more messages. Choosing a larger number requires you to scroll up or down more, while choosing a smaller number results in having to page through folders more frequently.

4. **Use the message previews menu to determine if previews are shown in the message list and how long they are.** The options are No, which displays only message subjects (no preview), Short, or Long. The Short option shows just one line from the message, while the Long option shows several lines. A longer preview shows more of a message's content without having to select it. But you have to scroll down to see more messages.

5. **To have images in HTML messages load automatically, select the Automatically load images in HTML messages check box.** If you don't select this option, you must click the Load button in HTML messages to see their images. If you do select this option, images appear automatically, which isn't always a good thing (such as when you receive spam messages that may contain offensive images).

Caution In addition to possibly exposing offensive messages, loading images can also tell the sender that your email address is valid and that you view messages sent to it. This might get you a lot more spam than if you don't load the images in a message.

6. **If you want to be able to see more information in the header area when you read a message, select the Enable "Show long headers" check box.** With this option selected, the Show Long Headers link appears in the reading pane. When you click that link, the message's full header information shows technical details about the path the message followed to reach you. If you don't select this option, this link doesn't appear.

7. **Click Save.** The dialog box closes, and your settings take effect.

Reading messages

Using the application to read messages is simple:

Note These steps assume the 3 panes option. If you use the 2 panes option, double-click the message you want to read. The message replaces the message list and reading pane, and you can read it. To move back to the previous folder, click the Back to *folder* link, where *folder* is the name of the folder where the message you are reading is stored.

1. **On the folder list, select the folder containing messages you want to read; to see new messages, select the Inbox (this is selected by default when you log in).**

2. **On the messages list, select the message you want to read.** The message appears in the reading pane at the bottom of the window, and if you hadn't read the message before, its blue dot (which indicates it is an unread message) disappears. At the top of the pane, you see the header information for the message including the sender, subject, date sent, and to address. If the message has attachments, you see the number of attachments and size just below the To line. Below that, you see the body of the message.

Genius
Because the email application is on the Web, email sent to you arrives almost instantaneously. If you want to check for new mail, click the Get New Mail button (the open envelope icon) on the toolbar.

3. **Read the body text.**

4. **If the message has attachments, click the right-facing arrow next to the paper-clip icon.** The list of attachments expands, and you see each attachment, as shown in figure 7.4.

Arrow to view attachments

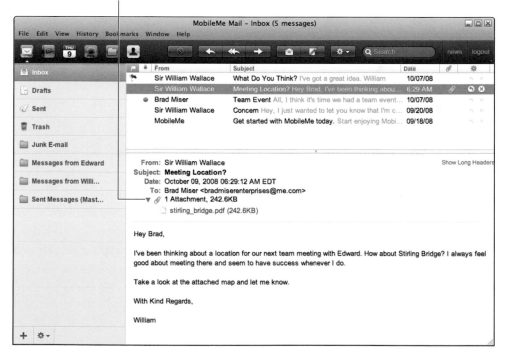

7.4 To expand the list of attachments for a message, click the arrow next to the paper clip so it points downward.

5. **To view an attachment, click its link.** You're prompted to open or save the file. The only difference between these options is that when you choose the save option, you can select a save location and you have to then open the file to view it. When you choose the open option, the file downloads to your default downloads location. It opens as soon as it is downloaded.

6. **If you've enabled the long headers link, click the Show Long Headers link to see detailed information about the path the message followed to reach you.**

When you're finished reading messages, you can deal with them in a number of ways:

- **Delete messages.** Select a message on the message list, and click one of the delete buttons. One is the red circle and slash in the toolbar; you can select multiple messages by holding down the ⌘ or Ctrl key and click this to delete multiple messages at the same time. The other is the "x" appearing at the far right end of the message on the message list; when you click this, only the related message is deleted. If you've configured the general preference so that deleted messages are saved, the message you deleted is moved to the selected folder. (The default is the Trash folder.) The deleted message remains there until you empty the folder by opening the Action menu on the toolbar. Then choose Empty Folder, and click OK or after 30 days since you deleted the message. You can retrieve the message by selecting the Trash folder (or the one you set as the delete folder) and dragging the message back to the Inbox or original folder.

- **Move messages to a different folder.** Drag a message from the message list, and drop it onto another folder on the folder list. The message moves into that folder. Another way to move a message to a different folder is to select it and choose the Move to Folder command on the Action menu.

- **Reply to or forward messages.** These actions are covered in more detail in a later section.

Creating and Managing Email Aliases

An email alias is an address that you create as an alternate to your primary MobileMe email address. When your contacts send email to this address, they address the message to the alias; and from their perspective, it works just like your primary address. However, the address just points to your primary MobileMe email address, so you receive any email sent to the alias and to your primary address.

In addition to your primary email address, you can have up to five aliases with your MobileMe account, giving you six email addresses that you can use at any time. And you can create and delete email aliases as you need to so they are very flexible.

You can use email aliases for many reasons. The following are two examples for using them for your small business.

One example is to use an alias as a sacrificial address for those situations in which an address is likely to get spammed, such as when you participate in public forums or when you register at Web sites. If you start receiving lots of junk mail addressed to an alias, you can simply delete the alias and the junk mail goes away with it. By shielding your primary business address from places that are likely to get it spammed, you can deal with spam easily.

The second example is to create an alias for a business marketing campaign. Suppose you want an ad in the local newspaper for your products or services. In the ad, you can provide an email address for people to get more information or to get a special discount. Instead of including your primary email address, you can use a customized alias so that you know exactly how many people are responding to the ad because you'll know exactly how many people sent messages to the alias address. So, you can judge how effective the ad was at getting people to communicate with your business.

You can be very specific and creative when you establish an email alias. Going back to the second example, you could create an alias like *mycompany_ad_feb_2@me.com* for an ad placed on February 2, and you can track the response to this one ad. Then, after reviewing the response, you can delete that address and create another one for another date.

Creating email aliases

To create an email alias, follow these steps:

1. **Open the Action menu (the gear icon) on the toolbar, and choose Preferences.** The Preferences dialog box appears.

Note You can't use email aliases with a free trial account. You can use them with Individual, Family Pack, and Family Member accounts.

2. **Click the Aliases tab.** The Aliases preferences appear.

3. **Click Create Alias.** A new alias line appears.

4. **Enter the email address in the Alias box.** You can use just about any text and characters as the alias. The alias must be unique — not just to your MobileMe account, but to all MobileMe accounts — but unless you choose something that is obviously likely to have been used by

someone else, you won't know if it is unique until you try to create it. Aliases can be from 3 to 20 characters.

5. **Enter the name you want to appear in the From field in the Name box.** You can use any text as the From identifier. If you are using the alias for business purposes, you might want to use either your business's name or your name as the From name.

6. **Select the color you want to be associated with messages sent to the alias by selecting that color's radio button.** These colors make it easier to identify email sent to each of your aliases; therefore, give each alias a unique color.

7. **Click Create.** The alias is checked for uniqueness and to ensure the text you entered doesn't violate any of the rules. If successful, you see the new alias in the table of aliases, as shown in figure 7.5. If the alias doesn't pass, you see an error message explaining the problem. If your choice is in use by someone else, you see suggestions for variations of the alias you created. Change the alias, and click the Create button until successful.

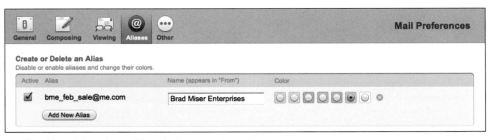

7.5 The alias address bme_feb_sale@me.com is ready to use.

8. **To add another alias, click Add New Alias and repeat steps 4 through 7.**

9. **When you're finished creating aliases, click Save.** The dialog box closes, and the aliases you configured are ready to receive email. You can send email from them, too.

Note Some changes to alias addresses, such as deleting them, can take time before they are processed. If you have five aliases and delete one, you can't create a new one until seven days have passed. During this time, the create button doesn't appear on the Aliases tab of the Preferences dialog box.

Managing email aliases

Email addressed to one your aliases is received and read in your Inbox just like messages sent to your primary address except that messages to aliases are color-coded based on your choices. You see the alias address in the To field, as shown in figure 7.6.

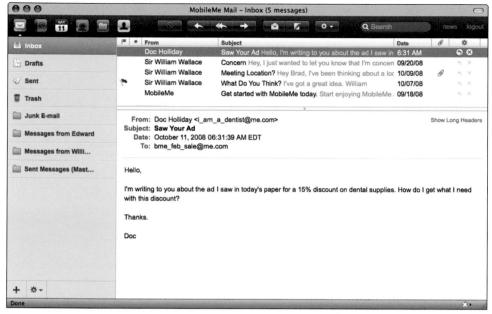

7.6 As you can see in the To field, the selected email was addressed to an alias.

Use these suggestions to manage email aliases:

- **Make aliases active or inactive.** You can create a bounce-back address, where email received at an alias is returned to its sender. Open the Aliases pane of the Preferences dialog box, and deselect the Active check box. When this box is unselected, an alias remains available to you, but email sent to the address bounces as if it is addressed incorrectly. You can select the box to make the address work again. This can be useful if an alias gets spammed, but you don't want to get rid of the alias permanently. Make the alias inactive most of the time. The spam (and other email) sent to the alias bounces. When you want to use it, make it active only for the time you need it.

- **Change the From name.** Change the text in the Name field to change the From name in messages you send from the alias.

- **Change the color.** Change the color associated with an alias by clicking the radio button for the color you want to use.

- **Delete an alias.** When you no longer want to use an alias, delete it by clicking its delete button, as shown in figure 7.7. You're prompted to confirm the delete by clicking OK. If you click OK, the alias is deleted from the list of aliases and is no longer usable. Any email sent to the alias bounces because the address is not valid.

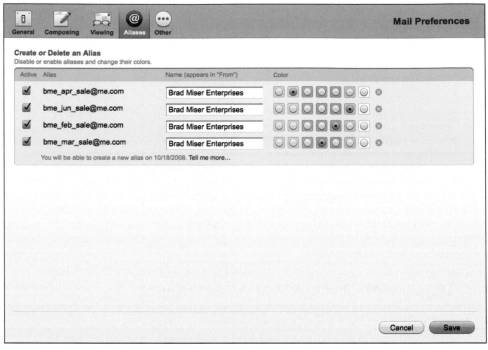

7.7 When you click an alias's delete button (x), it is gone for forever.

Note Deleting an alias isn't as dire as the prompt makes it sound because you can re-create an alias at any time. If you already had five aliases, you need to wait a week before you can create new aliases to replace those you deleted.

Working with an External POP Account

It's convenient to be able to get email from multiple accounts in one place, whether that is using an email application installed on your computer or using the MobileMe Web email application. You can add one of your POP email accounts to the MobileMe Web email application. Then you can use MobileMe to check email to that account.

Configuring a POP account

To add another account to the Web email application, follow these steps:

1. **Open the Action menu (the gear icon) on the toolbar, and choose Preferences.** The Preferences dialog box appears.

2. **Click the Other tab.** The Other preferences appear.

3. **Select the Check mail from an external POP account check box.** The account configuration fields appear.

4. **Enter a description of the account in the Description field.** This is text that helps you identify the account in various locations.

5. **Enter the user name for the account in the User Name field.** This is the part of the address before the "@."

6. **Enter the account's incoming server address in the Incoming Mail Server field.** This is usually something like pop.provider.com. You can get this information from the information you received when you obtained the account or from the provider's Web site.

7. **Enter the account's password in the Password field.**

8. **On the Destination menu, select the folder in which email sent to the added address should be stored.** You might want to create a distinct folder for the address (explained later in this chapter) and select it on this menu to have all its mail go into that folder automatically.

9. **Select the Leave messages on server check box, shown in figure 7.8, if you want email to remain on the server after you receive it.** This is useful when you want to be able to easily store email to this address on a specific computer as part of keeping email in sync. (This topic is discussed further at the end of this chapter.)

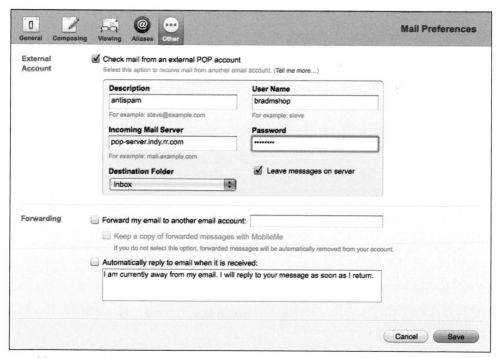

7.8 Adding a POP address to the MobileMe email application enables you to read messages sent to that address.

10. **Click Save.** The account is configured in the email application, and the dialog box closes. A link to check email to that account appears on the folder list.

Reading mail for a POP account

To check for email for the POP account you added to the email application, click the link for that account. This link, shown in figure 7.9, appears under the folder list and is labeled Check mail for *accountdescription* where *accountdescription* is the description of the account you entered. You see a status message stating that the external account is being checked.

When new messages are downloaded, they appear in the folder you selected on the Destination menu; you can see these messages by selecting that folder on the folder list.

7.9 Clicking the link for a POP account gets new mail for that account (Check mail for antispam, in this case).

Genius

To disable an external POP account, open the Other pane of the Preferences dialog box and deselect the Check mail from an external POP account check box. The settings you entered are hidden, and the account's link is removed from the folder list. You can re-enable the account by selecting the check box again.

Sending Email

You can use the MobileMe email application to send email from any of the MobileMe email accounts you've configured. Use the tool's composing preferences to tweak how its send functions work. You can then create email to send, and of course, reply to email you receive or forward it to a different address. Like other email applications, you also can attach files that you want to send along with your email messages.

Note

You can only receive email to a POP account you add to the email application. You can only send email from a MobileMe email account.

Setting composing preferences

To configure how the composing tools work, follow these steps:

1. **Open the Action menu (the gear icon) on the toolbar, and choose Preferences.** The Preferences dialog box appears.

2. **Select the Composing tab.** The Composing preference settings appear, as shown in figure 7.10.

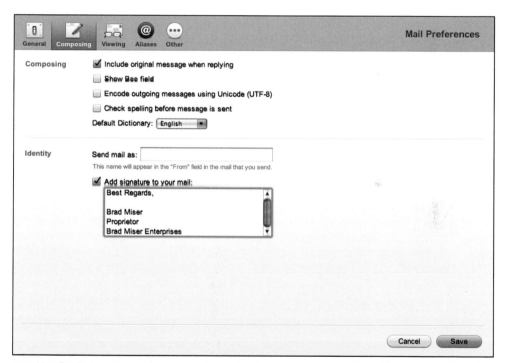

7.10 Use the Composing preferences to determine how you use the email application to send email.

3. **Select the Include original message when replying check box if you want the content of messages to which you reply to be pasted into the reply.** You should usually have this enabled so the context of your reply is included in the reply message.

223

4. **Select the Show Bcc field to be able to include Bcc recipients on messages you send.** Bcc recipients are hidden from the To and Cc recipients of a message.

5. **Select the Encode outgoing messages using Unicode (UTF-8) check box if you want to send email to people who use languages other than the one you use.** This option encodes your messages in a more universal format that is more likely to be interpreted correctly.

6. **Select the Check spelling before message is sent check box if you want to check spelling in messages you create when you send them.** If you leave this unselected, spelling is checked as you type.

7. **Choose the menu associated with the language you use to write email on the Default Dictionary menu.**

8. **Enter the name in the Send mail as box if you want messages you send to have a name in the From field other than the name associated with your MobileMe account.** You can use almost any text you want in this field, but you should use something that recipients of your messages should easily associate with you. If you leave this box empty, the full name for your MobileMe account (or email alias) appears in the From field.

9. **Select the Add signature to your mail check box and enter your signature in the box to automatically append a signature to messages you create.** You can add URLs to your signature, and those links are active, which can be very useful. For example, you can include the address of your business's Web site in your signature so that recipients of your messages can visit your site by clicking the link in your signature.

Note

You can't add images or other types of content to your signature; it can be text only. Of course, you can link to information by including a URL, which is even more useful.

10. **Click Save.** Your composing preferences are saved and take effect with the next email message you create.

Creating and sending email

Sending email in the Web email application is similar to sending email from other email applications. Follow these steps to begin the fun:

1. **Click the Compose New Message button (the pencil and paper icon) on the toolbar.** If you are using the 3 panes option, the new message window appears. If you are using the 2 panes option, the new message window replaces the message list and reading pane. Use

the Back to Inbox link to move back to the message list and reading pane. The rest of these steps assume the 3 panes option. If you configured a signature, it is pasted into the body of the message.

2. **Enter the To, Cc, and Bcc recipients for the message by entering email addresses in the respective fields in one of the following ways:**

   - **Type the email address in the appropriate fields, such as the To fields for the primary recipients.** As you type, the application attempts to match the email address with the one you've used previously and those in your Contacts application. If it finds a match, click it to enter that address. If not, continue typing the address until it is complete. To add multiple addresses to the same field, separate them with commas.

   - **Use the Contacts tool.** Click the Contacts button (the book with the @) on the new message toolbar. The Contacts dialog box appears. Use the dialog box to browse or search for the contacts you want to address the message to. Select the To, Cc, or Bcc check boxes to insert email addresses into those fields, as shown in figure 7.11. Click OK. The dialog box closes, and the selected addresses are pasted into the appropriate fields.

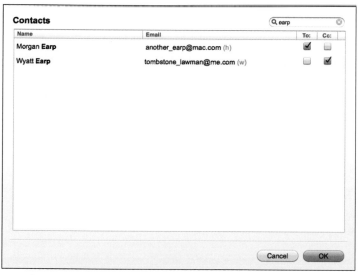

Name	Email	To:	Cc:
Morgan **Earp**	another_earp@mac.com (h)	☑	☐
Wyatt **Earp**	tombstone_lawman@me.com (w)	☐	☑

7.11 The Contacts dialog box makes adding addresses stored in the Contacts application easy.

Note

See Chapter 8 for information about the Contacts application.

3. **Enter the subject of the message in the Subject field.**

4. **On the Account menu, choose the account you want to send the message from.** You can choose your primary account, which is the default, or any of the active aliases. (This menu is enabled only if you have created at least one alias.)

5. **If you want to add attachments, perform steps 6 through 9; if not, skip to step 10.**

6. **Click the Attach a file link.** Depending on the browser you are using, either the Browse button appears (perform step 7) or you move directly to the Upload File dialog box (skip to step 8).

7. **Click the Browse button.** The File Upload dialog box appears.

8. **Move to and select the first file you want to attach, and click Open.** The file is uploaded to MobileMe and attached to the message. You return to the new message window, and the file you attached is shown next to the paper-clip icon. (In the current version, you can't attach multiple files at the same time.)

Genius

To save a draft of a message as you work on it, click the Save Draft button (the folded piece of paper icon) on the new message toolbar. A draft of the message is saved in the Drafts folder. You can close the message after you've saved it and move into the Drafts folder so you can open it to work on again.

9. **Click the Attach another file link, and repeat steps 7 and 8 to attach all the files you want to send with the message.** You see each attachment's size next to its file name and the allowed attachment size remaining next to the Attach another file link. You are limited to a total of 20MB of attachments per message.

10. **Type the text of the message in the body, above your signature if one was pasted in when you created the message.**

11. **Check the spelling of the message in one of these two ways:**

- **As you type.** With this preference enabled, words that the application thinks are misspelled are underlined in red. Open a misspelled word's contextual menu, and then use the commands on it to choose the correct spelling, add the word to the dictionary, and so on, as shown in figure 7.12.

- **All at once.** To check the entire contents of a message, click the Spell Check button (the ABC icon) on the new message toolbar. The message is checked, and a dialog box appears telling you how many misspellings were identified. Click OK. When you return to the new message window, each misspelling is red and underlined. Open a misspelled word's contextual menu, and use the commands to choose the correct spelling, add the word to the dictionary, and so on. When you have made corrections, click the Done button.

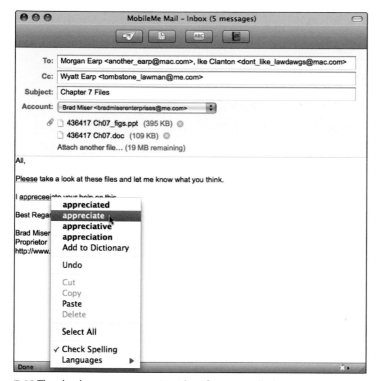

7.12 The check as you type option identifies misspelled words as you type them.

12. **Click the Send button (the paper airplane) on the toolbar.** The message is sent to the recipients and saved (or not) per the preferences you set on the General pane of the Preferences dialog box.

Note

A benefit of the 3 panes option is that the new message window is separate from the email application window so that you work with the application — to read a message, for example — while you are composing a new message. With the 2 panes option, you have to close the new message window to move to a message or other part of your .me Web site.

Replying to email with Quick Reply

The email application's Quick Reply is useful when you want to reply to a message with a simple text reply. If you want to add attachments or edit quoted text, you need to use the standard reply option as described in the next section. Quick Reply is easy to use following these steps:

1. **Select the message you want to reply to on the message list.** If you've enabled the Preview preference, you can read a portion of the message in the message list or read the entire message in the reading pane.

2. **Click the Quick Reply button (the curved arrow).** The Quick Reply dialog box appears.

3. **Type your reply.**

4. **Select the Reply All check box to send your reply to all recipients of the message, as shown in figure 7.13.**

5. **Click Send.**

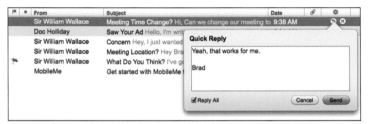

7.13 The Quick Reply feature makes replying to messages fast, but you can't add attachments to your reply.

Note Although you don't see it in the Quick Reply dialog box, your signature is pasted into your reply before it is sent.

Replying to email

When you want to add attachments to a reply or edit the quoted material, use the Reply or Reply All tools. Here's how:

1. **Select the message you want to reply to on the message list.**

2. **Perform one of the following:**

   - To reply only to the sender of the message, click the Reply button (single left-facing arrow) on the toolbar, open the Action menu, and choose Reply, or press Option+R on a Mac or Ctrl+R on a Windows PC.

   - To reply to everyone who received the message as To or Cc recipients, click the Reply All (the double left-facing arrows) button on the toolbar, open the Action menu, and choose Reply All, or press Shift+Option+R on a Mac or Shift+Ctrl+R on a Windows PC.

The reply message window appears in a separate window with the 3 panes option or in the same window with the 2 panes option. This message includes the content you are replying to. If you've enabled the signature preference, your signature is pasted above the quoted text. The message is addressed according to the kind of reply, and "Re:" is appended to the subject.

3. **Complete and send the message just like when you create a new message.**

Forwarding email

When you want to show someone else a message you've received, you can forward it. For example, suppose a prospective customer emails a question to you, but you need a team member's help to be able to answer it effectively. Using the Forward command, you can send the message to the team member while adding your information to it. Here's how:

1. **Select the message you want to forward on the message list.**

2. **Perform one of the following:**
   - Click the Forward button (the right-facing arrow) on the toolbar.
   - Open the Action menu, and choose Forward.
   - Press Shift+Option+F on a Mac or Shift+Ctrl+F on a Windows PC.

   The forwarded message window appears in a separate window with the 3 panes option or in the same window with the 2 panes option. The content of the message you are forwarding is pasted in the window. If you've enabled the signature preference, your signature is pasted above the quoted text. The message is not addressed unlike a reply, and "Fwd:" is added at the beginning of the subject line.

3. **Add you comments to the forwarded message.** For example, you can explain what you want the person to whom you are forwarding the message to do.

4. **Address and send the message just like when you create a new message.**

Forwarding email automatically

Automatic forwarding works even when you're not logged into your MobileMe account. It is a good way to have other people manage your email while you are unable to. For example, if you know you are going on vacation and don't want possibly important emails to sit in your Inbox, you can use automatic forwarding to get those messages to team members. You can have email automatically forwarded from MobileMe email to another email address by configuring the appropriate preference:

1. **Open the Other tab of the Preferences dialog box.**

2. **Select the Forward my email to another email account check box.**

3. **Enter the address to which email should be forwarded in the address field.**

4. **If you want to keep the email on the MobileMe server so you can access it with the MobileMe email application, select the Keep a copy of forwarded messages with MobileMe check box, as shown in figure 7.14.**

5. **Click Save.**

Caution You can't forward email to another MobileMe email account, which severely limits its usefulness if your business uses only MobileMe for email.

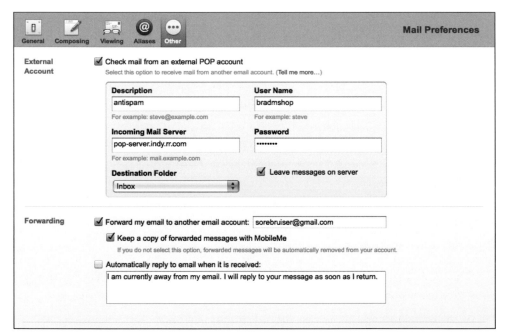

7.14 Automatic forwarding sends all email to another address.

Caution If you don't keep a copy of forwarded messages on the MobileMe server, those messages are deleted as soon as they are forwarded. They are not saved in the designated deleted folder, so they are gone for good.

Quoting Effectively

When you reply, the entire contents of the message you are replying to is pasted into the message along with the time and date of the original message. The quoted text is marked with the > symbol. Each time a reply is made, another > is added to the quoted material. Including the quoted text is useful because it gives the reader context for your reply. By default, the quoted text appears at the bottom of the message, and you type your reply at the top. However, to use quoting most effectively, you should delete all the quoted text except that which pertains to your reply. If you type your response immediately below the quoted text, the reply forms more of a conversation. This shows the reader exactly what you are replying to because it puts your response in a very specific context as opposed to just having your reply at the top of the message and relying on the reader to put it in the correct context. Quoting like this only takes a few moments longer, but if your goal is to communicate effectively, the additional time and effort pays off.

Managing and Organizing Email

Efficiency is even more important to a small business than it is to other kinds of organizations. You have a limited amount of bandwidth, and the more you can squeeze into the time you have, the better your business runs. While email is a critical business tool, it also can be a hugely inefficient waste of time. To keep your email time as efficient as possible, practice good organization habits for email. Fortunately, the MobileMe email application provides the tools you need to keep your email under your control.

Organizing email with folders

You can add folders to the folder list to organize your email:

1. **Click the Add Folder button (+) located at the bottom of the folder list, or open the Action menu and choose New Folder.** The New Mail Folder dialog box appears.

2. **On the Location menu, choose the location for the new folder.** The options are MobileMe, which adds the folder to the root level of the email application, or you can choose any of the current folders to place the new folder within (to create a nested folder).

3. **Type the name of the folder in the Name field, as shown in figure 7.15.**

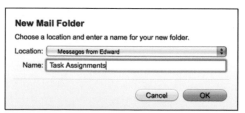

7.15 Use folders to organize email and work with it more efficiently.

231

4. **Click OK.** The folder is created in the location you specified.

Use these tips to keep your email organized in folders:

- When you create a nested folder, the folder in which it is contained has an expansion triangle next to it on the folder list. When this points to the right, click it to expand the contents so you see each folder it contains. When this points downward, click it to collapse the folder so the nested folders are hidden.

Caution Once created, you can't move folders around. To change the location of a folder, you have to delete it and re-create it in its new location. Of course, you need to move out the messages you want to save before deleting a folder.

- You can create a nested folder within a folder that is itself nested to create a multi-level folder hierarchy.
- To place messages within folders, you can drag them from the message list and drop them onto the folder you want to store them in.
- For another way to move a message, select the message you want to move. Open the Action menu to choose Move to Folder. The Moving message dialog box appears. Select the folder you want to move the message into, and click Move. The message is moved to the location you selected.

Managing folders

To organize your folders, open the Action menu on the toolbar or at the bottom of the folder list and choose Manage Folders. The Manage Folders dialog box appears. You see each of your folders and the total size of the messages stored in each one. Here, you can do the following:

- Rename a folder by selecting it and clicking the Edit button (the pencil icon). The folder's name becomes editable, and you can type a new name for it, as shown in figure 7.16. Press Return (Mac) or Enter (PC) to save the new name.
- Delete a folder by selecting it and clicking the Delete button (x). After you click OK at the prompt, the folder and all its contents are deleted.

Caution When you delete a folder, it and its messages are deleted immediately. They aren't moved to the Deleted folder, as are messages that you delete. When you empty a folder, its messages are deleted immediately as well. So don't perform either of these actions unless you are sure you don't need the related messages.

Manage Folders

Click a folder to rename or delete it.

Folder	Size	☼
🖥 Inbox	262 KB	
📂 Drafts	0.7 KB	
✉ Sent	519 KB	
🗑 Trash	667 KB	
📁 Junk E-mail	0.0 KB	
📁 Messages from Edward	0.0 KB	
📁 Expense Information	1.5 KB	
📁 2008 Cancel | Save	0.0 KB ✏ ⊗	
📁 Task Assignments	0.0 KB	
📁 Messages from William	0.0 KB	
📁 Sent Messages (Master Mob...	7.3 KB	

Folder Name [   ]   (New Folder)   (Empty Folder)

(Done)

7.16 You can rename folders using the Manage Folders dialog box.

- Create a new folder by selecting the folder you want to create it in, typing a name in the Folder Name field, and clicking New Folder.

- Delete the contents of a folder by selecting it and clicking the Empty Folder button.

When you are finished managing folders, click Done. The dialog box closes, and the changes you've made are shown on the folder list.

Genius

You also can empty a folder by selecting it on the folder list and choosing Empty Folder on the Action menu.

Using status information to manage email

The email application tracks various kinds of information about the messages with which you are working. You can use this information to help you manage your emails more effectively. Here are some pointers:

- Use flags to mark important messages for later action. To flag a message, select it and choose Flagged on the Action menu. The flag icon appears in the first column of the message list. You can sort by this column to have the most important messages at the top of the list. To remove a flag from a message, select it and choose Unflagged on the action menu. The keyboard shortcuts for these commands are Shift+Option+L (Mac) or Shift+Ctrl+L (Windows).

- Use the read/unread status marker (the blue dot) to help you know which messages you need to read. If you want to return a message to the unread status, select it and choose Unread on the Action menu. The keyboard shortcuts for this command are Shift+Option+U (Mac) or Shift+Ctrl+U (Windows).

- Sort the message list by any of the information shown by clicking the column by which you want to sort it. For example, click the Flag column to have all the messages you've flagged at the top or bottom of the window. Use a sort order that increases your efficiency when dealing with email.

Email Can Waste Lots of Time

As you operate your business, you'll probably receive lots of email. Some of it is important, while some of it is just a waste of time. You should deal with email as efficiently as possible. Some people are tempted to read all their new email first and then go back later to take action on it. This is inefficient because you have to spend time reading the message each time. Try to take action on each message as you read it. For example, if the message has no value, delete it immediately. If you need to reply to the message, reply as soon as you read it; when you're finished replying, delete the original or move it to a folder if you want to keep it. If you need to take some time to reply, create the reply, but don't add anything to it before saving it as draft. Deal with the original message, and when you have the time, move back to the draft reply and finish it. Or flag the message as needing action and move along.

Also, dealing with email is more efficient in batches. Be disciplined about working with email for short blocks of time; you'll spend less time than if you deal with new messages as soon as you receive them. For example, decide to handle email every hour or two.

Searching Email

Looking for specific email messages is something we all need to do. You can search your email by performing the following steps:

Genius

A good way to be able to find email is to keep it organized so you know where to look for it.

1. **Select the folder you want to search in.**

2. **Type the text for which you want to search in the Search field (magnifying glass icon) and press Return (Mac) or Enter (PC).** The messages that meet your search are shown on the message list.

3. **To limit the found messages to only those that contain the search text in a specific area, choose that field on the Show results from menu.** For example, to limit the results so the search text is only in the From field, choose From:, as shown in figure 7.17. Other options are All fields (default), To, and Cc. The list of messages is reduced to only those with the search text in the selected field.

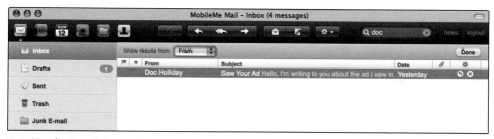

7.17 Use the Search tool to locate messages.

4. **When you're finished with the search, click the Done button or click the Delete button (x) in the Search field.**

Genius

To search within the body of a message you are reading, use the Web browser's Find command.

Setting Up Automatic Responses

Sometimes you can't respond to email in a timely manner. You may be on vacation (do people in small businesses really take vacation?), or you may not have time to respond to all your emails. Taking a long time to respond to email can be bad for business, especially if that email is from current or potential customers. For situations like these, it can be useful to set an automated response to your email. While not as good as a "real" response from you, an automated response is much better than no response at all.

To configure an automated response, follow these steps:

1. **Open the Other tab of the Preferences dialog box.**

2. **Select the Automatically reply to email when it is received check box.**

3. **Type the automatic reply in the text box, as shown in figure 7.18.**

4. **Click Save.**

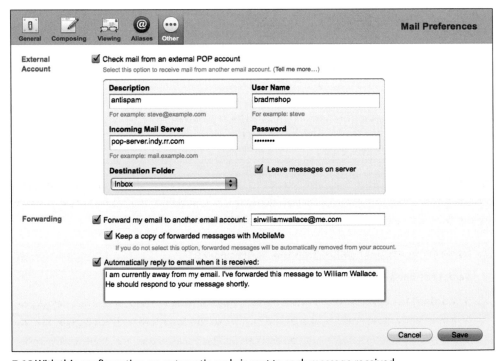

7.18 With this configuration, an automatic reply is sent to each message received.

Note

Your signature is not pasted into the response. If you want a signature block to appear in the automated response, include its text in Step 3.

Genius

You can combine this feature with automatic forwarding so you let people know someone will deal with your messages while you are out.

Managing Junk Email

One of the inevitable aspects of email is junk mail. In addition to being annoying or offensive, junk email can cause you to waste time, which you can't afford to do when you are involved in a small business.

The best way to manage junk email is to avoid it. Be careful where you provide an email address. For example, avoid public forums, Web sites that require you to register, and other scenarios that are likely to get an address spammed. When you do provide an email address in scenarios that might get spammed, use an alias. Then you can simply delete the address to deal with any spam it receives.

Even with good spam avoidance, your primary or alias addresses will probably receive spam messages from time to time. You can use the Junk mail tool to help you deal with spam.

Configuring junk mail filtering

The email application's junk mail tool flags email messages it thinks are junk by changing their color to brown and adds the text "MobileMe thinks this is Junk Mail" to the message header. Follow these steps to start the filtering process:

1. **Open the General tab of the Preferences dialog box.**

2. **Select the Enable junk mail filtering check box.**

3. **If you want the application to move email it flags as junk to the Junk folder, select the Automatically move messages marked as junk to the Junk folder check box, as shown in figure 7.19.** I recommend that you don't select this because then you have to remember to review the Junk mail folder. If you don't, important messages that are mistakenly flagged as junk and moved can languish in that folder.

Note Another good reason not to use the Junk folder option is that once the Junk folder is added to your folder list, you can't remove it, even if you disable the Junk mail tool.

7.19 The junk mail filter can be some help in the battle against junk mail.

4. **Click Save.** The dialog box closes. If you selected the check box in Step 3, the Junk folder appears on the folder list.

Managing junk mail

Here's how to deal with junk messages in the MobileMe email application:

- Review any messages you see that are brown. If the message is junk, delete it. If the message isn't junk, open it and click the Not Junk button. The message is no longer flagged as junk.

If you selected the Junk folder option, you need to periodically select that folder to review and deal with the messages it contains. Any messages in that folder are deleted after 60 days. It's more efficient to deal with new messages in the Inbox. There's also some chance that non-junk messages end up in the Junk folder where you might not read them in a timely way. That's why I don't recommend you use the Junk folder. If you do, make sure you review its contents regularly.

Note

When you select a message and choose the Mark as Junk Mail command on the Action menu, the message is marked as junk and moved to the folder (if the folder option is enabled). Of course, it's easier just to delete a junk message.

You can improve the MobileMe's spam mail filtering by reporting messages that should be flagged as spam. If the message you want to report isn't already flagged as junk, mark it as junk. Then click the Report as Spam button. The sender is reported to MobileMe as sending junk mail. While one report isn't enough to get a sender marked as a spammer, if many people report spam over time, the spammer gets blocked by the MobileMe email server and you never see its messages again. You can report a message as spam only once, but you can report the same sender multiple times.

Keeping Email in Sync

If you only use the MobileMe Web email application, you don't have to worry about keeping your email in sync because the same email is available to you regardless of the device you use to access your email. However, if you sometimes use an email application installed on your computer or the email application on an iPhone to access your email, it can get out of sync. That means you might not have messages you need in one location, or you have to deal with the same messages in multiple locations.

To keep your email in sync, decide upon one location as the "master" for email. This master might be the MobileMe email application or might be an email client installed on a particular computer. You want all email to end up in this location so you can save it in an organized way and you'll always know where you can get it.

In order to understand syncing, it is necessary to understand a little bit about how email works. There are two basic models.

In one model, email is received at a server associated with the account. To read that email, you use an email application to connect to the server and download the mail from the server to your computer. The email can be deleted from the server when you download it so it doesn't appear the next time you check email. It also can remain on the server from where it is downloaded the next time you check it from a different location. This model is primarily used with Post Office Protocol (POP) email accounts. Internet Service Providers and other organizations commonly provide POP accounts.

In the other model, email remains on the server. When you want to work with it, you use an application that connects to the server. But instead of downloading it to the computer, the message is read from and remains stored on the server. This means it is available to any email application on any device that connects to that account until the message is deleted from the server. At that point, it is no longer available to any device. This model is the Internet Message Access Protocol (IMAP).

MobileMe email is delivered using the IMAP model. So, when you check email using any email application, including the MobileMe email application, you work with the same emails until you move them from the server onto a device, such as storing them in a folder on your computer being managed in an email application. IMAP accounts are very easy to keep in sync.

Keeping IMAP email in sync

When you create folders to store email in, you can create them on the IMAP server or on a computer. The email messages you store in folders on the server are always available to you. Email messages you move from a folder on the server into a folder on your computer are available only when you use the email application on the computer.

Keep active email in a folder on the IMAP server so you can get to it from any location. When you no longer need to have easy access to a message, either delete it or move it from a folder on the server to one stored on the device that is the master for your email. For example, the master folder may be managed with an email application such as Mail or Outlook on a Mac or Windows PC. Remember that any email messages stored on the MobileMe server count against your allotted storage space on that server, so use that space efficiently.

See the earlier sections in this chapter for information about managing and organizing email messages using the MobileMe email application.

Keeping POP email in sync

Keeping POP email in sync is a bit trickier. You need to configure the application you use on the master device to remove email from the server when you check it. Configure the settings for that account on other devices not to remove messages when you check for email but to leave them on the server.

Each time you check for mail from a device that isn't the master, email messages are downloaded to that device so you can read them. This means you see the same message on each non-master device as a new message again, which can be confusing. Messages only stop being received as new messages when you check email from the master device. That's because when you check from there, the messages are downloaded from the server and then deleted from it.

To learn how to configure a POP account in the MobileMe email application, see the section on adding other accounts to the Web email application earlier in this chapter. To learn how to configure POP accounts in other applications, see the Help system for that application.

What Can I Do with the MobileMe Web Contacts Web Application?

Contact information for the people and organizations you interact with — be

they customers, prospects, partners, or vendors — is critical, no matter what

kind of business you operate. This information tends to be dynamic, chang-

ing as people change email addresses, phone numbers, physical addresses,

and so on. In Chapter 3, you learned how to keep contact information stored

on Macs, Windows PCs, and iPhones in sync with the MobileMe cloud. In this

chapter, you learn how to use the MobileMe application to access the cloud

so you can use and manage your contact information via the Web.

Exploring the MobileMe Contacts Application

Like most contact applications, the MobileMe Contacts application is based on the concept of a virtual address card or vCard. Unlike physical address cards, vCards are flexible and can store many kinds of information about each contact. Each vCard can have a different set of information so you see only the fields on a card that actually have information; for example, if a contact has only a name and email address, you see only those two fields on the associated vCard, whereas if another contact has ten different pieces of information, you see all ten on the vCard.

You can add cards to your contacts information in a number of ways, including creating a card using the MobileMe application, importing a vCard, and synching other contacts applications (Address Book or Outlook) with the MobileMe cloud.

You can organize your vCards into groups, for example, a group for your business's team members. Groups make it easy to find and work with multiple contacts.

To get an overview of the MobileMe Contacts application, log into your .me Web site and click the Contacts button the toolbar. The Contacts window appears. This window has three panes: groups, cards, and card detail, shown left to right in figure 8.1.

To work with a contact, select the group containing the contact on the Groups list. The default All group contains all of the vCards in the application. The cards contained in the selected group appear in the Cards pane. Cards are grouped by the first letter of the last name or first letter of the first name depending on your display preference (see the next section). Select the card you want to work with, and its detail appears in the far right pane.

Like the other MobileMe applications, the Contacts application has its own toolbar and Action menu at the top of the window. You also see the Search tool to the right of the toolbar.

At the bottom of the window, you see the Add (+) Group button along with the number of vCards in the selected group.

Contacts button   Selected card

          Groups   Cards   Detail for selected card

8.1 The MobileMe Contacts application uses a three-pane window; from left to right the panes are groups, cards, and card detail.

Configuring Contacts Preferences

The Contacts application has it owns set of preferences. Configure them using the following steps:

1. **Open the Action menu (the gear icon) on the toolbar, and choose Preferences.** The Preferences dialog box appears.

2. **Select First name Last Name or select Last name, First name, depending on how you want your contacts displayed.**

3. **On the Sort by menu, choose Last Name to have the cards sorted by the contacts' last names or First Name, depending on how you want your contacts sorted.**

4. **On the Address Layout menu, choose the format of the addresses shown on cards; the options are the most common formats, such as United States or Japan.**

5. **If you want the application to automatically and consistently format phone numbers, select the Automatically format phone numbers check box and choose the format you want on the menu.** You can choose from various formatting options, such as using hyphens or decimal points. When you choose any of the options, the country code for the number is added to it, as shown in figure 8.2.

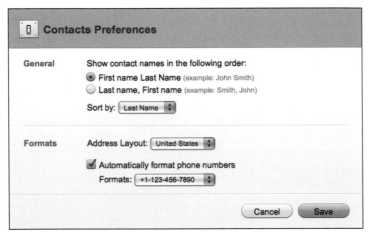

8.2 Use the Contacts Preferences dialog box to determine how contacts appear in the window, along with format options for addresses and phone numbers.

6. **Click Save.** The dialog box closes, and your settings take effect immediately.

Note

To see your format changes, refresh the card displayed by selecting a different card. Then re-select the card you were viewing when you updated your preferences.

Browsing and Searching Contacts

The first step to any action with a contact is to find the contact with which you want to work. There are two options: browsing and searching. Browsing is often faster, especially if you take advantage of groups to keep your contacts well organized. Searching is useful when you have a very large number of contacts and you want to locate a specific one without having to do a lot of scrolling.

Browsing for contacts

You can quickly browse the contacts in the application using these steps:

1. **Select the group containing the contacts you want to find.** To browse all of your contacts, select the All group. (In the current version of the application, you can select only one group at a time.) The contacts (vCards) contained in the group appear in the center pane.

2. **If necessary, use the scroll bar in the center pane to move up and down the list of vCards.**

3. **Select the vCard with which you want to work.**

Note

You can select multiple cards at the same time, but only specific actions can be taken on a group of cards. For example, when you select more than one card, only the card you most recently selected appears in the detail pane and some actions on the Action menu are disabled. However, some actions are enabled, such as the Export command (explained later in this chapter).

Searching for contacts

You can use the Contacts' application's Search tool to search for a specific contact. This is useful when you want to search by first name, last name, or company. However, in the current version of the application, these are the only fields for which you can search, which limits the value of the search tool considerably; likely, in a future version, you'll be able to search any field, including phone number, email addresses, physical addresses, and so on.

Performing a search is very simple:

1. **Select the group you want to search.** To search all your contacts, select the All group. (In the current version of the application, you can select only one group at a time.)

2. **Enter the text for which you want to search in the Search tool.** As mentioned earlier, the application only searches the first name, last name, and company fields. As you type, any cards that contain the text you enter are shown in the center pane. If you get so specific that only one card matches your search, that card is selected and its detail is displayed, as shown in figure 8.3.

3. **Select the card you want to work with.** Its information appears in the far-right pane.

To clear a search, click the Clear button (x) in the Search tool. The search term is deleted, and all the cards in the selected group appear in the center column.

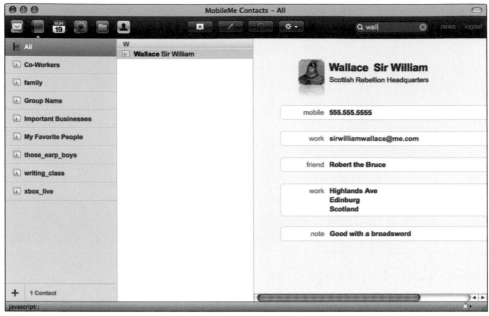

8.3 When you enter text in the Search tool, you see cards that contain that text in the name or company fields.

Creating and Managing Contacts

You can add contact information to the MobileMe Contacts application in a number of ways, including manually and by using vCards. After contact information is contained in the application, you can update that information as needed or delete it when you no longer want it.

Genius

If you have contact information stored in Outlook on a Windows PC, Address Book on a Mac, or on an iPhone, see Chapter 3 for the best way to get that information into the MobileMe cloud. By configuring synchronization among the devices you use, you also ensure that current contact information is available in all the synced locations.

Creating contacts manually

You can add contact information directly in the MobileMe Contacts information (and also to the MobileMe cloud), by doing the following:

1. **Click the New Contact button on the toolbar (the address card with the +).** An empty address card appears in the right pane of the window. Each field on the card contains a label for the field. For example, the field for first name contains the text "First Name."

2. **Enter the contact's basic information: first name, last name, and company in the appropriate fields.**

3. **If you are creating a contact for a company or other organization, select the Company check box.** The Company field moves to the top of the screen and becomes more prominent. You also can enter a first and last name for the contact or leave it at the organization level by leaving those fields empty.

Note

In the Cards pane, contacts for companies have icons that look like a group of buildings while contacts for individuals have the vCard icon. This is determined by whether the Company check box is selected.

4. **To add an image to the contact, click the Add link located under the image well to the left of the name and company fields.** The Add Photo sheet appears.

5. **Click the Choose Photo button.** The File Upload dialog box appears.

6. **Move to and select the image, and click Open.** You can use images in the GIF, JPG, or PNG formats that are less than 1MB. You return to the Choose Photo sheet, and the name of the file you selected is displayed.

7. **Click OK.** The image is uploaded, the sheet closes, and you return to the new contact and see the image you selected in the image well, as shown in figure 8.4.

8.4 You can add images to contacts on MobileMe; these images appear for certain actions, such as when you receive email from the contact in Mac OS X's Mail application.

8. **Using the menu next to the first Phone field, select the type of phone number (home or mobile) and enter it.** If you selected the autoformat preference, the number is formatted according to the option you selected. (For example, the country code is added to the number automatically.)

Genius

To add a type to the list available on the menu, open the menu and choose Custom. A text box replaces the menu. Enter the type in the text box. The information is labeled with that type.

9. **Repeat Step 8 for each phone number you want to enter; to remove phone numbers you aren't going to use, click the Delete button (red circle with -), or to add another phone number, click the Add button (green circle with +).**

10. **Repeat Steps 8 and 9 for email addresses, screen names, and physical addresses; when you enter screen names, choose the type of screen name on the menu, such as AIM for AOL Instant Messaging names.**

11. **Enter notes about the contact in the note field, as shown in figure 8.5.**

8.5 Configure an address card so it contains only fields in which you enter information.

12. **When the contact's information is complete, click Save.**

Note

You can use the Add Field menu to add a variety of other information for a contact. See the section on changing contact information later in this chapter.

Adding contacts with vCards

A vCard is a file format designed for contact information. You can add contact information to the MobileMe Contacts application using vCards, such as those that people email you. vCards have the filename extension ".vcf." To add a contact with a vCard, perform the following steps:

1. **Open the Action menu (the gear icon) on the toolbar, and choose Import vCard.** The Select vCard to Import sheet appears.

2. **Click Choose File.**

3. **Move to and select the vCard file you want to import, and click Open.** You move back to the Import sheet and see the file you have selected.

4. **Click Import.** The vCard is added to the Contacts application, and you can work with it just like cards you create. For example, you can change its information, add fields to it, and so on.

Updating contact information

As time passes, contact information Is lIkely to change. Or, you might want to add more information to or delete information from existing cards. You can edit address cards so they reflect the most current information and contain exactly the information you want them to. Here's how:

1. **Find and view the contact whose information you want to change.**

2. **Click the Edit button on the toolbar (the pencil icon).** The card moves into Edit mode in which it looks just like it did when you created it. All the fields become editable and the Add Field, Cancel, and Save tools appear.

3. **Change information in existing fields using the menus to change labels and by typing over the current information.**

4. **Add fields by clicking the Add button (green circle with +), or remove fields (used or empty) by clicking the Delete button (red circle with -) next to the corresponding fields.**

5. **To change the image associated with the contact, click the Change link under the contact's current image; use the resulting Change Photo sheet to select a different image file.**

6. **To add more types of information to the card, open the Add Field menu.**

7. **Choose the type of field you want to add to the card, as shown in figure 8.6.** (If an option is grayed out, that field is already on the card.) The field you select is added to the card.

8. **Select the label for the new field, and enter its information.**

9. **When you're finished making changes to the card, click Save.** Your changes are saved, and you see the updated card.

> Address
> Birthday
> Dates
> Department
> Email
> Instant Messaging
> Job Title
> Maiden Name
> Middle Name
> Nickname
> Phone
> Phonetic First/Last Name
> Prefix
> Related Names
> Suffix
> URL
>
> [Add Field... ▾]

8.6 The Contacts application supports many different types of fields, which can be added to a card.

Note There's currently no way to change the basic template for a contact. To add a field that isn't part of the basic template, you must add that field to each card you want to store it on.

Deleting contacts

To remove a contact from the application, perform the following steps:

1. **Find and view the contact you want to delete.**

2. **Click the Delete button on the toolbar (the red circle and slash).**

3. **Click Delete in the resulting warning prompt.** The contact's card is deleted from the application.

Caution When you remove a card from the Contacts application, it also is removed from all the locations synced to your MobileMe cloud the next time the sync occurs.

Using Contact Information

Generally, you simply view your contact information. However, many of the fields on address cards are active, meaning they are linked to actions. Following is a list of some of the uses for your contact information:

- **Send an email.** You can send a message to an email address on a card by clicking it. A new message window appears with the recipient's email address inserted into the To field, as shown in figure 8.7. Use the MobileMe email application to complete and send the message; see Chapter 7 for more information.

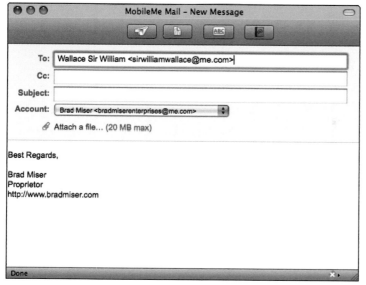

8.7 When you click an email address on a contact card, a new email message addressed to that card is created.

- **Visit a Web site.** When a contact card contains a URL, you can click that URL to visit it.

- **View an address's location on Google maps.** When you click a physical address, you see that address on a Google map, as shown in figure 8.8. Click the Satellite button to see a satellite image view of the address, or click Hybrid to see both the Map and Satellite views. To move to the Google Maps Web site, click Open in Google Maps. A new tab or window appears showing the address on the Google Maps Web site, where you can use tools to generate directions to the address.

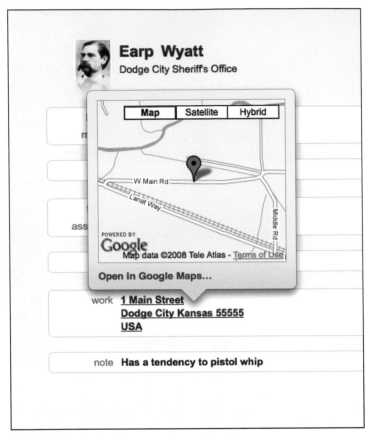

Earp Wyatt
Dodge City Sheriff's Office

Map | Satellite | Hybrid

W. Main Rd
Lanat Way
Middle Rd

POWERED BY
Google
Map data ©2008 Tele Atlas - Terms of Use

Open in Google Maps...

work **1 Main Street**
Dodge City Kansas 55555
USA

note **Has a tendency to pistol whip**

8.8 Click a physical address to see it on a Google map.

Note

Some active links, such as Web site addresses, are obvious because they are high-lighted in blue. Others, like physical addresses, aren't. You can only tell they are links by pointing to them; items that are active become underlined to indicate they are linked.

- **Print a contact.** View the contact you want to print, open the Action menu on the tool-bar, and choose Print. A new window opens showing the contact information in a print-able form, and the Print dialog box appears. Configure the dialog box, and print the contact's information. When you're finished, close the contact's print window.

Genius

You can send an email to multiple addresses by selecting each card containing the address to which you want to send a message (To select multiple cards on a Mac, press and hold the ⌘ key and click each card. To select multiple cards on a Windows PC, press and hold the Ctrl key and click each card). Then choose the Email Contact command on the Action menu. If cards you select have more than one address, the top address is used for that contact.

Working with Contact Groups

In the far-left pane of the Contacts window, you see the groups of your contacts. The All group contains all your contacts, but you can create other groups to collect specific cards together to make them easier to find.

Note

Currently there is no way to select a group and email every card in the group by addressing an email message to the group.

Creating contact groups

Creating a new contact group is simple:

1. **Click the Add button (+) at the bottom of the Groups pane.** A new group appears with its name highlighted, Indicating it is ready to edit.

2. **Type the name of the group, and press Return (Mac) or Enter (Windows).** The group's name is saved, and the group is ready for cards to be added to it. The group is stored on the list in alphabetical order.

Adding contacts to groups

To add cards to a group, follow these steps:

1. **Browse or search for the card you want to add to a group.**

2. **Drag the card's icon from the Cards pane, and drop it onto the group you want to place it in. The group becomes highlighted when the card is in position.**

3. **Repeat Steps 1 and 2 until you've added all the cards to the group that you want.**

4. **Select the group you added cards to.** You can see the cards it contains on the Cards pane, as shown in figure 8.9. The number of cards in the group is displayed next to the Add button at the bottom of the Groups pane.

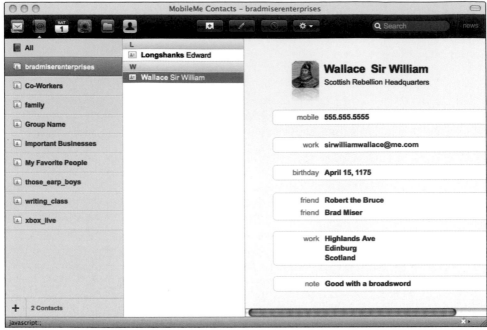

8.9 This group contains two address cards.

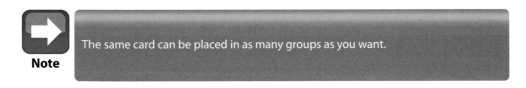

Note

The same card can be placed in as many groups as you want.

Changing groups

You can change your contact groups in the following ways:

- **Rename a group.** To rename a group, double-click its name. The field becomes editable. Type the new name and press Return (Mac) or Enter (Windows) to save your changes.

- **Remove cards from a group.** Select the group you want to remove cards from. Select the card you want to remove from the group, and click the Delete button on the toolbar. In the resulting prompt, click Remove from Group. The card is removed from the group, but it remains in the Contacts application. (You can delete the card from the application by clicking Delete at the prompt.)

- **Add cards to a group.** You can add cards to a group at any time using the steps in the preceding section.

- **Remove a group.** Select the group you want to remove, and click Delete in the resulting prompt. The group is deleted from the Groups pane, but the cards it contained are not changed.

Sharing Contacts with Other People

It's likely you want to share contact information with your team members. There are several approaches you can take, each having its own benefits and drawbacks.

Sharing contact information with vCards

The simplest approach to sharing contact information is to provide vCards to the people you want to share contact information with. After you've exported a contact as a vCard, you can email or share the vCard file to provide its information to others. The recipient can then add the vCard to his own contacts application.

The benefits of this approach are that it is easy to export and import vCards, and your team members do not have to share one contacts database. You will, however, need to create and provide the vCard to your team members. Also if you make changes to the vCard after you send it, you have to resend it because the updated vCard is not synchronized.

To create vCards, follow these steps:

1. **Select the cards you want to provide as vCards.**

2. **On the Action menu, choose Export vCard.** The Opening vCards dialog box appears.

3. **Choose the Save File option, and click OK.** Depending on the Web browser you are using, the vCard is saved to your default Downloads location or you're prompted to choose a Save location.

4. **If you're prompted for a Save location, move to it and click Save.** The vCard file is saved in the location you specified, as shown in figure 8.10.

Note If you select multiple cards in step 1, a single vCard file is created containing each of the cards you selected.

You also can store vCards in your Public folder so that people who can access that folder can download and import those vCards to their contact applications.

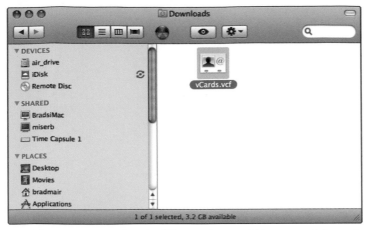

8.10 After you've created a vCard file, people can add its contact information to their contacts applications by importing the file.

Sharing a central contacts list using a single MobileMe account

If your business uses a single MobileMe account, you can easily share the same contacts data with all your team members. Each person with whom you want to share contacts data simply synchronizes his computer or iPhone to the same MobileMe account. Any changes made to contacts are reflected in all synced locations.

The benefit of this approach is that everyone has access to the same set of contacts. Changes made in one location are reflected in the other locations. However, a computer user account can be synced to only one MobileMe account at a time. That means everyone in your company has to use the same MobileMe resources. This can be a good thing in some situations, but is limiting in others.

It works well when team members don't need individual accounts, such as when they use another provider for email. Using the same MobileMe account ensures that everyone is accessing the same information. And everyone using the same account minimizes the cost of the MobileMe services to your business.

Caution When one account is used, any changes made to the data are made in that one database and then propagated to all the devices synced to it. Ensure data is backed up outside of MobileMe so that data isn't lost permanently if someone makes a mistake.

For example, your team members will have to use two contacts applications to have any contact information that isn't seen by the entire group: one application is synced via MobileMe while the other is not. Company contacts are stored in the synced application while personal contacts are stored in the unsynced application. And, unless you only want to use MobileMe email as a group, you'll have to use some other service for email because all team members would have access only to the same email account.

Note In Chapter 9, you learn about the MobileMe Calendars application. When you use a single MobileMe account or a Family Pack Member account for contacts information, these options benefit sharing calendars in similar ways.

Sharing a central contacts list using a Family Pack Member account

Another option is to use a Family Pack Member account to share contact information with a group of people. Because people can sync to only one MobileMe account at a time, they don't sync to the Family Pack account. Instead, you configure the Family Pack account with the "master" set of contacts you want people to share. Other people access these contacts by logging into the Family Pack account's Web site and using its Contacts application. They can then view and use the contact information or export vCards.

The benefit of this approach is that it does provide a central location for contact information. When team members need to get to the information, they simply log into the Family Pack account on the Web and use its Contacts application. After the contacts information is populated and each time a contact's information changes, you can update it in the Family Pack Member account. Then other people can access the updated information on the Web or download the updated vCard to update their own contacts.

You must maintain a Family Pack Member account for this purpose; if you have accounts you aren't currently using, this isn't a problem, but if you don't have accounts available, you'll have to add a new account.

Keeping addresses in sync with computers and other devices is a manual process; you change the information in the Family Pack Member account's Contacts application and then communicate the changes to others (who then have to manually add the information to their contacts data). Of course, if others only use the Web to access the contact information (as opposed to adding it to their own contacts applications), this isn't a problem because they don't have to actually move the information from the Web site to their computers or iPhones.

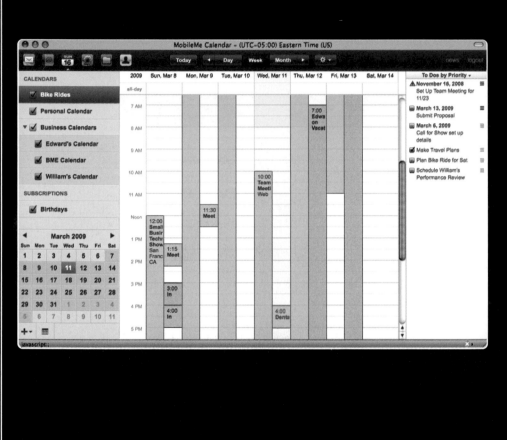

With the MobileMe Calendar application, you can access and manage your calendar via the Web, making your calendar available from any device running a supported browser with an Internet connection. For managing a personal calendar, this is convenient because you can easily view the same information from multiple devices. However, unless you are the only person involved in your business, you need to use a desktop calendar application to set up meetings and perform other calendar collaboration tasks. Through syncing, information you manage with a desktop application is also available in the Web application.

Exploring the MobileMe Calendar Application

To access the MobileMe Calendar application, log into your MobileMe account and click the Calendar button (the calendar icon that shows the current date and day of the week). The MobileMe Calendar application has up to three panes, which are the Calendar list on the far left, the Calendar itself in the center pane, and the To Do list in the far right pane, as shown in figure 9.1. (The To Do list is hidden by default so that you only see the first two panes. You can show this pane by opening the Action menu and choosing Show To Dos.)

Calendar list

Calendar button   Calendar   View controls   To Do list

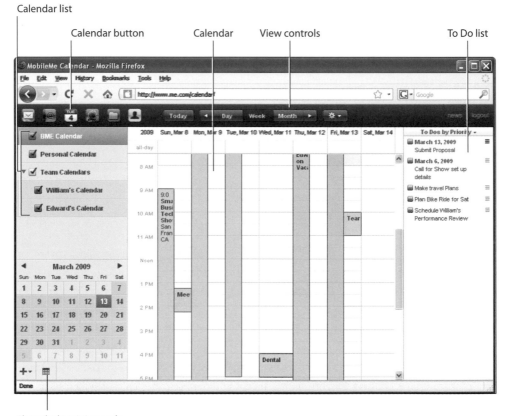

Show/hide mini-month

9.1 The MobileMe Calendar application has up to three panes, with the center pane displaying the calendar itself.

On the Calendar list, you see the calendars and groups of calendars being managed in the application. You can use multiple calendars to organize your events and To Dos. The obvious and often-used example is one calendar for your business life and another for your personal life. However, you can create calendars for less obvious purposes, such as for a major project. You also can organize calendars into groups; this simply places them within a container that you can expand or collapse to show or hide the calendars on the list. You can show or hide the events and To Dos associated with a calendar by selecting or deselecting its check box on the calendar list. Each calendar can have a color associated with it; this color is applied to the calendar's associated events and To Dos so you can more easily associate a calendar with the information it is being used to manage.

You can view and change the details for a calendar, such as its associated color, by selecting it and choosing Calendar Info on the Action menu. In the resulting sheet, you see the calendar's name, color, and description. You also can use this sheet to change any of this information.

Under the calendar list is the mini-month that shows you a month-at-a-glance view of a month you select. The month being displayed is shown in text at the top of the view and also by the shaded dates in the month. The date in focus is in blue (and also is shaded on the calendar). You can show or hide the mini-month by clicking the Show/hide mini-month button. You can change the month being displayed by clicking the arrow to the left or right of the month shown at the top of the mini-month. You also can click a date on the mini-month to jump to that date on the calendar.

Genius

To move to a specific date, open the Action menu and choose Go to Date. Enter the date you want to view and click OK. The calendar displays that date.

In the Calendar pane, you see a day, week, or month; the scope of what you see depends on the button selected at the top of the calendar. You can control the specific timeframe you see by clicking the left or right arrows to the left of the Day button and to the right of the Month button respectively. You can jump to the current date by clicking the Today button. The events shown on the days being displayed are color-coded based on the calendars with which they are associated. The amount of information you see for events depends on the view you are using. The Day view is the most detailed, while the Week and Month views show you increasingly larger spans of information. Compare figures 9.2 and 9.3 with 9.1 to see these differences. You'll likely switch between views for different purposes. In all views, the date currently selected is shaded.

The To Dos pane shows the To Do items associated with the calendars selected on the calendar list. This pane can be hidden or shown; when you log into your MobileMe Web site, the To Dos pane is hidden. To show the pane, open the Action menu and choose Show To Dos. To hide the pane, open the Action menu and choose Hide To Dos. You also can show or hide this pane by pressing ⌘+Shift+H on a Mac or Ctrl+Shift+H on a Windows PC.

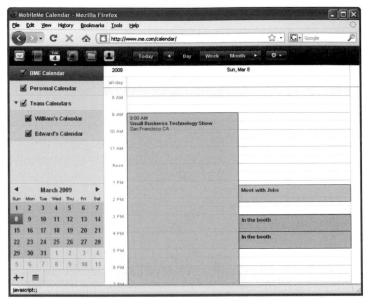

9.2 The Day view provides the most detail about a day's events, but only for one day at a time.

9.3 The Month view provides limited information about each day's events, but does give you a good idea of the fullness of your schedule.

Note In the current version of the Calendar application, the To Do list is hidden each time you move out of the Calendar application.

The To Do list can be sorted in different ways by opening the menu at the top of the list, as shown in figure 9.4. You can choose one of the automatic sort options (due date, priority, title, calendar) or choose Sort Manually and then drag To Do items up or down on the list.

To the left of each To Do item is the status check box; when you complete an item, select its check box to mark it as complete. When an item is due on or before the current date, this check box is replaced by a triangle containing an exclamation point so that you can easily tell the task is due or overdue. To the right of each To Do item is an indication of its priority; the more bars that are filled in for a task, the higher its priority is.

9.4 You can sort your To Do list by the options shown on this menu.

You can view the details for any event or To Do item by double-clicking it. The event's or To Do item's Edit sheet appears, where you can view or change details for the event or To Do item with which you are working, as shown in figure 9.5.

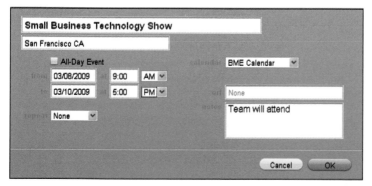

9.5 When you double-click an event or To Do item, you see its configuration sheet.

Configuring Calendar Preferences

You can configure a number of preferences for the Calendar application. These preferences are divided into two groups: General and Advanced.

Configuring general preferences

General preferences include those related to how your calendars appear and the date and time formats you use. To set these preferences, perform the following steps:

1. **Open the Action menu, and choose Preferences.** The Calendar Preferences dialog box appears.

2. **Click the General tab.**

3. **On the Days per week pop-up menu, choose 7 if you want your calendars to include all seven days in the week or 5 if you only want five days (the work week) to be shown.**

4. **On the Start week on pop-up menu, choose the first day of the week.** This is the day shown on the far left of the Week or Month views.

5. **On the Day starts at and Day ends at pop-up menus, choose the times at which your days start and end.** This simply applies a light shading to the times outside the times you set on these menus. I suppose it's a reminder when you're scheduling things beyond your time window. These settings are more for a traditional workday, such as an 8-hour day, but likely don't have much meaning in the context of a small business.

6. **On the Show pop-up menu, choose how many hours you want to display in the calendar window.** This setting determines how many hours are shown when the browser window is at full-screen size; when you reduce the size of the window, you see fewer hours regardless of this setting. Of course, you can always use the scroll bars to see the hours outside of those currently being shown.

7. **Select the Show time in month view check box if you want the start time for events to be shown when you view your calendar in the Month view.**

8. **Select the Show Birthdays calendar check box if you want to display a calendar of birthdays for contacts you're managing in the Contacts application.** This calendar takes the dates in the Birthday field on vCards in the Contacts application and presents them on the Birthdays calendar.

9. **If you usually add alarms to events, select the Add a default alarm to all new events and invitations check box, and enter the time before the event that the alarm should activate.** You can change the default for new events; if you don't use a default, you can always add an alarm to new events.

10. **Use the Date Format menu to determine how dates appear in the application.** For example, for the traditional U.S. format, choose MM/DD/YYYY.

11. **Use the Time Format menu to set the format of time information.** You can choose a 12-hour clock or a 24-hour clock.

12. **Use the Date Separator menu to determine which character is used to separate elements of dates.** You can choose / (slash), - (hyphen), or . (period).

13. **On the Time Separator menu, choose the character separating hours from minutes.** You can choose :(colon) or . (period).

14. **Click Save, as shown in figure 9.6.** Your preferences take effect immediately.

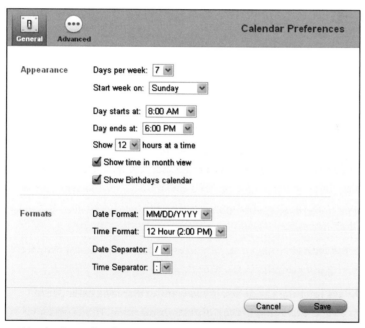

9.6 Use the General preferences to determine how date and time information appear on your calendars.

Configuring advanced preferences

The Advanced preferences include Time Zone support and To Do preferences. To set them, perform the following steps:

1. **Open the Calendar Preferences dialog box, and click the Advanced tab.**

2. **Select the Turn on time zone support check box if you want the Calendar application to account for time zones when you schedule events.** You can then associate events with specific time zones and change the time zone for which you are viewing events. This feature is most useful when you are using the application while traveling. As you change time zones, you can set the time zone you are currently in. Then the application adjusts the time for each event so it is appropriate to the time zone you are in. If you leave this check box unselected, time zone is ignored.

3. **If you enabled Time Zone support, choose the current base time zone on the Time Zone menu.** This adjusts all the events on your calendar to reflect the time zone change.

4. **Select the Hide To Do items with due dates outside the calendar view check box to hide any To Do items that don't need to be done during the period you are currently viewing.** This causes To Dos to be displayed only in the context to which they apply. For example, if you are viewing the current week, and a To Do is set to be due in a month, that To Do item doesn't appear on your list.

5. **Select the Hide To Do items days after they have been completed check box, and set the number of days that must pass until completed items are hidden.** With this option, completed To Do items are hidden, but not deleted, from your calendar after the set time has elapsed since you marked them as complete.

6. **Select the Delete events that are more than months old check box, and enter a number of days if you want expired events to be deleted from the calendar.** I don't use this setting because I like to use the calendar to recall when specific events occurred, so I leave events on the calendar indefinitely.

7. **Select the Delete To Do items days after they are completed, and enter a number if days if you want completed To Do items to be deleted from your calendars.** Again, if you like to use the Calendar to look at past items you've completed, you should leave this check box unselected.

8. **Click Save, as shown in figure 9.7.** The Preferences dialog box closes, and your changes take effect.

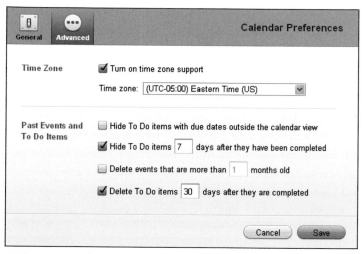

9.7 Advanced preferences control Time Zone support and how past events and To Do items are handled.

Working with Calendars and Calendar Groups

You learned earlier that the Calendar application can be used to manage multiple calendars for various purposes, which typically involve classifying the events and To Do items associated with those calendars, again with the obvious example of a calendar for your business and one for your personal affairs. You can create and manage calendars in the Calendars application, and you can organize your calendars in groups.

Creating calendars

You can create as many calendars as you need for whatever purposes you decide are important to manage as their own entities. On the other hand, you don't want to create so many calendars that they become unwieldy. In most situations, one to three calendars are ideal.

To create a calendar, follow these steps:

1. **Click the New Calendar button (+) located at the bottom of the calendar list.**

2. **Choose New Calendar on the resulting menu.** A new, untitled calendar appears on the calendar list with its name ready to be edited.

3. **Enter a name for the new calendar, and press Return (Mac) or Enter (PC).** The name can be just about anything you want, but in most cases, you want something that identifies the purpose of the calendar you are creating.

4. **With new calendar selected, open the Action menu and choose Calendar Info.** The Info sheet appears.

5. **Use the Color pop-up menu to choose a color for the calendar.** When you add events to the calendar, they appear in the color you select. Having different colors for different calendars is useful because you can easily see which events came from which calendar when you are viewing multiple calendars at the same time. The color also applies to To Do items.

6. **Enter a description of the calendar in the Description field.**

7. **Click OK, as shown in figure 9.8.** The changes you made are saved, and you see the calendar's name in the color you selected.

9.8 Use the Info sheet to configure new or existing calendars.

Working with calendars

As you use calendars, you can perform the following tasks:

- **Display a calendar's events and To Do items.** Remember that selecting a calendar's check box displays its events and To Do lists, while deselecting the check box hides a calendar's events and To Do items.

- **Change a calendar's information.** In the previous section, you learned how to configure a new calendar. You can use the same steps to change an existing calendar's name, color, and description.

- **Change a calendar's name.** Double-click a calendar's name to change it.

- **Change the order of calendars.** To reorder the calendars on your list drag calendars up or down until the list is organized as you prefer.

- **Delete a calendar.** To remove a calendar, select it, open the Action menu, and choose Delete. After you click OK in the resulting warning prompt, the calendar, its events, and its To Do items are removed from the Calendar application.

Creating and configuring calendar groups

You can use groups to organize your calendars. A calendar group simply places calendars together in one collection and enables you to show or hide those calendars by showing or hiding the group in which they are contained. To create and configure a calendar group, do the following steps:

1. **Click the New Calendar button (+) located at the bottom of the calendar list.**

2. **On the resulting menu, choose New Calendar Group.** A new group appears on the calendar list.

3. **With new group selected, open the Action menu and choose Calendar Info.** The Info sheet appears.

4. **Enter a name of the group in the Name field.**

5. **Enter a description of the group in the Description field.**

6. **Click OK, as shown in figure 9.9.** The changes you made are saved.

7. **To add calendars to the group, drag them onto the group.** The calendar moves under the group and is indented on the list to show its relationship to the group.

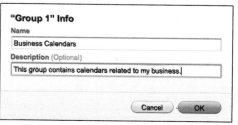

9.9 The Info sheet for a group is similar to the Info sheet for a calendar.

Managing calendar groups

You can manage your calendar groups with the following tasks:

- **Display a group's calendars.** When you select a group's check box, all the calendars it contains (whose check boxes are selected) are displayed. When you deselect a group's check box, its calendars are hidden.

- **Expand or collapse a group.** Click a group's expansion triangle to collapse it or expand it. When collapsed, you see only the group's name on the calendar list.

- **Change a group's name or description.** Use the Info sheet to change this information for a group.

- **Remove a calendar from a group.** To remove a calendar from a group, drag it outside the group and place it on the calendar list where you want it to be located. (You can also delete a calendar that you no longer need to remove it from a group.)

- **Reorganize calendars in a group.** To change the order in which calendars are listed in a group, drag them up or down within the group.

- **Delete a group.** To remove a group, select it, open the Action menu, and choose Delete. After you click OK in the resulting warning prompt, the group, along with all the calendars it contains (and the events and To Do items on those calendars), is removed from the Calendar application.

Creating and Managing Events

In Calendar terminology, an event is simply a period of time about which you want to record information for planning or other purposes. Events can be appointments, meetings, or maybe just a period of time you want to set aside for a specific purpose. The Calendar application enables you to create and manage events on your calendars. In addition to the basics of time and date, you can include other useful information for events, such as associated URLs and notes.

Creating events

To add an event to a calendar, perform the following steps:

1. **Select the calendar on which you want the event to appear.** It becomes the active calendar and is highlighted on the calendar list.

2. **Do one of the following tasks:**

   - On the mini-month, select the date on which you want the event to occur; that date moves into view on the calendar, and it becomes highlighted. Open the Action menu, and choose New Event. A new event appears on the calendar with its title selected. By default, the event is an all-day event and appears at the top of the selected date. The name of the event is highlighted.

   - On the Action menu, choose New Event. A new event appears at the current time and date. The name of the event is highlighted indicating its name can be edited.

   - Place the cursor at the approximate time and date of the event, and drag for the length of time of the event; as you drag, the start and end times are shown at the top and bottom of the event. A new event appears on the calendar with its name selected.

3. **Type the name of the event.**

4. **Press Return (Mac) or Enter (PC).** The event name is saved, and it appears in the color of the calendar with which it's associated. When selected, the event appears in a darker shade of the calendar's color to indicate it is the active event. Figure 9.10 shows several events on a calendar. If that's all the information you want to include for the event, you're finished and can skip the rest of these steps. But to fully configure an event, march on.

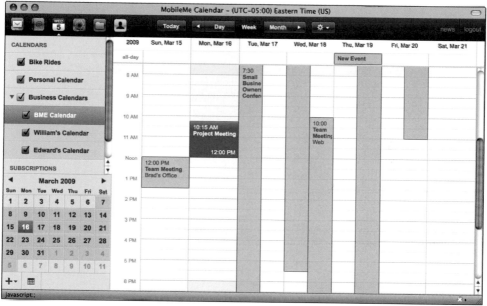

9.10 At their most basic, events include a date, period of time, and title.

Note

These steps assume that the time zone support feature is turned on. If not, just ignore any time zone information you read or see here.

5. **Double-click the event.** Its Info sheet appears. Here, you see the detailed information for the event and can input or edit it as needed.

6. **Enter information about the location of the event in the Location field.**

7. **If the event is an all-day event, select the All-Day Event check box.** This fixes the duration of the event to be the 24-hour period on which it occurs, or if it occurs over multiple days, the 24-hour periods for each day are blocked off. When you check this, time tools disappear because they don't apply, and you can skip the following step.

273

Caution

The Calendar application is very specific about date and time information you enter. Dates must be entered in the MM/DD/YYYY format, and you must enter times as HH:MM. You can't leave any digits out, or you see an error message.

8. **If you want to set specific start and end dates and times for the event, use the from and to fields to set those dates and times.** When you click in one of the date fields, you can enter a date manually or use the pop-up calendar to select dates. Note that an event can span multiple days, and don't forget to associate AM or PM with the event's times.

9. **Choose the time zone for the event on the time zone pop-up menu.** This is important because it associates the event with a specific time zone. As you change the overall time zone for the calendar, the event's time information is shifted according to the time zone with which it is associated. For example, if the overall time zone is Eastern Time (US) and you associate an event with Pacific Time (US & Canada), it is shifted on the calendar to show the times relative to the associated time zone, so it would appear 3 hours earlier on the calendar than the times you configure for the event.

10. **If you want the event to repeat, use the repeat pop-up menu to determine when it repeats.** You can choose a standard frequency for the event, such as Daily or Weekly, or select Custom to set a custom frequency.

11. **If you made the event repeat, use the end pop-up menu to choose an end date for the repeating event.** This becomes the last date on which the repeating event occurs. Choose never to repeat the event indefinitely, on date to set the end date, or after to number of times the event should repeat.

12. **If you selected on date or after, enter the end date or the number of times the event should occur, respectively.** (If you selected never in step 11, skip this step.)

13. **If you want to change the calendar with which the event is associated, choose a different calendar on the calendar pop-up menu.**

14. **If a URL is associated with the event, enter it in the url field or copy and paste it there.**

15. **Enter any notes about the event in the note field.**

16. **Click OK, as shown in figure 9.11.** The event's details are saved, and your calendar is updated accordingly.

Genius

When you are creating or editing events or To Do items and the Web browser's spell checker is active, you see red underlines under terms that aren't recognized. You can manually correct errors, use the spell checker to do so, or just leave them as is.

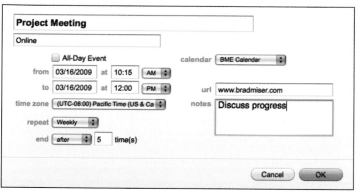

9.11 You can configure an event in more detail via its Info sheet.

Managing events

Check out these event tidbits:

- Events in the Calendar application are more limited than events in a desktop calendar application. For example, you can't set alarms for events, and if you are memory challenged like me, not having an alarm for events makes them much less useful.

- If you need to invite other people to an event, you need to use a desktop calendar application to create it. You can only view the people who were invited to an event using the MobileMe Web application.

- Unless you are the only one involved in an event and you are pretty sure you'll remember it, I recommend that you use a different application to create and manage your events, specifically iCal on Macs, Outlook on Windows PCs, or the Calendar application on iPhones. With these applications, you can set alarms, invite others, and generally do all the things you need to for meaningful and useful events. You can then use the MobileMe Calendar application to view the events you create with a different tool.

- You can change the details for an event by double-clicking it. Its Info sheet opens, and you can make changes to the various data fields as you do when you create an event.

- You can change the time and date of an event by dragging it from the current location on the calendar to when you want the event to occur.

  You can change the start time or end time for an event by dragging the top or bottom borders respectively. As you drag, the current start or end time is displayed; when you stop dragging, the time is set to the value displayed.

275

You can change the calendar with which an event is associated by dragging it from the calendar window and dropping it onto the new calendar. The event occurs on the same date and at the same time, but it's moved onto the new calendar.

- When you can't open an event's Info sheet by double-clicking it, that event was created in another application and its field's aren't editable using the MobileMe Calendar Web application. This also means you may not be able to see details for the event, such as who else is invited, and there doesn't appear to be a way to tell when you can view the details for an event and when you can't. You just have to try opening an event to find out. When you try to open an event that was created in another application, you see a message stating that the event is Read-only. You have to use a different application to see the event's detail.

- When you receive an email invitation to an event, you can't add that event directly to the MobileMe Calendar application from the MobileMe Email application. You have to download the event from the email message and add it to your desktop calendar application (such as Mail or Outlook). The event becomes visible in the MobileMe Calendar application the next time your information is synced (with the limitation that you can't see its details because it was added in a desktop application).

- If you enabled the Delete events preference, events are deleted automatically after they are older than the number of months you specified.

- To manually delete an event from the calendar, select it and press the Delete key. The event is deleted, but be aware that you don't see a warning prompt.

Caution You can drag events that were created by a desktop application around the MobileMe calendar to change the date or time for them. However, changes you make won't be moved into the creating application calendar when the information is synced, so the events appear at different times in the MobileMe Calendar application and in the desktop calendar. You should change events created in a desktop application only in that application.

Creating and Managing To Do Items

As you know, To Do items are tasks that you need to accomplish. You can use MobileMe Calendar To Do items to track just about any kind of action for which you are responsible. The To Do tools are similar to the event tools so after you understand one kind of element, you can work with the other easily enough. For example, you associate To Do items with a specific calendar. In this section, you learn how to create and manage your To Dos, including how to complete them — and by that, I mean how to mark them as complete; you're on your own to actually do the work.

Creating To Do items

Creating a To Do item is similar to adding an event, as you see in the following steps:

1. **Select the calendar with which you want to the To Do item associated.**

2. **Do either of the following:**

   - Open the Action menu, and choose New To Do.

   - Press Ctrl+K.

   If the To Dos pane isn't shown, it opens. A new, untitled To Do item appears; the item's name is selected indicating that you can edit it.

3. **Type the name of the To Do item.**

4. **Press Return (Mac) or Enter (Windows PC).** You've completed the basic To Do information. But, why stop there?

5. **Double-click the new To Do item.** The Info window appears, as shown in figure 9.12. You can configure additional details for the To Do item using this window.

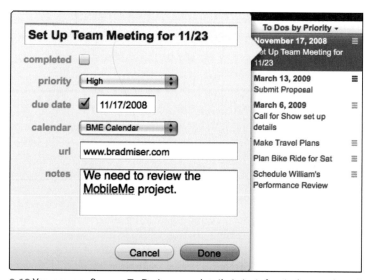

9.12 You can configure a To Do in more detail via its Info window, such as the item's priority.

6. **Use the priority pop-up menu to set the To Do item's priority.** You can choose None, Low, Medium, or High. You can use To Do item priorities to sort the items on your list.

7. **If the To Do item has a due date, select the due date check box.**

Caution You can't set alarms for events, so you have to review the To Do list to see your To Do items, their priority, and when they are due.

8. **Use the date fields that appear to set the due date.** You can either type the date in directly (using the DD/MM/YYYY format) or choose a date from the calendar that pops up when you click in the due date field.

9. **To change the calendar with which the To Do item is associated, select a calendar on the calendar pop-up menu.**

10. **If a URL is associated with the To Do item, enter it in the url field.**

11. **Enter notes for the To Do item in the notes field.**

12. **Click Done.** The changes you made to the To Do item are saved. If you entered a due date for the To Do item, it appears above the To Do item's name on the To Do list. If the list is sorted, the item appears on the list according to the sort order, as shown in figure 9.13.

Managing To Do items

You manage your To Do items in the To Do pane, which appears on the right side of the Calendar window. As you work with To Do items, keep the following points in mind:

To Dos by Priority ▾
☐ **November 17, 2008** ≡ Set Up Team Meeting for 11/23
☐ **March 13, 2009** ≡ Submit Proposal
☐ **March 6, 2009** ≡ Call for Show set up details
☑ Make Travel Plans ≡
☐ Plan Bike Ride for Sat ≡
☐ Schedule William's ≡ Performance Review

9.13 Changes you make to a To Do item are immediately reflected on the To Do list.

Note If you don't see the To Do pane, open the Action menu and choose Show To Dos or press ⌘+Shift+H (Mac) or Ctrl+Shift+H (Windows).

⦿ Sort the order in which To Do items appear on the list using the To Do pop-up menu at the top of the To Do pane. You can sort the list by due date, priority, title, calendar, or manually. After you make a selection, the list is ordered accordingly. By due date is useful to see which To Do items are required to be done in chronological order. If you choose Manually, you can drag items up or down the list.

- When To Do items don't have the information by which the list is sorted, such as priority, they appear at the bottom of the list sorted by title.

- When you sort the list by priority, items with the same priority are sorted by due date.

- When the due date for an item is the current date or the due date has passed, its complete check box becomes a warning icon to indicate that the item is due or overdue, as shown in figure 9.14. You can check the warning icon to mark the item as complete.

- The priority of a To Do item is indicated by the number of bars that appear to the right of its name on the To Do items list. A high-priority item has three bars in the color of the calendar with which it is associated, a medium-priority item has two bars, and a low-priority item has one bar. Items without a priority have all the bars shown, but none of the bars are highlighted with the associated calendar's color.

To Dos by Priority ▾
⚠ **November 16, 2008** ≡ Set Up Team Meeting for 11/23
☐ **March 13, 2009** ≡ Submit Proposal
☐ **March 6, 2009** ≡ Call for Show set up details
☑ Make Travel Plans ≡
☐ Plan Bike Ride for Sat ≡
☐ Schedule William's ≡ Performance Review

9.14 To Do items marked with a caution icon are due today or are overdue, such as the top item on this To Do list.

- You can change the priority of an item by clicking its current priority setting. Choose the new priority on the resulting menu; the current priority is marked with a check mark on the menu.

- You can change any of an item's information by double-clicking it. Its Info window appears, and you can change its data just as when you create a new To Do item.

- You can change an item's title by selecting it and pressing Return (Mac) or Enter (Windows). The item's name becomes highlighted, and you can change it.

- When you have completed a To Do item, mark it as complete by selecting the box next to its name on the To Do list or by selecting the completed box on the Info window, as shown in figure 9.15. Depending on the preferences you set, it may remain on the list for the amount of time you set, or it may be removed immediately if you configured the preference to hide completed To Do items immediately.

⊙ If the due date for a To Do item is outside of the current view — perhaps because you are viewing the current week and an item is due next week, and you've set the related preference — the To Do item doesn't appear on the list until you are viewing its due date on the calendar.

Sharing Calendars

When it comes to sharing information, the MobileMe Calendar application is less useful for running a business because it isn't really designed to collaborate with others, which is a requirement for most small businesses. However, you can share calendar information with your team members in some ways; the best way is to use a desktop application such as iCal, but you do have a couple of options using the MobileMe Calendar application.

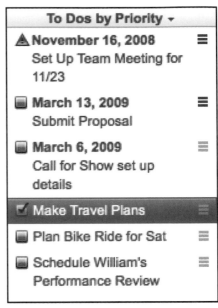

9.15 To Do items marked with a check mark (the Make Travel Plans item in this example) are complete.

If all your team members use Mac computers, using iCal's Publish and Subscribe feature is the way to go because it's very easy to share your calendar with your team and to access your team members' calendars within iCal. If not, you have to find some combination of techniques that work for your business. For example, if some team members use Outlook, they can add an extension that enables them to subscribe to published iCal calendars.

Sharing calendars using iCal

Mac OS X's iCal calendar application's Publish and Subscribe feature is designed to work with MobileMe. You can easily publish calendars so other people can subscribe to them and vice versa. Calendars to which you've subscribed appear on your list of calendars so you can easily view the events and other information they contain.

Even if a team member doesn't use iCal, he can still view a published calendar on the Web.

Publishing calendars using iCal

To make your calendar available to other iCal users, publish it by performing the following steps:

1. **In iCal, select the calendar you want to publish.**

2. **Select Calendar ⇨ Publish.** The Publish sheet appears, as shown in figure 9.16.

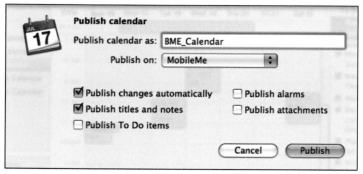

9.16 Use the Publish sheet to share a calendar with other iCal users and to publish it to the Web.

3. **In the Publish calendar as field, type the name of the calendar as you want it to appear to someone with whom you share it.** By default, the calendar's shared name is the same as its name in iCal, but you can change this if you want to.

Genius

It's a good idea to remove any spaces in the calendar's name because in the URL for a calendar, spaces are replaced by %20, which makes the URL harder to deal with than it needs to be. If you don't want the words in the name to run together, use underscores instead of spaces.

4. **Select MobileMe on the Publish on pop-up menu.**

5. **If you want changes you make to your calendar to be published automatically, select the Publish changes automatically check box.** In most cases, you should select this so your published calendar is always up to date.

6. **If you want both the title and notes associated with an item to be published, select the Publish titles and notes check box.**

7. **If you want To Do items to be included in the published calendar, select the Publish To Do items check box.**

8. **If you want the calendar's alarms to be published, select the Publish alarms check box.**

9. **If you want attachments to events included in the published version, select the Publish attachments check box.**

10. **Click Publish.** When the calendar has been published, you see the confirmation dialog box, as shown in figure 9.17. This dialog box provides the following information and tools:

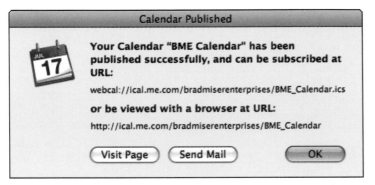

Calendar Published

Your Calendar "BME Calendar" has been published successfully, and can be subscribed at URL:

webcal://ical.me.com/bradmiserenterprises/BME_Calendar.ics

or be viewed with a browser at URL:

http://ical.me.com/bradmiserenterprises/BME_Calendar

(Visit Page)   (Send Mail)   (OK)

9.17 This calendar can be viewed on the Web or subscribed to in iCal.

- The URL someone can use to subscribe to the calendar in iCal
- The URL to view the calendar on the Web
- The Visit Page button that takes you to the calendar on the Web
- The Send Mail button that creates an email message you can send to iCal users to enable them to subscribe to your calendar
- The OK button that closes the dialog box

Caution

One limitation of publishing a calendar via MobileMe is that you can't protect it with a password. Anyone who can access its URL can see the calendar.

Consider these additional points when publishing your calendars:

- When a calendar is published, the published icon (which looks like radiating waves) appears next to the calendar's name on the list of calendars in iCal.

- If you open a published shared calendar's contextual menu in iCal, you see several interesting commands. These include Unpublish, which removes the calendar from the Web; Send Publish Email, which enables you to send an email announcing the published calendar and its URL; Copy URL to Clipboard, which copies the calendar's URL to the

Clipboard so you can paste it into documents; Refresh, which publishes any changes you have made to the calendar; Refresh All, which updates all your published calendars; and Change Location, which enables you to move the calendar to a different site.

⊙ You can change a shared calendar by selecting it and then choosing the Get Info command on its contextual menu. Use the tools in the calendar's Info sheet to make changes to the calendar's publishing and other settings.

Subscribing to published iCal calendars in iCal

You can subscribe to calendars being published via MobileMe to add them to the iCal window:

1. **Select Calendar ➪ Subscribe.** The Subscribe sheet appears.

2. **Enter the URL for the calendar to which you want to subscribe.** The URL has the form webcal://ical.me.com/*membername*/*calendarname*.ics, where *membername* and *calendarname* are the user's MobileMe member name and the calendar's published name, respectively.

Genius The easiest way to subscribe to a calendar is using its publish email because that email has a link that the user clicks, preventing the need to type the URL. To send a publish email, open a published calendar's contextual menu and choose Send Publish Email. When you receive a publish email, click its subscribe link and skip to step 4.

3. **Click Subscribe.** The Subscribing configuration sheet appears, as shown in figure 9.18.

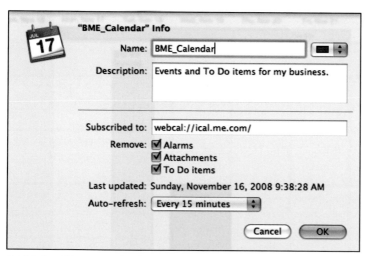

9.18 Subscribing to a calendar enables you to view its events and other information.

4. **Enter the title that you want to be used for the shared calendar in iCal.** Typically, this is the same as the published name, but you can change it if you prefer to see it under a different name.

5. **Choose a color for the calendar using the Color pop-up menu.**

6. **Enter a description of the calendar in the Description field.**

7. **If you don't want the calendar's alarms to have any impact, deselect the Alarms check box.**

8. **If you don't want the calendar's attachments included in your version, deselect the Attachments check box.**

9. **If you don't want the calendar's To Do items to show up in your iCal window, deselect the To Do items check box.** You usually don't want to display the To Do items on a calendar to which you are subscribing unless you have To Do items on it.

10. **If you want the calendar's information to be refreshed automatically, select the frequency at which you want the refresh to occur on the Auto-refresh pop-up menu.**

11. **Click OK.** The calendar is added to the SUBSCRIPTIONS section of your iCal window, and you can view it just like your own calendars; you can't make any changes to the calendar (if you try, you see an error message). If you configured the calendar to be refreshed automatically, iCal keeps it current.

Genius

If you don't set a calendar to which you are subscribed to be refreshed automatically, you can refresh it manually by opening its contextual menu and selecting Refresh.

Subscribing to published iCal calendars in Outlook

Subscribing to published iCal calendars is not supported in Outlook by default. However, you can find extensions to Outlook enable you to subscribe to published iCal calendars similar to iCal. One example is iCalendar for MS Outlook, which is available at www.keener-price.com/icalendar.

After the extension is installed, you configure it similarly to how you subscribe to a published calendar in iCal, as shown in figure 9.19. For example, you configure the extension to access the published calendar's URL, set the refresh cycle, and so on. After it's configured, the published calendar appears in Outlook, where you can view its events and other information.

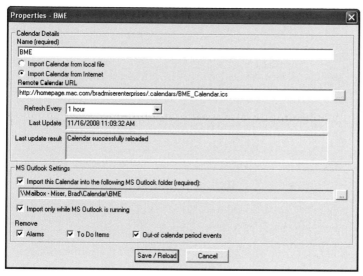

9.19 Using an extension to Outlook, such as iCalendar for MS Outlook, you can subscribe to published iCal calendars so that you can view their information within Outlook.

Note

When you configure iCalendar for MS Outlook, use the browser URL (the one beginning with http) for the published calendar rather than the subscribe to URL (beginning with webcal).

Viewing published calendars using a Web browser

If you want to share a published calendar with someone who doesn't use iCal, just provide the published calendar's browser URL to the person with whom you want to share it. A published calendar's URL has the form http://ical.me.com/*membername*/*calendarname*, where *membername* and *calendarname* are the user's MobileMe member name and the calendar's published name, respectively.

Genius

You can easily share a published calendar's browser URL with someone by using the calendar's contextual Send Publish Email command. The resulting email includes both the subscription URL and the browser URL.

To view a published calendar, simply visit its browser URL, as shown in figure 9.20. To make it easy to move back to the calendar at any time, set a bookmark or favorite to the calendar's URL.

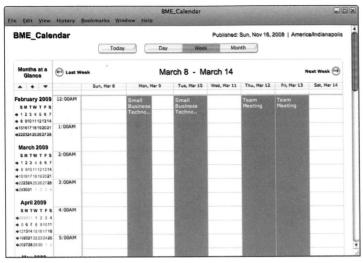

9.20 You can view a published calendar from iCal using any Web browser.

Sharing calendars using a single MobileMe account

If you share a single MobileMe account among all your team members, it's easy to share calendars. Create a calendar for each team member; when you access the MobileMe Calendar application, you see each calendar on the Calendar list and you can work with them just as with calendars you've created.

This approach has the benefit of being simple to implement (you learned earlier in the chapter how easy it is to create additional calendars). It also has the benefit of calendars being easily synced among different devices. For example, one team member can use iCal to manage her calendar while another uses Outlook to manage his. As long as both have their computers synced to the same MobileMe account, their calendars are available via the MobileMe Calendar application and also are synced on desktop applications and iPhones.

That being said, you can only sync a computer with one MobileMe account per user account at a time. This means that all team members must share the same account, which limits the usefulness of email, iDisk, and other MobileMe functions. Also, team members must maintain separate calendars in other applications to have any private information because any information they enter in their synced calendar applications is posted to the MobileMe cloud, where it is visible to anyone who accesses the account or is synced to the account's cloud.

Sharing calendars using Outlook

For team members who use Outlook, the process to share calendars is complicated because it depends on the version of Outlook being used and how the team member's computer is connected to a local network. To share calendars over the Internet, you must use Outlook 2007. To share calendars over a local network, you can use older versions.

Note If the Windows PC running Outlook is connected to a Microsoft Exchange server, that server determines how information can be shared. In some cases, you can't share calendar information outside the Exchange network.

Sharing calendars over the Internet using Outlook 2007

Outlook 2007 allows you to publish calendars to the Internet in a couple of ways.

You can publish calendars via a Windows Live, Hotmail, or MSN account. View the calendar you want to share, and click the Publish My Calendar link. Follow the onscreen instructions to sign into or create a Windows Live or other account and publish the calendar; because these accounts are free, you can do this for no additional cost. At the end of the process, you see a URL to the published calendar. Provide this URL to the people with whom you want to share the calendar.

If your entire team uses Windows computers, this is the best method for you because you can obtain the required accounts for free. However, if some of your team uses Macs, you should try the following option instead.

You can publish Outlook 2007 calendars using WebDAV (Web-based Distributed Authoring and Versioning) extensions to the HTTP protocol. You can't use the MobileMe servers as the WebDAV server to which to publish an Outlook calendar, so the published calendar can't be accessed using MobileMe. However, Mac OS X's iCal can publish calendars to a WebDAV server, so if your team uses a mix of Windows PCs and Macs, using a WebDAV server can be a good option for your company.

In order to share calendars over the Internet using WebDAV, you need to have a WebDAV server available to which you and your team members can publish their calendars. There are such services available on the Internet; some have costs associated with them, and some don't. These services tend to be a bit flighty, especially the free ones, so I can't really recommend a specific service for you and be sure that service will still be available when you read this. One service that was available when I wrote this was at www.icalx.com.

Genius

To use a WebDAV server with iCal, open the Publish calendar sheet and choose a Private Server on the Publish on menu. Then configure the WebDAV server's information in the resulting fields, which include URL, username, and password.

To gain access to a WebDAV server, you need an account on that server. If the account is free, you simply need to create an account with the service managing that server. If the account isn't free, you need to provide a credit card and other personal information to gain access to it. When you obtain a WebDAV account, you get a URL, username, and password for that account.

In Outlook, right-click the calendar you want to share and choose Publish to Internet. Then choose Publish to WebDAV Server. Following the onscreen instructions, enter your WebDAV server's information and complete the rest of the configuration for the shared calendar, such as how often you want the information refreshed, which specific information you want to be available online, and so on. At the end of the process, the calendar is shared on the Internet.

To enable others to subscribe to the calendar, right-click the calendar that is published and choose Publish to Internet; then choose Share Published Calendar. Send the resulting email to the people with whom you want to share the calendar, including Outlook and iCal users. Those users can then subscribe to the published calendars in Outlook and in iCal.

Note

Older versions of Outlook allow calendars to be saved as HTML pages that can then be published via a MobileMe Web site, but this is a static process and must be repeated when calendar information changes, so it isn't really a practical solution for the long term.

Sharing calendars over a local network using Outlook

If Windows computers are on the same local network, you can share Outlook calendars within the Outlook application; you can't share with iCal users, so if the network includes Mac computers, share the calendar over the Internet instead. To share a calendar over a local network, perform the following steps:

1. **Right-click the calendar you want to share.**

2. **Choose Sharing.** The Properties dialog box for that calendar appears with the Permissions tab selected, as shown in figure 9.21.

3. **Click Add.**

4. **Move to and select the people with whom you want to share the calendar.**

5. **Select the first person whose access you want to configure.**

6. **Choose the permissions they have to the calendar; in most cases, you should select only the Read Items check box.**

7. **Configure each person's permissions to the calendar.**

8. **Click OK.** The dialog box closes, and the shared calendar becomes available to the people you selected. (They can access the shared calendar within Outlook.)

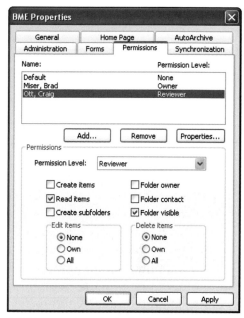

9.21 You can share Outlook calendars over a local network using the Permissions tab of the calendar's Properties dialog box.

Appendix A

How Can I Use MobileMe to Display Images on the Web?

In addition to all the great features of MobileMe you learned about in this book's chapters, the service has one more trick up its digital sleeve — the MobileMe Gallery. Using the Gallery, you can publish photos and other images to the Web, where they can be viewed using any Web browser. You can allow viewers to download photos from your gallery, and you can even allow viewers to upload images to your gallery.

Exploring the Gallery Application

The MobileMe Gallery application enables you to publish photos and other images to the Web. You can have multiple albums within your gallery; each album has a link so you can direct viewers to them individually. You also can configure features for an album, such as which information is displayed, if its contents can be downloaded, or if viewers can upload their images to your gallery. And you can protect the contents of albums with a username and password.

To access your Gallery, log into your MobileMe Web site and click the Gallery button, which is the flower icon. The Gallery window has two panes. In the left pane is the Source list that has two sections. My Gallery contains all the albums you've published. When you select My Gallery, those albums appear in the right pane of the window, as shown in figure A.1.

To the right of the buttons on the Gallery toolbar, you see the URL to the gallery, which is http://gallery.me.com/*membername*, where *membername* is your MobileMe member name. If you click this link, you move to your gallery's home page on the Web. (Viewing your gallery on the Web is covered later in this chapter.)

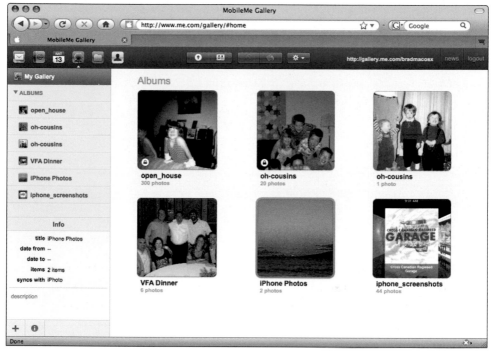

A.1 My Gallery shows you all the albums you've published.

For each album, you see a thumbnail showing the key photo (which you can set) for the album along with its title and the number of photos it contains. You can move through the photos in an album by dragging across its thumbnail; as you drag, you move through the images in that album. The faster you drag, the faster you move through the images. When you move away from an album's thumbnail, its key photo appears again.

When an album displays the lock icon, that album is protected with a username and password; that information must be provided to be able to view the album's contents using a Web browser.

If you select an album and click the Info button (the "i" within a blue circle at the bottom of the Source list), you see information about the album in the lower-left pane of the Source list. The information you see depends on the kind of album you've selected, but it typically includes the album name, date range of the photos it contains, number of images, and a description. If the album is synced with iPhoto, you also see the text "syncs with iPhoto."

Below My Gallery, you see the ALBUMS section, which shows each album you have published. You can expand or collapse this section by clicking its expansion triangle.

When you select an album, you see thumbnails of the images it contains in the right part of the window, as shown in figure A.2. Under each thumbnail, you see the image's title (if the album is configured to display it). You can scroll in this window to view all the album's images. Change the size of the thumbnails by dragging the slider, located in the lower-right corner of the window, to the right to increase their size or to the left to decrease it.

A.2 When you select an album, you see the images it contains in the right pane of the Gallery window.

To focus on an image, double-click it. The image fills the Gallery window. Use the left- and right-facing arrow buttons at the bottom of the window to move through the images. Click the Actual Size button in the lower-right corner of the window to see the image at its full size. Click the Scale to Fit button to return to the previous size. Click the Back to Album link at the bottom of the window to move back to the thumbnail view.

On the right of the Gallery toolbar, you see the URL to the album. This is the same as the URL to your gallery except that it has the album's reference number (created by MobileMe) appended to it. You can click this link to view the album on the Web (more on this later in this chapter).

Like the My Gallery item, you can view information about an album in the Info pane. When you select an image's thumbnail, the Info pane shows information about the image rather than the album.

You can get detailed information about an image by selecting it, opening the Action menu, and choosing Show Detailed Info. In the resulting Details window, you see specific information about the selected image, including its name, date, size, URL, and so on, as shown in figure A.3.

A.3 Use the Show Detailed Info command to get even more detailed information about images.

You can create albums in your gallery using iPhoto or with the Gallery Web application. You can use the Gallery Web application to manage your albums. You (or any one else, which is the point of using the Gallery) can use any Web browser to view your albums.

Note

If you're wondering why this is an appendix instead of chapter, the reason is that the Gallery isn't quite as useful for business as the other MobileMe features. For business purposes, you are probably better off using your Web site to publish photos because you can include additional information along with the photos, such as your contact information, a text description of what's in the photo, links to other Web sites, and so on. Even so, you may find creative ways to incorporate the Gallery into your business.

Publishing a Gallery Album Using iPhoto

With a MobileMe account and Apple's iPhoto application, you can quickly and easily publish photos to your gallery on the Web, where they are viewable in any Web browser. Because MobileMe is integrated into iPhoto, as it is in iWeb and other applications, creating and managing your online galleries is a seamless process.

Note iPhoto is available only on Mac computers. If you use only Windows PCs or have a Mac but don't use iPhoto for some reason, you can create gallery albums using the MobileMe Gallery Web application (you learn how later in this appendix).

Creating and publishing an album using iPhoto

Making photos available on the Web is a straightforward process. Follow these steps:

1. **In iPhoto, create a photo album that includes the images you want to publish.**

Genius Place the image you want to be the key photo for the album in the top-left position in the album. This becomes the album's thumbnail when it is viewed on your gallery page.

2. **With the album selected, click the MobileMe button.** The Gallery sheet appears, as shown in figure A.4.

3. **On the Album Viewable by pop-up menu, choose one of the following options:**

   - **Everyone.** Makes the album available to everyone who visits your gallery's Web site.

   - **Only Me.** Limits access to the album to you (it won't appear on your gallery's Web site).

   - **Edit Names and Passwords.** Lets you protect an album by requiring a username and password to view it. When you choose this option, use the resulting sheet to create usernames and passwords. After you create a username and password, the username appears on the Album Viewable by pop-up menu.

   - **User name.** Limits access to the album to a username you select.

4. **To allow visitors to be able to download photos from the album, select the Downloading of photos or entire album check box.**

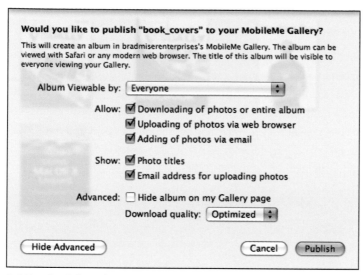

Would you like to publish "book_covers" to your MobileMe Gallery?

This will create an album in bradmiserenterprises's MobileMe Gallery. The album can be viewed with Safari or any modern web browser. The title of this album will be visible to everyone viewing your Gallery.

Album Viewable by: [Everyone ▼]

Allow: ☑ Downloading of photos or entire album
☑ Uploading of photos via web browser
☑ Adding of photos via email

Show: ☑ Photo titles
☑ Email address for uploading photos

Advanced: ☐ Hide album on my Gallery page
Download quality: [Optimized ▼]

[Hide Advanced]   [Cancel] [Publish]

A.4 Use the Gallery sheet to publish an iPhoto photo album to the Web.

5. **To permit people to upload photos to the album via the Web, select the Uploading of photos via web browser check box.**

6. **To allow viewers to add photos to the album by sending with an email application, select the Adding of photos via email check box.**

Note Allowing people to add images to an album (view the Web or email) is a great way to make your gallery sites interactive. For example, you could allow customers to upload images of themselves using your products.

7. **To display titles on the gallery, select the Photo titles check box.**

8. **If you selected the check box in Step 6, select the Email address for uploading photos check box to display the email address on the album's Web page.**

9. **Click the Show Advanced button.** Additional, advanced options appear.

10. **To hide the album on your gallery's Web site, select the Hide album on my Gallery page check box.** With this selected, the only way to move to the album's Web site is by using its URL.

11. **Use the Download quality pop-up menu to choose one of the following options:**

   ● **Optimized.** To allow faster uploading while providing photos that print at good quality up to 16 x 20 inches.

- **Actual Size.** To upload images at their actual size, which means they will be at their maximum quality, but can take longer to upload.

12. **Click Publish.** iPhoto publishes the photo album to the Web. Next to the album's name in the MOBILEME GALLERY section, you see a progress indicator show how the upload process is moving along. When you select the album being published, you also see a progress bar in the upper right corner of the iPhoto window along with the pending status on the thumbnails of any images that haven't been uploaded yet. Publishing occurs in the background so you can go about your business while it is being done. When the publish process finishes, click the album's URL located at the top of the iPhoto window to view it on the Web (see figure A.5).

A.5 Albums you publish can be viewed in any Web browser.

Note If you allow people to add images via email, you see the email address to which photos can be sent in the top-right corner of the iPhoto window. Any images emailed to this address are added to the album.

Telling people about a gallery album using iPhoto

After you've published an album, you want to make it available to people to view. Here's how:

1. **Select the published album in the MOBILEME GALLERY section of the iPhoto source list.**

2. **Click the Tell a Friend button.** Your email application opens, a new message is created, and information about the album is pasted into the message. This includes the key image from the album along with View Album button that the recipient can click to view the album on the Web.

3. **Address the message, make changes to its default content, and send it.** Recipients can use the View Album button in the message to view the album's Web site.

Genius

A gallery album can be a great way to show off products or services your company provides. For example, you can publish a gallery containing photos of your products and include a link to that gallery in emails you send to prospective customers. If your company provides services, you can include images, such as scans of covers of documents you have created, and use the gallery to show viewers what you have done.

Publishing a Gallery Album Using the MobileMe Gallery Web Application

You can create and publish an album using the Gallery Web application. After it's created, you add images to and configure it. Then tell people about it so they can visit its Web site to see the images.

Creating an album with the Gallery Web application

To create a new gallery album, perform the following steps:

1. **Access the Gallery Web application.**

2. **Click the Add button (+) at the bottom of the Source list.** The Album Settings sheet appears.

3. **Enter the album name in the Album Name field.**

4. **To allow visitors to be able to download photos from the album, select the Downloading of photos or entire album check box.**

5. **To permit people to upload photos to the album via the Web, select the Uploading of photos via web browser check box.**

6. **To allow viewers to add photos to the album by sending with an email application, select the Adding of photos via email or iPhone check box.**

7. **To display titles on the gallery, select the Photo titles check box.**

8. **If you selected the check box in step 6, select the Email address for uploading photos check box to display the email address on the album's Web page.**

9. **To hide the album on your gallery's Web site, select the Hide album on my Gallery page check box.** With this selected, the only way to move to the album's Web site is by using its URL.

10. **Use the Syncs with to select iPhoto or Aperture to choose the application with which you want the album to sync.**

11. **Click Create.** You see the new album, which is selected on the source list and is ready for you to add images, as shown in figure A.6. In the upper-right corner of the window, you see the URL to the album.

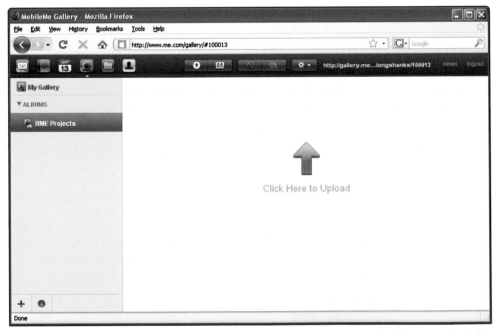

A.6 After you've created an album, you can add images to it by clicking the Upload button or the link shown in this window.

Adding images to a gallery album

To publish images, you add them to a MobileMe gallery. Follow these steps:

1. **Select the album to which you want to add images.**

2. **Click the Upload button (the up arrow) on the Gallery toolbar.** The Upload dialog box appears.

3. **Click Choose.**

4. **Move to and select the images you want to add to the album, and click Select (Mac) or Open (Windows).** The files you select are uploaded and added to the album.

5. **Repeat Steps 3 and 4 until you've added all the images to the album.**

6. **Click Done.** You move back to the album and see the images you've added. Under each image, you see its title. You're ready to configure the album.

Caution Any albums you created using the MobileMe Gallery Web application are available to anyone who can access the album's URL. To be able to protect an album with a user-name and password, you must publish it with iPhoto (or Aperture).

Configuring a gallery album

To configure an album, perform any or all of the following tasks:

- To change the publish settings for the album, click the Settings button (the switches) the Gallery toolbar. The Album Settings sheet appears. Use the controls on this sheet to configure the album as you do when you create a new album.

- To delete an image from the album, select it and click the Delete button (circle and slash) on the Gallery toolbar and then click OK in the resulting warning prompt.

- To change the orientation of a photo, select it and click the Rotate button (photo with curved arrow).

- To change the order of the images, drag them around the window. Images appear on the Web (and in a slideshow) in the order in which they appear in the Gallery window starting at the top-left corner.

- To change an image's title, click it and type the new title.

- To set the album's key photo, select the image you want to use, open the Action menu, and choose Set Key Photo. (The Key Photo is the one that appears in the album's thumbnail within the Gallery application and on the Web.)

- Select the album (deselect an image if one is currently selected), open the Info pane, and enter information about the album, such as its title and description, as shown in figure A.7.

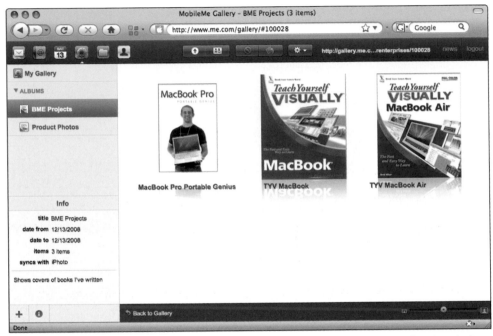

A.7 As you make changes to an album in your gallery, those changes appear on the album's Web site immediately.

Genius

As you configure an album, click its URL located to the right of the Action menu to preview it in a Web browser.

Telling people about an album's Web site

The whole point of publishing an album is to get people to view the images it contains. Here's how to get the word out:

1. **Click an album's URL.** You move to the album's Web site, as shown in figure A.8.

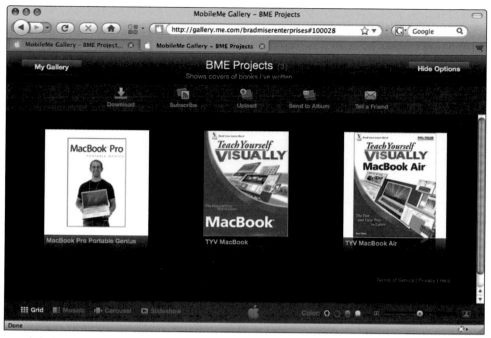

A.8 Click the Tell a Friend button on an album's Web site to publicize it.

2. **Click the Tell a Friend button.** The Tell a Friend sheet appears. Along with the fields you complete to send a message, you see the album's Key Photo.

3. **Enter your email address in the From box.**

4. **Enter the email addresses of the people you want to view the site in the To box (separate addresses with commas).**

5. **Enter text for the message in the Message box.**

6. **If you enabled email uploads to the album, select the check box if you want to include the address for adding images to the site in the email message.**

7. **Enter the security characters in the bottom box.**

8. **Click Send, as shown in figure A.9.** The recipients you entered in Step 4 receive a message that includes the key image from the album along with the View Album button that the recipient can click to view the album on the Web.

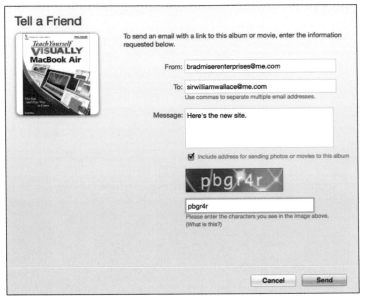

A.9 Use this form to send a message about an album's Web site.

Viewing MobileMe Galleries and Albums with a Web Browser

Earlier, you learned how to view the contents of your gallery with the MobileMe Gallery application. In this section, you learn the details of viewing a gallery or album using a Web browser, which is what the people with whom you share your gallery and albums will do.

Viewing a MobileMe gallery with a Web browser

To view a gallery the Web, move to its URL, which is http://gallery.me.com/*membername*, where *membername* is the member name of the account associated with the gallery. You see the gallery in a Web browser. Within the gallery's window, you see each of its visible albums; remember that albums can be hidden within a gallery. Following are some things to know about viewing a gallery, as indicated in figure A.10:

- For each album, you see its title, number of images, and Key Photo.
- To preview the images in an album, drag across its thumbnail.

- If you don't see an album's Key Photo and it has the Lock icon, that album is protected with a username and password. You need that information to be able to view the album.

- To view an album, click its thumbnail (see the next section for information about viewing albums).

- If you use an RSS (Really Simple Syndication) reader, you can subscribe to a gallery so you are notified when its contents change. To do so, click the Subscribe to Updates link in the upper-right corner of the gallery window. You see a sheet containing the address you use to subscribe to the gallery.

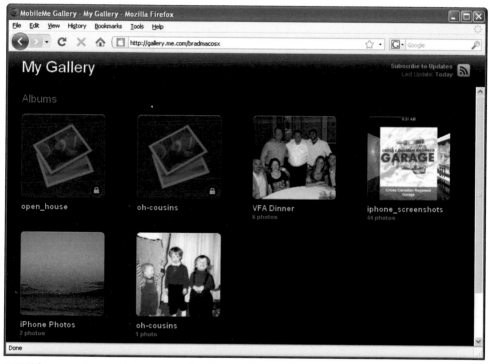

A.10 When you view a gallery, you see the albums it contains (but you don't see albums that are hidden).

Viewing a MobileMe album with a Web browser

To view an album with a Web browser, you can move to it in the following ways:

- Enter the URL for the album (http://gallery.me.com/*membername/album#*, where *membername* is the member name of the account associated with the gallery and *album#* is the number of the album assigned by MobileMe).

- Move to the gallery in which the album is stored, and click its thumbnail.
- Click the View Album button in an email message announcing the album.

Note No matter which method you use, if the album is protected by a username and password, you have to provide that information when prompted to do so before you can view an album.

At the top of the album's window, you see its title and the number of images it contains. Within the window, you see thumbnails of the images in the album along with their titles, as shown in figure A.11.

A.11 Many tools and options are available to you when you view an album.

You can view and work with an album in a number of ways. The following list describes all possible options being enabled for an album. If a specific feature isn't enabled, such as downloading images, you won't see the related button when you view that album.

- Scroll in the window to browse all the album's thumbnails.

- Change the size of the thumbnails with the slider located in the lower-right corner of the window.

- To change the background color of the album, click one of the Color radio buttons located next to the size slider.

- To download all the images in an album, click the Download button in the album toolbar. You see the download sheet explaining that all the images in the album will be compressed into a ZIP file. Click Download. The ZIP file is downloaded to your computer. Uncompress the file and you can work with the images in the album.

- If you use an RSS reader, you can subscribe to an album so you are notified when its contents change. To do so, click the Subscribe button in the album's toolbar. You see a sheet containing the address you use to subscribe to the album.

- To add images to the album via the Web browser, click the Upload button. You see the Upload sheet. Provide your name, email address, and enter the security code displayed at the bottom of the sheet. Then click Choose Files and select the files you want to add to the album.

- To add images to the album via email, click the Send to Album button. You see a sheet containing the email address for uploads to the album. Click the address, and a new email message is created in your default email application. Attach the images you want to add to the album, and send the email.

- If you want to tell other people about the album, click the Tell a Friend button. (See the section on telling people about an album's Web site earlier in this chapter.)

- To move to the gallery in which the album is stored, click the My Gallery button.

- To hide the album's toolbar, click the Hide Options button. To show the toolbar again, click the Show Options button.

- To view an image, click its thumbnail. The image appears in the window along with its title, as shown in figure A.12. When you move the cursor, a toolbar appears below the image. Click the Download button (downward facing arrow) to download the image to your computer. Click the left or right arrows to move to the previous or the next image in the album. Click the Info button ("i") to view information about the image. Click the Back to Album button to return to the image's album.

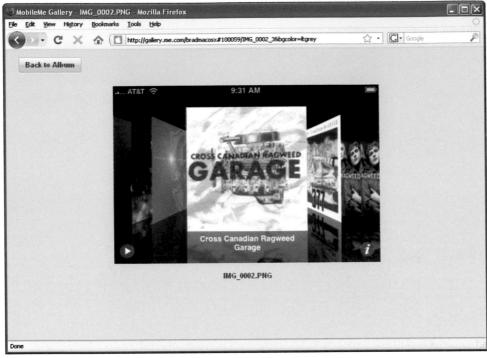

A.12 When you click an image's thumbnail, it appears by itself in the album's window.

● To be able to see thumbnails of an album's images and a large view of a selected image, click the Mosaic button at the bottom of the window. Along the right side of the window, you see smaller thumbnails of the album's images. Select a thumbnail, and you see a large view of the image in the left side of the window.

● To see images that you can "flip" through, click the Carousel button. You see thumbnails of images fanned out across the window. (This view is similar to viewing the iPod function on an iPhone when it is in landscape mode). The image in focus appears larger at the center of the window. Scroll through the images by dragging the slider to the left or right. To scroll through the images automatically, click the Play button at the left end of the slider. To focus on an image, click its thumbnail.

● To view images in a slideshow, click the Slideshow button. A new, maximized window appears, and the album's images begin playing, as shown in figure A.13. When you move the cursor, the slideshow toolbar appears at the bottom of the screen. To download the current image, click the Download button (downward facing arrow) to download the image to your computer. Use the left- or right-facing arrows to move back or ahead in the slide show. Use the Play/Pause button to start or stop the slide show. Use the return button (two arrows pointing to each other) to close the slide show window and return to the previous album view.

A.13 You can view the images in an album in a slide show.

Glossary

Address Book Mac OS X's contacts application. You can synchronize contact information stored in the Address Book with other devices via MobileMe.

AdSense An ad network run by Google where the ad server automatically examines the content of your page and generates one or more ads that are related in some way to that content. You can use the Add Web Widget tool in iWeb to add AdSense ads to your Web sites.

AIM America Online (AOL) Instant Messenger is an application that you can use for text, audio, and video chat. AIM is available for Macs, Windows PCs, and iPhones.

allocating disk space Your total MobileMe disk space is shared between your iDisk and email storage. You can allocate disk space between these two areas so that you have enough space in each area.

Aperture Apple's high-end photo application. You can sync photos from Aperture with your MobileMe Gallery.

bookmark An Internet site saved so that you can access the site quickly in future browsing sessions.

buddy A person with whom you chat using iChat or AIM.

buddy list The list of people you've configured as buddies in iChat or AIM.

chat room What you create when you invite more than one person to a text chat using iChat or AIM. Each person in the chat room can read what anyone else writes. People can leave a chat room at will.

chat status An indication of whether a buddy is available for chatting. When you look at your buddy list, you see the status of your buddies, such as Available or Away, and your buddies see your status on their buddy lists.

domain The "area" where an Internet resource is stored. On the Internet, all resources are located in a specific domain that is linked to the organization providing that resource. Domains are identified by an IP address or a domain name.

domain name A means to identify a domain that uses text instead of an IP address. For example, apple.com is the domain for Apple Computer.

domain registration The process of defining a domain by location (IP address) and name. You can register your own domain name so that your MobileMe Web site address is www.your-name.com instead of web.me.com/member-name. Registering a domain requires that you pay a fee and that your domain name is unique.

email alias An email address you create that points to your primary MobileMe email address, but that hides it from other people. You can have up to five email aliases that you can use for various purposes, such as to guard against spam or for special offers for your business.

Entourage Microsoft's email, contacts, and calendar application for Macs.

event A defined date, time, and other information being managed on a calendar, such as a meeting.

Exchange Microsoft's system for managing email, contacts, and calendars for groups of people over a local network. Exchange is used by many organizations because it provides many features that are designed to support an organization. It also is very expensive and requires significant hardware, software, and technical resources to support. For many small businesses, MobileMe is much less expensive and a simpler alternative that provides similar functionality.

Family Member account A MobileMe account that is provided through a Family Pack account. You can create Family Member accounts for a group of people, such as team members in your business.

Family Pack account A MobileMe account that includes an individual account and up to four Family Member accounts. A Family Pack account is a great way to provide MobileMe accounts to a group of people for less cost than buying an individual account for each.

fetch When a device, such as an iPhone, requests email or other data from another device, such as an email server, on which the data is stored. The client (such as the iPhone) requests the data from the server and gets the data from the other device, thus initiating the data transfer. The opposite is push, where the providing device drives the transfer.

Firefox A free Web browser application that is very popular because of its speed and excellent features. It is available for both Macs and Windows PCs and is one of the two Web browsers that fully support MobileMe (Safari is the other).

free trial You can create and use a MobileMe account for up to 60 days at no charge.

Gallery The MobileMe service whereby you can easily publish photos and other images on the Web. You can use the MobileMe Gallery Web application to do so, or if you have a Mac, you can use iPhoto or Aperture.

HomePage The tool you could use to create Web pages under the previous version of MobileMe (called .Mac). While HomePage is still available, it isn't easy to get to, and with iWeb, there's really no reason to use it anymore. If you published pages under HomePage, they continue to be available under MobileMe.

HTML See *Hypertext Markup Language.*

Hypertext Markup Language A collection of codes — called tags — that define the underlying structure of, and to some extent the formatting on, a Web page.

iCal Mac OS X's calendar application. You can synchronize calendar information stored in iCal with other devices via MobileMe.

iChat Mac OS X's text, audio, and video chatting application. It also supports online file and desktop sharing. A MobileMe account includes an iChat account.

iDisk Virtual disk space that you access over the Internet. You can access your iDisk from a Mac or Windows PC desktop or using the MobileMe iDisk Web application. Your MobileMe account includes a specific amount of online disk space that is shared between

your iDisk and email. You can upgrade your accounts to get more disk space. All the data you use for MobileMe, including content for your Web sites and Gallery, is stored on your iDisk, along with any files you choose to store there.

IMAP account An email account that uses the Internet Message Access Protocol. An IMAP account is designed to store messages on the server, where they are read by — but not downloaded to — an email client application. The benefit of an IMAP account is that the same set of messages can be accessed from any device running an email application. A MobileMe email account is an IMAP account.

individual account A MobileMe account designed to be used by one person. It includes email, an iDisk, a .me Web site, and so on.

instant messaging Also known as IM or chatting, where you communicate with someone in real time (thus the term *instant*) via text.

Internet Explorer The default Windows Web browser application produced by Microsoft. It does not fully support MobileMe functionality, so you need to use either Safari or Firefox to get the most out of MobileMe services.

IP address The Internet Protocol address that is a series of numbers, such as 10.0.1.256, that defines a resource's location on the Internet. Fortunately, you typically use a domain name, such as apple.com, instead of the IP address. All locations on the Internet must have a unique IP address.

iPhone Apple's revolutionary smart phone that provides extensive functionality and an extremely intuitive interface. You can access MobileMe services using an iPhone, and you can synchronize iPhones with other devices via the MobileMe cloud.

iPhoto One of Apple's photo managing applications. You can use iPhoto to import images from a camera or from your desktop. You can then organize, edit, and create projects from those photos. MobileMe is integrated into iPhoto, so you can easily publish images to the Web.

iSight Web cameras built into all Macs except Mac Pros.

iWeb Apple's Web site creation application. You build Web sites based on templates that you modify with your own content. MobileMe is integrated into iWeb, so you can publish Web sites with a single mouse click.

junk mail MobileMe's name for spam email, which is any email you don't request and don't want. You can use tools in the MobileMe Email Web application to manage junk mail. You also can use email aliases to limit your exposure to junk mail.

.Mac The previous name of MobileMe services when they were available for Macs only and had less capability.

Mail Apple's email application, which is installed on all Macs by default. You can synchronize email in Mail with other applications using MobileMe.

me.com The Web site you use to access your MobileMe Web applications and to manage your MobileMe accounts.

member name The name associated with your MobileMe account. This name is important because it appears in your email address and the URLs for your Web sites and other online resources. You choose a member name when you sign up for a MobileMe account.

MobileMe Apple's set of online services that provide email, contacts, calendars, online images, virtual disk space, and synchronization. You can access these services via a Web browser and on desktop applications on Macs and Windows PCs along with iPhones.

MobileMe account You need a MobileMe account to be able to access MobileMe services. Several types of accounts are available, with different fees associated with each.

MobileMe cloud The name given to the area where information is stored via MobileMe services. You can access information stored in the MobileMe cloud using a computer or iPhone. Data is synchronized by first copying it to the cloud and then copying it to synchronized devices.

MobileMe control panel The software you use to configure MobileMe on a Windows PC.

Monthly data transfer The amount of data that can be moved across your MobileMe account per month. This is important if you have lots of activity on your Web site because it

311

could limit the amount of information that can be provided. You can upgrade your account in this area.

Outlook Microsoft's email, calendar, and contact application, which is dominant on Windows PCs. You can synchronize email, calendar, and contact information stored in Outlook with other applications using MobileMe.

POP account An email account that uses the Post Office Protocol. A POP account is designed to download messages from the email server into an email application. Many ISP email accounts are POP accounts. You can configure one POP account in the MobileMe Email Web application.

Public folder A folder on your iDisk that can be accessed over the Internet by anyone who knows its address. The Public folder is useful for sharing files with other people. You can determine whether people can write files to your folder along with being able to read files stored there. The URL for your public folder is public.me.com/*membername*, where *membername* is your MobileMe member name.

push When a device that stores email or other data, such as an email server provided by an ISP, automatically moves data onto a device that is configured to receive that data, such as an iPhone, when there are changes (such as a new email being received). The device providing the data drives the data transfer process

while the receiving device merely receives the data pushed to it. This is the opposite of fetch, where the receiving device drives the data transfer process.

rich text Text that includes formatting features such as fonts, colors, and styles.

RSS Really Simple Syndication, which is a technology for presenting dynamic information in various applications. For example, you can use RSS to subscribe to changes to someone's Gallery so you know when the images it contains change.

Safari Apple's Web browser application. It is installed by default on all Macs. It also is available for Windows PCs. It is one of the two Web browsers that fully support MobileMe (Firefox is the other).

synchronization A process that ensures that data such as contacts, email, files, and other data is the same on multiple devices, including Macs, Windows PCs, and iPhones. With MobileMe, you synchronize via the MobileMe cloud.

System Preferences application You use the MobileMe pane of this application to configure MobileMe on a Mac.

To Do item A task that needs to be completed. You can manage To Do items in iCal, Outlook, and the MobileMe Calendar Web application.

URL Uniform Resource Locator is the address you use to access an online resource, such as a Web site. For example, the URL for the MobileMe Home page is http://www.mobileme.com.

vCard A Virtual Card, which is a file that contains a person's or company's contact information. You can use vCards in most contact applications, including Address Book, Outlook, and MobileMe's Contacts Web application.

Web cam A camera that connects to a computer and transmits images over the Internet. These are useful for video conferencing using iChat or AIM.

WebEx An online conferencing service (www.webex.com) that allows an unlimited number of people to communicate via audio over the phone and by viewing content on their computers. It is ideal for online presentations and collaboration. The service requires a fee to use, but can be very valuable for business with remote customers, potential customers, or team members.

Web widget Small applications that you can add to your Web sites using iWeb's Web Widgets tool. For example, you can add Google maps or AdSense Ads.

Index

G

H

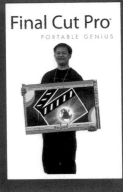